*An Analysis of Malay Magic*

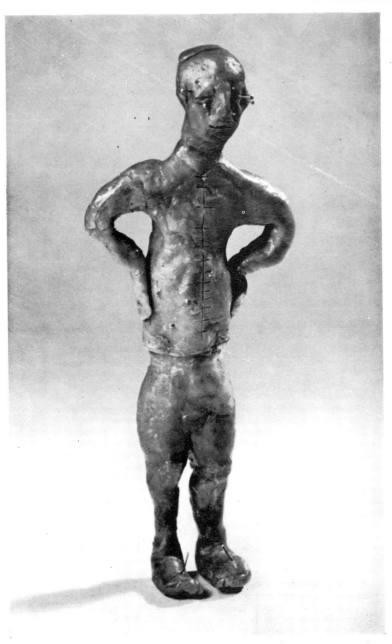

Wax figure stuck with pins to cause illness.
See Skeat's *Malay Magic*, p. 570 and plate 28, fig. 1. Height 24.3 cms.

# An Analysis
# of Malay Magic

KIRK MICHAEL ENDICOTT

KUALA LUMPUR
**OXFORD UNIVERSITY PRESS**
OXFORD NEW YORK MELBOURNE

*Oxford University Press*

OXFORD  LONDON  GLASGOW
NEW YORK  TORONTO  MELBOURNE  WELLINGTON
KUALA LUMPUR  SINGAPORE  HONG KONG  TOKYO
DELHI  BOMBAY  CALCUTTA  MADRAS  KARACHI
NAIROBI  DAR ES SALAAM  CAPE TOWN

● *Oxford University Press 1970*
*First published 1970*
*Second impression 1981*

ISBN  0 19 582513 6

*Printed in Malaysia by Sun U Book Co. Sdn. Bhd., Kuala Lumpur
Published by Oxford University Press, 3, Jalan 13/3,
Petaling Jaya, Selangor, Malaysia*

To

MY PARENTS

# PREFACE

CONSIDERABLE information on the Malay folk religion has been published. The subject seems to have fascinated Europeans almost from the beginning of the British involvement in Malaya. Reports by colonial administrators of interesting beliefs and rituals began to appear in print, especially in the *Journal* of the Straits Branch of the Royal Asiatic Society, during the second half of the last century. These reports, based on observations of many different groups at different times, were inevitably fragmentary and were seldom related to other beliefs and rituals of the same people. A number of studies since the end of the 19th century have improved the situation considerably. Some of these have brought information together, arranging it by topics or by historical origins and sequences, while others, based on more or less extended periods of fieldwork, have gone more deeply into the beliefs of particular groups. The present study is an attempt to tie the published information together in terms of the apparent patterns in the beliefs themselves. It is necessarily speculative and in some respects may be wrong, but I think the attempt is justified if it makes only a small step toward a fuller understanding of this complex and fascinating body of ideas.

My major source of information has been W. W. Skeat's *Malay Magic* (1900), an extensive exposition of Malay beliefs and magical practices, especially those in and around the state of Selangor shortly before the turn of the century. The book consists of much material collected by Skeat himself—most notably magical spells, which are very hard to obtain—and lengthy quotations from the work of previous authors. I have drawn heavily also on Annandale and Robinson's *Fasciculi Malayenses* (1903 and 1904), probably the most thorough and clear report of the beliefs and rites of a single group, namely, the peasants and fishermen of Patani in southern Thailand, and the voluminous works of R. O. Winstedt have been used extensively. Some of the information contained in Winstedt's books is drawn from earlier published works, but he gives it added interest by showing the various historical influences on the Malay beliefs and practices. The reports of Jeanne Cuisinier on the Malays of Kelantan (1936 and 1951) have also been very valuable. Their rich detail reflects intensive investigation on the spot. Wilkinson's *Malay-English Dictionary* (1900 and 1964) has been especially valuable in translation and in gaining understanding of difficult Malay concepts. The works of many other authors have been used to a lesser degree, and these are enumerated in the bibliography. I have also acquired useful ideas and information from conversations and correspondence with Geoffrey Benjamin, James Fox, and William Wilder, and I thank them very much for their help and interest.

This book was originally written as a thesis for the degree of Bachelor of Letters at Oxford, and only minor changes have been made in the present version. The basic approach of the study was inspired by Evans-Pritchard's *Witchcraft, Oracles, and Magic among the Azande* (1937), and by F. D. K. Bosch's *The Golden Germ* (1960). The particular method of interpretation used was influenced by Rodney Needham, who supervised the writing of the thesis, and by the works of Arnold van Gennep, Mary Douglas, Edmund Leach, Claude Lévi-Strauss, Victor Turner, Louis Dumont, and many more. The ideas and understanding gained from these sources are greatly appreciated.

I should like to thank all my teachers, especially Professor David French who guided me through my undergraduate work at Reed College and encouraged me to continue in anthropology, and Dr. Needham who supervised my work at Oxford. Dr. Needham's help went far beyond his formal obligations; he encouraged me and generously gave the extra time and work required to help me finish the thesis under very difficult conditions (including the necessity of returning to the United States in the middle of the preparation). For this I am extremely grateful.

I wish also to thank my wife Mette for keeping up my morale during the entire operation. Finally, my deepest thanks go to my parents, Charles and Margaret Endicott of Eugene, Oregon. They financed, in large part, my formal education, often at considerable personal sacrifice, but never attempted to tell me what my educational goals should be. Furthermore, they contributed immeasurably to my education in the deeper sense, encouraging me to learn and attempting to teach me to think clearly.

K. E.

# CONTENTS

# I

## INTRODUCTION

### I. AIM OF THE STUDY

THE aim of this study is to find some order in the body of magical beliefs and practices of the Malays of the Malay Peninsula. The main obstacle to this is the extreme complexity of the Malay folk religion, a complexity bordering on chaos. This probably derives basically from two conditions: the heterogeneity of the Malay population in the Peninsula and the large number of religious traditions that have influenced the area of western Indonesia.

Except for the peoples of Kedah and Patani, states located on ancient trade routes between China and the West, the bulk of the so-called Deutero-Malays in Malaya are relatively recent immigrants from various parts of Indonesia. Until the establishment of the important trading port of Malacca, this modern Malay racial type was probably represented in the rest of the Peninsula by only a few scattered coastal villages of pirate-fishermen and occasional colonies of gold and tin miners inland. These were apparently preceded by the Negritos, Senoi (or 'Sakai'), and the Jakun. The last are generally believed to be proto-Malays, an earlier wave of migration from the Malay homeland in Yunnan, though much work is needed before this can be accepted as fact. The recent (since 1400) influx of Deutero-Malays has originated in a number of geographically and culturally distinct regions. For example, the mixture of peoples in Selangor, Perak, and Negri Sembilan in the late 1800's included numbers of Menangkabu, Batak, Rawa, Korinchi, Mandailing, and Achehnese from Sumatra, Bugis from Celebes, and Javanese.[1] While sharing some common cultural heritage, significant differences are apparent, and these are recognized by the people.

My decision to make the field of study the Malays of the Malay Peninsula is obviously quite arbitrary, determined as much by

[1] Gullick 1958, p. 25.

practical considerations as by theoretical ones, and it is certainly not meant to imply that this accidental assemblage of peoples constitutes a homogeneous society or culture. I do assume, however, that, despite the cultural differences among the people to be examined, there is some order to be found at some level of analysis. The fact that the unit of study is a conglomerate of Malay peoples (speaking the Malay language) actually increases the possibility that the analysis will have application beyond the boundaries of the Malay Peninsula, to those related cultures in the surrounding islands from which most of the immigrants came.

An adequate account of the succession of religious influences on the modern Malay, the other main factor complicating the data, must necessarily treat the region as a whole rather than restrict itself to the Malay Peninsula. The islands of Sumatra and Java are most important in this connection, being the immediate source of most of the Malays presently in Malaya.[1] The earliest religion of the Deutero-Malays is known only through 'survivals'. Reconstruction of that religion is clearly conjecture; interpretations vary from writer to writer. Winstedt (1961b) compares modern Malay beliefs with those of the Khasi of Assam and the Moi of Indo-China, and assumes that the features common to two or all three were present in their early common forerunner. These features include beliefs in an all-pervading vital or effective force similar to *mana* (*sĕmangat* for the Malays), a personal soul which may persist after death as an ancestor-ghost or malicious demon, a vast assortment of nature spirits presided over by a Father Sky and Mother Earth, practices of sacrifice to supernatural beings, and shamanistic séances to further control them.[2] The historian Moorhead seems to attribute to the earliest Malay religion those features of modern belief that are not obviously taken from one of the more recent traditions. He asserts that the early Malays were animists, populating all of nature with spirits that were mostly malevolent; they believed in a 'soul energy' that lay behind practices of cannibalism and head-hunting, and they worshipped their ancestors and nature gods, especially the sun. They also regarded mountains as sacred, one of several indications of their basic similarity in belief to the

---

[1] Moorhead says that 'the Malays, properly so called, are immigrants from Sumatra and Java, though, of course, they also trace their descent from the populations who came originally from the north' (1957, p. 24).

[2] Winstedt 1961b, pp. 18–25.

pre-Aryan Indians.[1] It would be impossible to determine precisely the nature of the early Malay religion, and these statements provide a rough picture, adequate for present purposes, and a sense of the uncertainty of our knowledge. I think a truly accurate reconstruction would have to take into account the relatively recent influences of a 'primitive' sort coming from the aboriginal peoples in the places where the Malays settled.

The major Indian religions to affect the Malays were Brahmanism and Mahayana Buddhism, the branch of the faith that makes Gautama a god and retains a substantial proportion of Brahman belief.[2] Of somewhat lesser importance were Hinayana Buddhism, which rejects the ritual and beliefs of Brahmanism and the doctrine of Gautama's divinity, Sivaism which exalts Siva over Brahma, and Tantrism with its emphasis on magical power. Islam should also be considered as at least partially Indian in the form that reached the Malays. It was transmitted as much through Indian converts, especially traders from Gujerat, as through the Arabs.

The earliest spread of the Indian faiths into Sumatra and Java probably came via Indian missionaries and traders, and Malay traders who were converted while in India.[3] Inscriptions have been found in Kedah and Province Wellesley indicating the presence of Buddhism in northern Malaya as early as the fourth century A.D.[4] This may have been introduced by Indian traders who crossed the Peninsula in that area or by impulses from the Indianized states developing in mainland Southeast Asia. Funan, the legendary empire based in the Mekong Delta which was sometimes Buddhist and sometimes Brahmanist, appears to have controlled the fledgling states on the Malay Peninsula from about A.D. 225 to A.D. 540[5]. Meanwhile, Mahayana Buddhism took hold in southeastern Sumatra and parts of Java and Shaivite Brahmanism in other parts of Java. Some form of Brahmanism appeared in East Borneo about A.D. 400 and probably also in Bali.[6]

Once established, the influence of the various religions expanded and contracted according to the political fortunes of the royal houses that followed them. Control of the Malay Peninsula eventually passed from Funan to Sri Vijaya, a Mahayana Buddhist kingdom based in Palembang on the southeastern coast of Sumatra

---

[1] Moorhead 1957, pp. 26–27, 69.　　[2] ibid., pp. 29, 65.
[3] ibid., pp. 34–35.　　[4] ibid., p. 51.
[5] ibid., pp. 45, 52–53, 62.　　[6] ibid., pp. 51–52, 62.

(and later in Malayu just to the north). Its expansion began about
A.D. 680, and its power endured until the late thirteenth century
when its control over Malaya was taken by the Thai of Siam (a
Hinayana Buddhist people) and its position in the southern part of
the Straits of Malacca usurped by the East Javanese whose leader
was a Tantric Buddhist.[1] The latter occurrence marked the beginning of the rise of the Javanese 'Empire' of Majapahit which, by
conquest and diplomacy, was able to unite most of the states of
Sumatra, Java, Bali, and Malaya against Kublai Khan in China
and his allies the Thai.[2] By the end of the fourteenth century, the
kingdom and confederation of Majapahit had disintegrated, and
control over the Straits had shifted to the young port of Malacca
on the southwestern coast of the Malay Peninsula.[3] This had been
founded by a refugee nobleman from Sumatra and had prospered
because of its favourable location for trade and the decline of
Majapahit power in the Straits. In 1414, the ruler of Malacca was
converted to Islam by Arabs, who had become important in the
spice trade and had previously established themselves in the kingdoms of Pedir and Pasai in northeastern Sumatra.[4] The power of
Malacca gradually increased in the Peninsula at the expense of the
Thai, and eventually most of the Malays in Malaya became avowed
Muslims.

These, very briefly, are the ingredients of the Malay folk
religion and the order of their incorporation into the mixture. This
is obviously oversimplified but it also, in some respects, makes the
picture more complicated than it need be. For one thing, the
essential features of Mahayana Buddhism, Brahmanism, Sivaism,
and Tantrism are not vastly different; it is mainly the emphases
that distinguish them. Furthermore, many of the religious influences on the Malay states have been filtered through a single
place, namely Malacca. And, while the religions of the rulers have
changed or the rulers themselves been replaced a number of times,
the religion of the common people—which is the foundation of the
magic—has probably changed more slowly because of lack of
interest and imperfect education in the pure forms of the great
religions. All these factors would simplify the effects of the major
religions on Malay magic and moderate the impact of the quite
rapid changes from one to another.

[1] ibid., pp. 55, 94–95, 97.          [2] ibid., pp. 96–97, 105–114.
[3] ibid., pp. 114–115.                [4] ibid., p. 123.

Still, it would be impossible to predict from historical considerations alone the proportions of the various ingredients that make up the living folk religion of the modern Malays. No thoughtful student of the culture history of this area implies that the historical layers of belief composing the folk religion are complete religions or sets of beliefs accumulated haphazardly. The underlying assumption is that there are criteria of compatibility among beliefs that determine which new beliefs can be incorporated with the old and which must be modified or rejected. If this is a valid assumption, as I think it is, then it follows that there is some order in the body of Malay religious and, more narrowly, magical beliefs at any given time despite the diverse historical origins of the beliefs themselves. The order presumed to underlie, at some level, recent Malay magical beliefs and practices is what I seek to discover in this analysis.

## II. FORM OF THE ANALYSIS

I think it is useful to distinguish two kinds of order in a study of this sort. One is found at a low level of abstraction, in the content of a particular culture and very likely unique to it. It is formed of a people's specific beliefs and ideas and the specific relations among them. I call this the traditional order. The other is the order derived from an abstract analysis of the traditional order. It translates the specific categories and relations of the traditional order into formal and universal ones and seeks out their overall form. This more abstract order should illuminate the content of the particular culture from which it is extracted and should be capable of acting as a framework for comparison of that content with the content of other cultures. It should, in other words, be a structural model.

I do not mean to imply that the traditional order is any more 'real' than the structure; both are the product of inquiry and speculation. It is only by means of the assumption that order exists in the data that one can say that the traditional order is discovered rather than created. Many of the inferences one must make in seeking the traditional order can never be fully validated because they take place at a level of which the people themselves are unaware. If, for example, one accepts the proposition that only ritual specialists are qualified to expound fully the meanings of certain symbols, it is impossible to escape the conclusion that there is no one in the society capable of explaining the underlying assumptions on which those specialists base their interpretations. It is almost a matter of definition that a people's basic assumptions are ones of which they are unaware, things they take for granted, having never considered that alternatives were possible. Thus, it would be more accurate to say that traditional order will be treated *as if* it were in the content. The structural model, on the other hand, while obviously brought to the data by the analyst, is logical and carries with it any claims to objective reality that can be attached to logic because of its seemingly universal correspondence to the evidence of the senses. Such relations as identity, homology, analogy, inclusion, and complementary opposition have been found to apply to virtually all kinds of cultural ideas regardless of the use—myth, ritual, social groupings, etc.—to which the ideas are put. Thus, the two kinds of order differ in the points of view from which they are derived and in their level of abstraction, but not in the sense that one is real and the other imaginary.

It must be emphasized that structural analysis, as I use the expression, only makes sense in conjunction with and appended to a cultural analysis. Properly speaking, a structural analysis must include an analysis of the traditional order; it does not replace content but extracts from it an abstract order.[1] The notion of structure makes possible the translation of particular categories of culture into the universal categories of logic. Thus, it guides comparison by showing which items of two cultures are of the same type and therefore comparable and which are simply irrelevant to each other. It also furthers understanding of a particular culture by exposing the principles of organization behind the traditional order. Structure alone is meaningless and, consequently, is not the end of the analysis but the means by which valid comparison can be achieved and one kind of cultural understanding attained.

This analysis, then, will consist of two related operations, one based on the other. The bulk of the work will be an attempt to discern the specific patterns in Malay magical thought, to discover and describe the important concepts and the ways they are interconnected. The other phase of the analysis will be an attempt to put these patterns of concepts and relations into structural terms

[1] Cf. Nadel, who claims (1957, p. 155) that a structural analysis succeeds to the extent that it falls short of its aim, which is, he implies, to rid itself of content.

and to work out the implications of their logical characteristics. What comparison I shall make of the results of this analysis will not be thorough or even very systematic, as I have chosen to make an intensive analysis of Malay ideas rather than an extensive comparative survey. However, I shall put my conclusions in such form as should make possible valid comparison with the results of similar analyses made on other cultures. I shall not attempt to make any broad generalizations except in the form of very tentative suggestions.

### III. BASIC CONCEPTS

The meanings I attach to the terms 'structure' and 'traditional order' have been outlined above. It is necessary to explain my use of a few other terms, not so much to define them, because the terms themselves are not often used, but to make explicit certain basic assumptions and ideas that lie behind the analysis. In the interest of clarity I shall use, as far as possible, the most widely accepted and least controversial meanings for terms. In the following cases, where little consensus exists, I can only explain the way in which I use the expression and attempt to justify the definitions by showing the reasoning on which they are based. In these circumstances, my aim is to produce a set of definitions that is internally consistent and which clarifies the subject matter to which it refers. How well this is achieved must be judged, ultimately, by how well the definitions serve the analysis.

### Magic

The meaning I attach to the word 'magic' is not completely orthodox, as I use the term to designate a particular segment of Malay culture, not as an analytical term of wide applicability. By magic I mean, following Skeat (1900), the popular or folk religion of the Malays—as distinct from orthodox Islam. This especially concerns practices designed to affect the world (as the Malays see it) through non-physical means and includes the body of ideas behind the practices. I am interested in Islam only to the extent that it has become embedded in this generally held body of ideas. I appreciate the fact that this definition of magic is somewhat vague and makes no profound, universal distinctions, but using the term simply to delineate the field of study does not demand the rigorous definition required of an analytical tool.

*Meaning* (inherent, relational, symbolic)

The traditional order, as I see it, is made up of meaningful objects and connections, determined by their meanings, among those objects. I shall briefly explain my view of meaning in general and the way that cultures project it on to things. I shall then describe the three kinds of meaning—inherent, relational, and symbolic—that I find it useful to distinguish. There are many possible ways to divide meaning; the divisions I make are based on differences in the way the meaning is attached to its referent.

The meaning of something, in the summary acceptation I adopt here, is basically its effect on people, or, more accurately, its potential effect. These potential effects may be stored in the mind for varying lengths of time, and during this period may come into contact with other temporarily latent effects. The eventual effect on a person is a product of interaction among a lot of potential effects, some from the immediate environment and some from sources far removed in time and space. While the meaning of a tiger is immediately registered on a person if he is confronted with one, the effect of a lesson learned in childhood may continue throughout life or not become manifest until a much later date. Meaning, then, is in the mind, and it is manifested through its effect on a person's attitudes and actions.

However, meanings are frequently cultural, shared among a group of people. Things usually affect people in the ways that they are taught to be affected. In our society, for example, girls are expected to be afraid of mice while boys are not, and this is usually the case though there are no sex-linked physiological reasons for it. When the potential effect of something is standardized in this way, it is convenient for people to treat it as if it were in the object itself. This is actually done, as we well know. Even as a child is being taught the concept that defines a thing, he is also taught what his proper reaction to it is, how it should affect him—in a word, its meaning. The classifications that cultures impose on the world create the objects and discrete actions in it and, at the same time, regularize the meanings of them in the minds of the people. In this way cultural meaning can be said to be attached to things, specifically to the shared concepts of things, and reference need not be made to the reactions of individuals.

## (a) INHERENT MEANING

Inherent meaning is the meaning seen as constituting the essential defining properties of a thing. These properties set it off as a discrete entity, a member of a class of such entities, and serve to identify it from one situation to the next. In other words, the inherent meaning of a thing is distinctive and enduring. I must emphasize that the meaning is attached to the concept of the thing, not directly to the referent of the concept. Concepts are distinctive and enduring though their referents may not be. Thus 'lightning' and 'running' have inherent meanings just as do 'rock' and 'tree'. 'Real' and 'imaginary' things need not be distinguished either in the matter of inherent meaning. As concepts these all have the same status, the same formal properties, and they must have some inherent meaning or they would merge into other concepts or disappear between situations.

It might be objected that it is persistent qualities, not necessarily meanings, that give a thing its continuing identity. This would be partially true. However, qualities are only really 'things' when considered in themselves, as when classifications of qualities are being examined. When seen as attributes of other things, the inherent meaning of the quality becomes part of the inherent meaning of that thing. Even so, the total inherent meaning of something is more than the sum of the meanings of its qualities; they help to identify it, but in so doing they help activate its own unique identity and the meanings implied in that.

## (b) RELATIONAL MEANING

Relational meaning is the meaning a thing acquires from other things by virtue of their conjunction in a system of relationships, either a concrete system—an integrated situation, or an abstract one—a classification. The interaction of meanings confers an added layer of meaning on the component parts of the system. Relational meaning, in other words, is picked up by a thing from its environment, and it varies, therefore, unlike inherent meaning, from one situation or classification to the next.

A new level of meaning is also created in that the network of relations may be seen as having, by virtue of its power to confer meaning on things, an independent existence and meaning of its own, meaning which can be imposed on things to adjust their total meaning in order to uphold the consistency of the system. Insofar as inherent meaning and the needs of systems are incompatible, some balance of priority between them must be established. This seems to vary in general with different cultures as well as in particular with different things. Our society emphasizes inherent meaning, essences, in the face of almost all changes with context. For example, if my car is painted red, I shall probably consider it red even at night when, scientifically speaking, it is black, the absence of colour. Some painters (for example, impressionists) try consciously to overcome this bias against seeing what is there, against recognizing the differences light conditions and juxta-position of colours make on the values of the colours themselves.[1] Most Oriental and non-literate peoples are habitually more aware of such variations; their cultures emphasize the integrity of the situation even at the expense of consistency of inherent meaning in things appearing in different contexts. Sometimes the attributes of a thing appear flatly contradictory as, for example, with Aiyanar, a Hindu god. Dumont (1959) demonstrates that the contradictory meanings in this case are due to the god's participation in two types of ritual situation and two systems of concepts—the high gods and the impure demons. Another effect of emphasizing the system over the content is that more substitution of particular components of systems can take place, since the meanings of the alternative components can be adjusted to fit. For example, the Malays will substitute a chicken for a goat or an egg for the chicken in a sacrifice, whereas such substitution in the materials of the Catholic communion would probably be resisted. The substi-tutions mentioned for the Malay sacrifice would hardly change the meaning of the rite as a system, in the matter of relational meaning, though it would, as I shall explain, change some symbolic mean-ings.

## (c) SYMBOLIC MEANING

Symbolic meaning, as I shall employ the notion here, is the meaning of a thing acquired from another thing by virtue of an analogy between them, their having similar positions in different classifications or systems of concepts. The members of such a relationship can be said to 'stand for' each other, not as simple

---

[1] Cf. Whitehead 1927, p. 3.

alternatives, but as representatives of each other in different classifications. Usually these different classifications operate in different concrete situations, so symbolic associations cut across both. Sometimes, however, things symbolically associated are brought together, as in ritual; the result is the condensation of the meanings of several classifications into layers in a single situation following an orderly set of correspondences defined by analogy. The symbols do not merge into each other or the result would be a monstrous redundancy; rather they supplement each other and charge the ritual with a level of meaning beyond that normally reached by the combined inherent and relational meanings of a situation.

Symbolic meaning is built upon inherent and relational meaning. A classification is a system of abstractions; the connections among categories confer relational meaning on their content. The patterns of relations determine whether two classifications are comparable and may, if there is some formal asymmetry, indicate what particular categories will align with each other. The position of particular things in classifications is usually determined by their inherent meanings, and inherent meanings of content may also come in to align the categories of similar classifications when there is no necessary formal correspondence among them. For example, if a group saw 'sun and moon' and 'man and woman' as forming two dual classifications, and if they brought the two classifications into symbolic association, the particular alignment of categories would probably be determined by the inherent meanings of their content. The alignment would depend, in other words, on which, between the sun and moon, was considered more masculine and which more feminine. If the inherent meaning of sun and moon were to change, the symbolic associations could switch without disrupting the formal correspondence of the two classifications. Thus symbolic meaning is built upon relational and inherent meaning, but the synthesis is a new dimension, adding further meaning to things and to situations in which several classifications of things are brought together.

I would divide meaning, then, according to the different modes of attachment of meaning to object. Inherent meaning is seen as the essential defining properties of a thing, relational meaning is added via relations in a classification of things, and symbolic meaning is acquired by analogy and similarity from things in other classifications. I have chosen this division of meaning because it makes the kinds and degrees of distinction that are useful for the present analysis; whatever wider value it might have is left open for further investigation.

# II

## OUTLINE OF MALAY MAGIC

THE Malay word for magic is *ilmu* which also means 'knowledge' or 'science'.[1] This chapter concerns the ways in which this knowledge is acquired and made effective and the general areas of life in which it is applied.

### 1. THE MAGICIAN

The Malays have two words for men who practice magic as a profession: *pawang* and *bomor*. Usually the words are treated as interchangeable, though one may be more favoured in a particular region. Sometimes, however, the distinction signals a division between the curer—called the *bomor*—and other practitioners of the magical arts.[2] This is only one of a number of functional divisions of the profession which are not always marked by different terms of reference but which are nevertheless clearly recognized by the people concerned.

Malay magicians are specialists; the body of knowledge necessary for the professional is extensive, and most magicians concentrate their efforts and learning in one area, such as fishing magic, rice agriculture magic, or divination. Similarly, the magic of conducting babies into the world is such a specialty, and there is every reason to regard the midwife as a minor, part-time, magician.

Other kinds of distinction within the profession are made. In Perak and Kelantan the ordinary magician (*pawang*) is distinguished from the *bĕlian*, the shaman. The shaman is distinguished by his method of operation; he carries out his work, which includes curing epidemics and extreme individual illnesses, divination, and

---

[1] The term *ilmu* is Arabic. *Ilmu jahat* is the black art; *ilmu pasti* is mathematics; *ilmu perbintangan* is astrology; *ilmu 'l hayah* is astronomy; *ilmu batin* is esoteric learning generally, mysticism; *ilmu kejadian* is physics (Wilkinson 1964, p. 98).

[2] Hugh Clifford, quoted in Skeat 1900, p. 56 n.

general spirit propitiation,[1] by means of spirit-raising séances called *běrhantu* or *běrjin*. By contrast, the ordinary magician must rely on recitation of spells and performance of ritual actions using special materials. Another distinction sometimes made is between hereditary magicians (*bomor pesaka*) and initiated ones (*bomor belajar*). In some unusual cases a person will be considered a *bomor pesaka* even though no magician ancestors are known. This happens when someone experiences an unsolicited revelation from the supernatural, a certain sign of magical heritage.[2] Hereditary magicians consider themselves superior to initiated ones; they are more respected, and their magic is thought to be more effective. Similarly, the magic of shamans is considered superior to that of the ordinary practitioner, and the distinction between those two categories often corresponds to that between hereditary and initiated magicians.[3]

### Acquisition of Magic

I find it impossible to construct, from the material in the literature alone, a clear and complete description of the process by which one becomes a magician. Most sources touch only lightly on the subject, and I find the most detailed of them, Cuisinier's *Danses magiques de Kelantan*, quite difficult to follow and understand. Consequently, I am forced to depart somewhat from the printed sources, and this, of course, involves some speculation. I try to stay close to the form of the Malay ideas but cannot know for certain how far this is accomplished.

To become a magician one must somehow acquire *ilmu*—magical knowledge. The most obvious way this can be done is through formal training. A person may attach himself as a student or disciple to an established magician, and by going through a ceremony of initiation he obtains the right to use the *ilmu* of his master and the line of magicians through which it has passed.[4] The ceremony features prominently a payment by the initiate to the original *guru*[5] in the line of transmission (this is actually

---

[1] Cuisinier 1936, p. 39; Winstedt 1961a, p. 7; 1961b, p. 23.
[2] Cuisinier 1936, pp. 3, 6.      [3] Winstedt 1961a, p. 7.
[4] Cuisinier 1936, p. 12.
[5] The term *guru* is from Sanscrit. In Malay it means basically 'a teacher' (Wilkinson 1964, p. 88), though Cuisinier claims that it also means 'ancestor' (1936, pp. 7, 67).

received by the living magician, of course).[1] The initiate is brought into a particular magical tradition and is sworn to secrecy regarding its contents.[2] A prospective magician may study with more than one master, but this is unusual. The son or grandson of a magician may study under his own relative, although he usually prefers to be taught by someone else, perhaps even someone from outside the area.[3] Apparently initiation is not always required for a descendant of magicians; Cuisinier implies that there are only some cases in which custom demands it.[4] If this is so, it would probably be required when the training is acquired outside the family. Cuisinier says that initiation creates artificially a right to use *ilmu* analogous to the right transmitted naturally by heredity.[5]

Another way to obtain *ilmu* is through *tuntut*, seeking after it by practices such as praying, fasting, and reciting the Koran until a revelation comes in a dream or spell of temporary madness.[6] Cuisinier calls *tuntut* 'à la fois tendre à la connaisance [presumably *ilmu*] et y parvenir'.[7] Skeat describes a procedure for obtaining magical powers which entails sitting on the grave of a murdered man,[8] paddling with a palm leaf midrib as if paddling a canoe, and requesting the dead man to assist in a journey to 'the saints of God, And I desire to ask for a little magic' ('*elmu sadikit*).[9] 'In a little while the surrounding scenery will change and take upon itself the appearance of the sea, and finally an aged man will appear, to whom you must address the same request [for *ilmu*] as before.'[10] Winstedt reports that the aspiring magician may 'sit fasting and shrouded to hear the prayers for the dead read over him and he would repeat the name of Allah 5,000 times until hysteria brought nightmare visions of tiger or serpent to be succeeded by visions of angels and saints instructing him in mystic knowledge'.[11]

[1] Cuisinier 1936, p. 7.  [2] ibid., p. 14.  [3] ibid., pp. 6–7.
[4] ibid., p. 12.  [5] ibid., p. 7.
[6] Cuisinier 1936, pp. 3, 27; Winstedt 1961a, p. 73; 1961b, p. 37.
[7] Cuisinier 1936, p. 27.
[8] Possibly this is a Tantric echo (Cf. Pott 1966, p. 77).
[9] Skeat 1900, pp. 60–61, 61 n.
[10] Skeat 1900, p. 61. Among the Sakai tribes of the Perak-Pahang border, 'a dead shaman is never buried; he is placed in a raised hut or otherwise held up above the ground so that the tiger, his familiar, may tear open his body and release the soul. His son and successor should be present at this time to receive from the tiger himself or from the two attendant fairies full instruction in the dead man's magic' (Wilkinson 1932, p. 127).
[11] Winstedt 1961a, p. 73.

Any magician must obtain *ilmu*; shamans must also acquire a spirit helper (often called a familiar). It seems that a spirit helper can only be inherited, usually patrilineally ('en règle générale l'exercice de la magie se continue de père en fils'),[1] though it seems possible for it to pass from either parent to a child of either sex.[2] Blagden says 'the *Pawang* keeps a familiar spirit, which in his case is a *hantu pŭsaka*, that is, an hereditary spirit which runs in the family, in virtue of which he is able to deal summarily with the wild spirits of an obnoxious character'.[3] One may become aware of the inheritance and establish communication with the spirit helper through *tuntut*. Winstedt states that 'a Malay shaman gets possession of a familiar spirit by inheritance from another shaman, becoming sensible of the gift in a dream or in a trance beside a grave'.[4] Formerly a prospective shaman 'kept vigil beside an open grave or waited in the dark forest for the coming of a tiger familiar'.[5] Cuisinier relates the case of a man who, in a seizure of madness, was lost in the jungle for over two years. Afterwards he recalled having stayed in a hidden village where tigers walked about in the form of men, and this experience led him to become a *bomor bĕlian* as several of his ancestors had been.[6] The tiger-village in the jungle contains the *hantu bĕlian* that 'possess' shamans to aid them in their work.[7] It seems that the man mentioned became aware of a tiger spirit helper in his madness; significantly, he said he had seen the tiger village again often in his dreams.[8]

It seems likely that the being who conveys *ilmu* through *tuntut* and the spirit helper are different aspects of the same creature. They are both contacted by the same means and reveal themselves in the same way, sometimes even in the same mystical revelation. Cuisinier says the revelation is obtained through a dream, or sometimes the recluse simply feels that a spirit is entering him, protecting or dominating him; he thus realizes that 'le pouvoir de cet esprit lui est dévolu et se sent autorisé à se dire son délégué et à agir comme tel'.[9] The spirit combines the functions of helping (protecting, giving power to) the magician and of giving him *ilmu* and the right to use it. Cuisinier emphasizes the fact that the

---

[1] Cuisinier 1936, p. 6.
[2] See Zainul-Abidin bin Ahmad 1922b, p. 384.
[3] Quoted in Skeat 1900, p. 59.          [4] Winstedt 1961b, p. 23.
[5] Winstedt 1961a, p. 73.          [6] Cuisinier 1936, pp. 5–6.
[7] Rentse 1933a, p. 248; Skeat 1901, pp. 26–27.
[8] Cuisinier 1936, p. 5.          [9] ibid., p. 3.

magician is the 'délégué' of a magical tradition, that the *ilmu* is only entrusted to his safekeeping.[1] It is likely, furthermore, that the 'dream *guru*-spirit helper' is the ghost of one of a person's magician ancestors. Winstedt says that the tiger (spirit helper) 'is in fact a dead ancestral shaman who becomes his successor's guide and helps him now in the trance when he is possessed by spirits'.[2] Gimlette claims that the office of *bomor* is 'only inherited if the soul of a dead *bomor*, in the form of a tiger, passes into the body of his son'.[3] Cuisinier mentions a belief that the soul of a *bomor bĕlian* is reincarnated in the body of a tiger after death.[4] I show in a later chapter that the part of the 'soul' remaining on earth after death becomes a ghost, which is simply one kind of spirit (*hantu*). I would interpret the belief cited by Cuisinier as meaning that the form taken by the ghost of a shaman is that of the tiger spirit, *hantu bĕlian*. Wilkinson says that the term 'blian' is an old Indonesian word for 'shaman'[5]; *hantu bĕlian* might mean 'the shaman's spirit', but it might just as well mean 'the shaman spirit'—or both at once. If the *guru* or spirit helper that reveals itself in *tuntut* is in fact a shaman ancestor, it is easier to understand why the ability to succeed in *tuntut* is regarded as a certain sign of magical heritage. It must be that ancestral shamans contact only their descendants, and the only beings who initiate such revelation are ancestral shamans.

The Malays consider three things in evaluating magicians: *tuntut*, *pesaka* (the fact of hereditary transmission) and *baka* (that which is inherited).[6] The hereditary factors seem to weigh more heavily than *tuntut* as such, though, if it is spontaneous, *tuntut* has the value of indicating heredity. Most respect and confidence is granted to the hereditary magician who has had a revelation, next to the hereditary *bomor* who has not had one, then to the non-hereditary *bomor* who has had a revelation following an attack of madness (presumably not spontaneous *tuntut* since that would place him in the first rank), and only then to the *bomor* by instruction (alone).[7] Revelation can skip one or several generations of hereditary magicians, and, if this is the case, the person skipped can combine his heredity with instruction.[8] The slight deficiency

[1] ibid., pp. 6, 12.  [2] Winstedt 1961a, p. 13.
[3] Gimlette 1929, p. 21.  [4] Cuisinier 1936, pp. 39–40.
[5] Wilkinson 1932, p. 128.
[6] See Cuisinier 1936, p. 27; Wilkinson 1964, pp. 17, 209.
[7] Cuisinier 1936, pp. 12–13.  [8] ibid., p. 6.

in prestige for such a person is probably due to a belief that *ilmu* transmitted directly from the ancestors is more valuable (perhaps more 'pure') than that obtained through fallible human transmission. The Malays emphasize *pesaka* even over *baka*,[1] probably because the content of *baka* is variable, but the meaning of *pesaka* is clear. The existence of heredity (*pesaka*) from magicians means that one has inherited a spirit helper and guardian, that he is a shaman, while the inheritance (*baka*) may or may not include *ilmu*. The initiated magicians who seek revelation probably do so not so much to get *ilmu*, but to establish that they have what cannot be transmitted by their teachers, namely, a spirit helper. Their claims to success are usually not believed by the public and especially not by magicians of manifest magical heritage.[2]

It is possible now to summarize. *Ilmu* can be acquired through two kinds of transmission: learning from unrelated magicians and learning from relatives, either living or dead. In the former case a right to use *ilmu* must be established by ceremony; in the latter it is inherited. The lines of transmission of *ilmu* will sometimes coincide with the patrilines of magicians, but this is by no means necessary. A magician who has inherited *ilmu* may transmit it only to initiates, and a hereditary magician may get all his *ilmu* from unrelated magicians. Rights to magic due to heredity may be activated or left residual, and rights by initiation may be established arbitrarily. It is best to view *ilmu* as a tradition handed down through a series of magicians who may or may not be linked by heredity; one's magical antecedents may be his ancestors, but they probably are not. The invocation of ancient magicians at the beginning of a séance is not ancestor worship. Cuisinier mentions a case of a *bomor bĕlian* who did not include his own father in his invocation; he said his father was a *pengantin* (questioner), not a *bĕlian* and that they were two separate groups, the *bĕlian* having their origin in Mecca and the *pengantin* in Medina.[3]

What is inherited are spirit helpers, the possession of which makes one a shaman. Spirit helpers are probably the ghosts of ancestral magicians;[4] it is not possible to control the transmission

---

[1] ibid., p. 27.        [2] ibid., p. 13.
[3] Cuisinier 1936, pp. 56 and n.
[4] In a case recorded from Negri Sembilan, a woman inherited her spirit helper as well as the art of medicine from her husband who had died many years before. 'Many people believed that the husband turned into a tiger after his death . . . and that the tiger-*akuan* was no other than himself' (Zainul-

of them, but one can increase the significance of it by seeking to make contact with the spirit to get *ilmu* and supernatural guidance. In any case, a magician by heredity can count on the assistance of a spirit helper in his work, which increases the efficacy of his *ilmu* whatever its source.

## Problem of Secrecy

I have implied throughout the discussion that *ilmu* is effective in itself, though of course possession of a spirit helper greatly expands the number of ways in which it can be used and increases the chances of success. Cuisinier claims, however, that *ilmu* is without power (*kuasa*) unless it is kept secret and the person using it is initiated (presumably if he does not have a hereditary right to it).[1] The Malays, she says, consider secrecy an external but nevertheless necessary condition for success.[2] She explains how spells are protected by such techniques as mumbling, silent recitation, chanting, distortion, and the use of foreign languages and private symbolisms.[3] And the initiation of a magician features a swearing to secrecy of the initiate as a condition for being given the right to use the *ilmu* of a particular tradition,[4] just as the hereditary magician is required to guard the *ilmu* of his line jealously.[5]

I certainly would not deny that magicians try to maintain secrecy surrounding their *ilmu*, but I do not think it is a necessary condition for magic. Much of what must be regarded as magic is public knowledge because it is of continuing concern to nearly everyone. Few people are ignorant of the methods for protecting one's house from vampires, the prohibitions on expectant mothers and their husbands, and the way to combat the yellow sunset glow. Being widely known does not seem to diminish the potency of these procedures. The reason secrecy is maintained is probably much more mundane than Cuisinier imagined, namely, professional jealousy. It is the business of magicians to know what other people do not know, and sharing the knowledge would diminish their importance and the demand for their services. Cuisinier

---

Abidin bin Ahmad 1922b, p. 381). Perhaps inheritance of a spirit helper through affinal as well as descent relationship is a possibility in all places, but the principle of descent in Negri Sembilan is matrilineal, and this may be a special adaptation.

[1] Cuisinier 1936, pp. 3, 12, 14.          [2] ibid., p. 28.
[3] ibid., p. 15.          [4] ibid., p. 14.          [5] ibid., p. 6.

mentions that powerful rivalries among magicians exist.[1] Rather than secrecy being a necessary condition for the efficacy of one's magic, I suggest that it is precisely because *ilmu* is believed to work for anyone that it is jealously guarded. And if, as Cuisinier claims,[2] formal initiation were needed to make *ilmu* effective, there would be no need for secrecy at all.

## II. PRACTICE OF MAGIC

The ordinary *bomor belajar* can perform most of the everyday magic needed in Malay villages. There is generally 'no need for a shaman in order to deal with the rice-baby, or teach the appropriate spell for catching a crocodile or the tabus to be observed by collectors of camphor and honey'[3]. The ordinary magician knows spells to propitiate or intimidate the spirits and to gain control of errant souls. He knows the equipment and medicines that are needed for the various ceremonies he conducts. He knows what offerings the spirits demand and the way they would have them prepared. He knows what actions he must perform and what he must have the other participants and the spectators do. His method is straightforward and direct. He speaks to the supernatural forces, performs for them, and gives them things. In return he expects straightforward results. By virtue of his *ilmu* and his magical equipment he expects to be able to deal with the supernatural, to confront it, and even to control it.

The procedure of the shaman is more complex, as befits the more critical nature of his work. There are different types of shaman's séance, but the basic outlines are the same. The participants must include a dancer or performer, usually the shaman, a questioner, and at least one musician to beat a drum, the questioner sometimes doubling in this rôle. With the aid of aromatic plants, incense, sometimes opium, the pounding drum, and chanted songs, the dancer is driven to a state of *lupa*, forgetfulness, during which he becomes a medium for a spirit. The questioner addresses the spirit through the shaman who either reports for the spirit or becomes his organ of speech. Ordinary spirits[4] can be summoned

---

[1] ibid., p. 13.      [2] ibid., p. 12.      [3] Winstedt 1961a, p. 8.

[4] The exact relationship between the shaman and the spirits called in is not clear. Zainul-Abidin bin Ahmad refers to them as being 'owned', just as the spirit helper is, and calls both types of spirit *akuan* or 'spirit friends' (1922b,

to forecast events or diagnose an illness and prescribe a cure. The shaman's special spirit helper, usually the tiger spirit, can be called up to help combat spirits of disease or misfortune. The ceremony is ended with the return of the dancer to his normal condition, and rites are performed to break off connections of all concerned with the spirits.

There is some disagreement among writers, and apparently among the Malays as well, as to whether or not the spirits called up actually 'possess' the performer. The Malays say that the dancer 'changes his body' (*tukar badan*),[1] and the climax of many séances comes with the shaman growling, leaping about and even licking the patient's body in response to some intimate connection with his tiger spirit helper.[2] Yet Cuisinier says that the spirit only directs the unconscious body of the shaman, sitting on his shoulders.[3] Most of her informants said that the spirit's entering the dancer's body would cause him serious illness.[4] One would assume that the information of Cuisinier, who has gone deeply into this matter, is accurate; it is accepted as being so by Winstedt.[5]

The full relationship between the shaman and the tiger is not clear. The usual spirit helper of the shaman, as I have mentioned, is the tiger spirit, *hantu bĕlian*. As suggested above, this is probably the form taken by the ghosts of shamans. I mentioned also the belief that the souls of *bomor bĕlian* are reincarnated in tigers' bodies and suggested that this may mean that their ghosts are *hantu bĕlian*. It seems likely also that the creatures inhabiting the tiger village in the jungle are *hantu bĕlian*, ghosts of former magicians who may be contacted through *tuntut*. This all fits fairly well with what has been presented so far; what follows does not. Some of Cuisinier's informants said that the chief dancer must have the power, during life, to become a tiger;[6] he must, in other words, be a were-tiger. And the tiger form of the *bomor bĕlian* (called *halak* in Kelantan; *hala* is the Senoi and Semang word for sorcerer) leaves a mark of five claws instead of four,[7] a characteristic strikingly reminiscent of a common distinguishing feature of

p. 378). However, the shaman's relationship with his 'familiar' seems more intimate, personal, and enduring than that with the *pĕnggawa* or 'control spirits' (see Gimlette 1929, p. 87) that are occasionally called in for consultation.

[1] Cuisinier 1936, p. 35.    [2] See e.g. Skeat 1900, pp. 442–443.
[3] Cuisinier 1936, pp. 35–36.    [4] ibid., p. 36.
[5] Winstedt 1961a, p. 59.
[6] Cuisinier 1936, pp. 39–40.    [7] ibid., pp. 40–41

'sacred' tigers (*rimau kramat*), having one foot smaller than the rest.[1] Furthermore, some people think that a real tiger prowls around when a *bomor bĕlian* is performing a séance, but others say it is a were-tiger.[2] My own interpretation is that it is neither; rather it is the *hantu bĕlian* of the *bomor* which, like all spirits, can make itself visible. I also think that the were-tiger and the *bomor bĕlian* are quite distinct concepts in Malay thought and that the combining of them is due to Negrito or Senoi influence, much of which is in evidence in the shaman's séances of Kelantan.[3] Negrito shamans are believed to be were-tigers.[4] I think that bringing the two ideas together in the Malay context is not to be taken as literal fact, but as having a symbolic significance; it indicates the similarity between the metamorphosis of the were-tiger and the metamorphosis involved in 'changing the body' to become a medium for a spirit. It seems that the Malays do not take this literally. Cuisinier says the obligation for the *bomor bĕlian* to have the power to become a tiger is not a very strict one, if indeed it is even taken into account.[5] The tiger appears in a number of classifications, and it is not too surprising that a number of other tiger-beings are dragged into what is essentially, I suggest, the realm of the spirit tiger, the ghost of shamans. Why the association between shamans and tigers should exist at all is a difficult question. Part of the answer may be that the two creatures hold similar positions in their respective societies, one being the most powerful (or dangerous) of men and the other the same for the jungle beasts.

The power of the shaman among men recalls another fact that should be mentioned, the often noted similarity between the shaman and the king in Malaya. Specific similarities are numerous: 'both hold offices that ideally are hereditary and in any event require some form of consecration; both are masters of an archetypal world; both have insignia baleful to the profane; both have been credited with the possession of familiars and with supernatural ability to injure and to heal and to control the weather; both have been honoured by tree-burial'.[6] The sultan may actually act as a shaman, for example, in important ceremonies when it is necessary to call up the genies of the state.[7] Winstedt

---

[1] See Skeat 1900, pp. 70–71.          [2] Cuisinier 1936, p. 41.
[3] See e.g. ibid., p. 38.          [4] Skeat and Blagden 1906, pp. 227–229.
[5] Cuisinier 1936, p. 43.
[6] Winstedt 1961a, p. 9; see also Skeat 1900, pp. 23–42.
[7] See Skeat 1900, p. 446.

even goes so far as to suggest that the political leader (chief) and the shaman were probably one until the Malays came under the influence of the Hindus[1]. There may very well be a genetic relationship between the two rôles; it is quite certain that their analogous positions—one being supreme in relations with the supernatural and the other in relations among men—reinforce the similarities between them.

The two basic kinds of Malay magician—hereditary shaman and initiated practitioner—differ, then, in their power, their presumed effectiveness in performing magic. The symbolic associations of the shaman express his superior power. It is quite clear, however, that both types of magician operate within the same system of magic. Their differences are ones of degree; the shaman has stronger influence over the supernatural by virtue mainly of having an accomplice there, a spirit which can protect him, help him deal with other spirits, and convey to him the most effective *ilmu*.

### III. AREAS OF LIFE IN WHICH MAGIC IS APPLIED

Malay magic has many forms due, in part, to the many areas of life in which it is applied. A brief survey of those areas will provide valuable background.

#### Economics

Probably the most common means of gaining a living among the Malays is rice agriculture. Magical practices are interwoven with all the practical processes in the agricultural cycle. Divination is used to find the propitious time to begin each activity and the best place to clear if a new field is to be developed. A ceremony for driving the evil spirits from the fields is performed before planting. Then, for irrigation farming, a nursery plot is prepared, the seed is planted and a ceremony performed entrusting it to the care of the spirits of the soil. After 44 days the sprouts are removed to the main fields where they are planted, in most regions with further ritual. When the crop is ready for harvest, the spirit pests are magically driven out, and selected ears of rice are taken with elaborate ceremony, usually by the village midwife, and borne back to the home of the field's owners, exactly as if they were a new-born baby. This is the rice-soul that will form the nucleus of

---

[1] Winstedt 1961a, p. 9.

the seed-rice for the next year. After several days the harvest begins in earnest, and, when the grain is in, a general feast is held. Similar ceremonies are used with dry-rice farming, which is not so common with the Malays. Less elaborate magical complexes surround the cultivation of other traditional crops such as sugar cane, bananas (plantains), and coconuts.

Fishing is the livelihood of many coastal Malays, and much magic is used to make the work safe and fruitful. Some *pawang* specialize in fishing magic: knowing when and where to go, locating the fish once in the proper area, and enforcing the taboos the fishermen must observe. Magic is also used to control the weather, especially the wind which is important to all navigators whatever their occupation. A good deal of fishing is done with traps that are set out or built with appropriate ceremony and which are the scene of repeated offerings to the spirits controlling the fish.

Tin mining and, especially in ancient times, gold mining have been important industries for the Malays. Malay tin mines are usually open pits used for extraction of alluvial gravels. The gravel is washed and the tin ore trapped in sluice boxes. Magic is used when a mine is constructed to get rid of harmful spirits and to propitiate the ones that persist. During a mine's operation, a mining *pawang* will periodically perform rites to attract tin ore, which is believed to wander around underground, or to detain it if it appears to be leaving the mine.

Hunting is of minor economic importance for the Malays, but there exists an elaborate body of magical techniques to ensure success. Rites exist for attracting one's prey, making the equipment used (traps, snares, etc.) effective, and for combating the dangerous influences (*badi*) in the carcases of the animals killed.

The gathering of valuable jungle resources is also accompanied by magic and ritual prohibitions. Certain magicians specialize in finding such things as eagle-wood, gutta-percha, and camphor; they also know how to propitiate the spirits that guard these products, and they enforce the use of special vocabularies by members of the gathering expeditions.

### Building

Just as magic is required when a field or mine is cleared, it is employed to prepare the way for the building of a house or similar structure. Divination is used to select the best site and the propitious time to begin the process, rites are performed to clear out noxious spirits, and offerings are made to the ones that remain.

## Human Life Cycle

Even before birth, one is affected by magic. During pregnancy, both the future mother and her husband observe prohibitions designed to save the child from mishap or deformity. Ritual is performed to ensure a smooth delivery. During birth, extensive precautions are taken to ward off birth demons that would attack mother and child. Rites are performed over the newly born child to protect it and ensure it a good future. On the seventh day it is formally named and the head shaved (except for one lock for boys); a goat is sacrificed for a girl and two goats for a boy. The mother is isolated for 44 days at the end of which the baby is ceremonially introduced to 'Mother Earth and Father Water'. It is symbolically given power over domestic animals, food plants, the products of the forest, and the creatures of the water to prepare it for a successful life.

Certain rites of passage occur during childhood and adolescence. Boys are circumcised at a propitious time between the ages of six and twenty; magical precautions are taken and the boy's future divined. Both sexes formerly had their teeth filed down and blackened at puberty, and girls' ears are bored at puberty or in early childhood. Rites accompanying these ceremonies protect the child from evil spirits and protect all concerned from the dangerous influences unleashed by the operations.

The Malay marriage rites are taken largely from Hinduism. The central features are an exchange of food between bride and groom, their walking around an inverted rice-mortar (possibly a symbol of Mount Meru), and the sitting in state of the bride and groom as if they were royalty. This essentially Hindu core is embroidered, however, with many typically Malay rites of protection and pro-pitiation of the spirits.

The Malays have adopted the Muslim funeral customs with little alteration. The corpse is ritually washed and is buried with the head to the north, on the right side, facing Mecca. Feasts and prayers are conducted by the grave three, seven, fourteen, forty, and one hundred days after the burial, and a final ceremony takes place after a year. A few traces of pre-Muslim ideas remain in the details of the rites and in extra precautions taken, for example, to avoid leading the ghost back to his former home.

## Curing

Malay 'medicine' is almost entirely magical; even when procedures of real medical value are used, the reasons given are magical. The term *ubat* applies equally to remedies that work by magic and those working by chemistry. It means 'a drug, a medicine, a chemical, a magic simple, a philtre'.[1] Diagnosis is divination, the causes of disease are supernatural forces, and their cures are the magical methods by which those forces can be controlled. Any of a large number of magical practices can be used for treatment of disease, depending on the cause of the affliction—invasion of a spirit (wild, or a sorcerer's familiar), loss of part of one's soul, decrease in the soul's vitality, etc. The especially serious nature of disease undoubtedly lies behind the fact that curing is the major concern of the shaman.

## Entertainments

To a large extent Malay entertainments are competitive (gambling, cock fighting, buffalo fighting, etc.), and magic is often used to improve one's chances against opponents. Some of what must be called entertainments are the magical rites and feasts themselves, rites whose primary purpose is something other than amusement. The shaman's séance is especially popular and bears an interesting resemblance to the most elaborate of Malay entertainments, the shadow play. Malay shadow plays closely copy the Hindu ones developed in Java; they include rites to protect the human troupe and invocations to spirits to descend and possess the shadow-puppets.

## Forecasting Events

Most formal methods of divination used in Malaya are borrowed complete from Indian, Chinese, and Arabic sources. Only a few experts understand and follow the dictates of astrology, magic squares, and tables of propitious times, but most magicians

[1] Wilkinson 1964, p. 300.

know how to read signs from the spirit world, and many laymen are familiar with simple omens.

## Personal Life

A minor species of magic, performed mainly by amateurs, involves ways of improving one's person as a means to desired ends. This consists of spells, charms, and rituals intended, most commonly, to make oneself invulnerable or more desirable to the opposite sex.

## Interpersonal Relations

The Malays have an extensive body of love magic, a reflection of one of their major interests. Most of the techniques aim to gain control of a person's will by operating on his soul, so he will be inescapably attracted to the executor of the magic. Rites similar in form are used to harm one's enemies. This 'black magic' works directly on the victim's soul or through spirit intermediaries, for example, 'familiar' spirits.

This rough sketch shows the major areas of life in which the Malays use magic. It also provides a broad outline of the Malay way of life, since there are few areas untouched by magic.

# III

## MALAY WORLD-VIEW: SOME THEORIES

THE world-view is both a major part of Malay magic as I have defined it and the proper context in which to view specific magical practices. This subject has been approached by previous writers from several points of view leading to descriptions of various conceptual types. Skeat's 'all pervading Animism'[1] is a basic assumption underlying his descriptions of specific beliefs. Cuisinier's 'culte de la vie' is the theoretical end product of her search for the meaning of *sĕmangat*, the Malay 'soul substance'. Sufism, the doctrine of a Moslem sect described by Winstedt as a 'mystic pantheism',[2] is merely a branch of Moslem belief that has so flourished in Malaya as to suggest a basic sympathy with pre-Moslem Malay ideas.

Though no single one of these approaches can be said to give a full and balanced picture, taken together they act as several sources of light illuminating different aspects of their common focus—the Malay world-view. I shall begin my search for the traditional order of Malay magical ideas, therefore, with a discussion and evaluation of the interpretations put forward by the writers mentioned.

### I. SKEAT'S ANIMISM

Skeat says that the Malay 'has arrived at the idea of a generally animated nature' and that this 'Malay theory of Animism embraces, at least partially, the human race, animals and birds, vegetation (trees and plants), reptiles and fishes, until its extension to inert objects such as minerals, and "stocks and stones, weapons, boats, food, clothes, ornaments, and other objects"'.[3] For Skeat the nature of this animation is simple and obvious, so he does not set out explicitly its form or the signs by which it may be recognized. Nevertheless, it is not difficult to discover what he means by the term animism.

---

[1] Skeat 1900, p. 579.    [2] Winstedt 1922, p. 261.
[3] Skeat 1900, p. 53.

One important indication of Malay animism, according to Skeat, is the widespread occurrence of anthropomorphic ideas about things in nature. In fact, in one place he refers to the 'extraordinary persistence of anthropomorphic ideas about animals, birds, reptiles, trees, if not of minerals' as the 'theory of Universal Animism'.[1] Evidence for this theory, I take it, includes the innumerable folktales describing how human beings have sometimes been changed into animals, birds, trees, and even rocks or landmarks of various kinds. These origin tales are usually used to explain peculiarities in the behaviour or physical characteristics of a plant or animal. For example, the marks on the legs of deer are supposed to be traces of an abscess suffered by a man who, on dying of the condition, was changed into a deer.[2] Often the distinctive qualities of a bird's call are associated with the sound of the particular Malay phrase that was supposedly being uttered by a person at the time he was changed into a bird. I do not know if man-like characteristics are ever thought to occur where there is no history of human origin or if all things that originated as men retain traces of their former identity. Skeat regards anthropomorphic attributes and the 'theory of Human Origin' as so closely related as to be virtually one belief.[3] It is likely that there is a tautology in Malay belief on this point: physical and behavioural traits not believed to be tied to a human origin are not considered man-like.

Another anthropomorphic belief is the idea that some natural objects are really men in another form. The best known example of this is the were-tiger. Some men, especially certain Korinchi Malays from Sumatra, are thought to have the power to change into a tiger and back again at will. Such tigers can be recognized by their unusual behaviour, and they are greatly feared (more even, I presume, than ordinary tigers). The belief that some men can temporarily take the form of tigers is quite distinct from ideas of the type previously discussed. This is in addition to beliefs that tigers act in some ways like men—for example, they divine who their future victims should be—and to tales that they were originally human.[4]

Further anthropomorphic ideas are held regarding tigers and elephants. Both are believed to have a city of their own, far off in

---

[1] ibid., pp. 53, 54.　　[2] ibid., p. 171.
[3] ibid., pp. 53–54.　　[4] ibid., pp. 158–160.

the jungle, where they go about in human shape and live as human beings. Whenever they leave their city, they resume their animal form. I have shown that it is not physical tigers, but tiger spirits that inhabit the tiger village, and it is likely that the creatures in the elephant village are also spirits which take their identity from a type of animal.[1]

As evidence of a general anthropomorphic view of natural objects, I think Skeat would cite the fact that these things are frequently addressed 'exactly as if they were human beings'.[2] This implies two things. First, it indicates that such things as animals, plants, and even some minerals have the same desires, feelings, and interests as men, and, therefore, similar techniques of persuasion will be effective with both. For instance, the hunter coaxes the deer into his snare by describing the nooses as bracelets, rings, and necklaces offered for the adornment of their necks and feet.[3] Secondly, the notion that one can communicate with the non-human things at all is probably to attribute to them some form of consciousness. While this is not too startling regarding the higher animals, consciousness is not the most obvious characteristic of trees, rocks, and weapons and, in them, might be termed an anthropomorphic trait.

This implied consciousness of things in nature seems to be connected with what I would regard as Skeat's other major indicator and ingredient of Malay animism: the possession by most things of souls. In a sense this too is an anthropomorphic idea since Skeat regards the idea of animal, mineral, and vegetable souls as a natural extension from the theory of human souls.[4] Yet the importance of the Malay conception of the soul—Skeat calls it 'the central feature of the whole system of Malay magic and folklore'[5]—demands that it be treated separately.

The root idea of the Malay world-view, according to Skeat, is 'an all-pervading Animism, involving a certain common vital principle (*sĕmangat*) in Man and Nature, which, for want of a more suitable word, has been here called the Soul'.[6] This *sĕmangat* becomes differentiated into the full range of human, animal, vegetable, and mineral souls.[7] As to the form of these souls, Skeat says 'speaking generally, I believe the soul to be, within

---

[1] See ibid., pp. 151–3.     [2] ibid., p. 171; see also pp. 181, 249.
[3] ibid., p. 171.     [4] ibid., p. 52.     [5] ibid., p. 579.
[6] ibid., p. 579.     [7] See ibid., p. 53.

certain limits, conceived as a diminutive but exact counterpart of its own embodiment'.[1] It is insubstantial in nature—shadowy, vapoury, or filmy—so it can enter and leave physical objects without causing displacement. It normally remains in the body of its possessor but can wander in sleep, trance, or sickness. As long as its absence is temporary, there is no particular danger, but prolonged absence can cause illness and even death. Consequently, a major part of Malay medicine is designed to retain an escaping soul or recover one that has already departed. Though life depends on the presence of a soul, many non-living things have souls as well.

The soul, as I suggested above, possesses 'the personal consciousness and volition of its corporeal owner'.[2] While this, I think, refers specifically to the human soul, it probably applies also to non-human souls. It would be strange if the conscious part of a non-human thing that is addressed by means of charms were something in addition to the soul, while it is specifically the soul in human beings that is addressed in this way. Thus, the practice of magic consists partially of dealing with souls, both of people and of things, and a fundamental principle of these dealings is that 'if you call a soul in the right way it will hear and obey you'.[3] There are ways to induce a person's soul to leave his body and come into one's own possession, giving one power over that person. There are also ways to make the soul of the pigeon obey one's command and cause the wild pigeon to come into a snare. Thus, not only understanding of the world, but an important source of power in it depends for the Malay on an understanding of the soul.

An animistic world-view, then, following Skeat, consists of two related ideas: anthropomorphic notions about non-human things, and a belief in the presence of souls throughout the natural world. Unfortunately, this formulation suffers from serious deficiencies that severely limit its usefulness.

By grouping as anthropomorphic ideas a number of quite distinct types of relation between man and nature, Skeat directs attention away from the systems of relations of which they are part. For example, the notion of a human origin for non-human things, which Skeat elevates to the level of a theory in the minds of the Malays, is really just a special case of a general belief that things may originate in the metamorphosis of something else.

[1] ibid., p. 52.    [2] ibid., pp. 47–48.    [3] ibid., p. 49.

Many examples of this found in the folklore do not involve human beings at all. For instance, one species of squirrel is thought to have developed from a type of caterpillar.[1] Also, there is a type of mollusc that is said to have originally been a mouse and a fish that sprang from a cat.[2] This fish is said to squall like a cat when harpooned and to have very fine white bones like a cat's hairs. Though this belief shows a remarkable resemblance to those which make up the 'theory of Human Origin', since it falls outside Skeat's notion of animism, he is forced to regard it as another of many 'strange beliefs' about animals.[3] His formulation makes quite meaningless any attempt to discover the common conditions of metamorphosis-origins or to get at the meaning of the 'anthropomorphic' examples by reference to the non-human ones.

Skeat's category of anthropomorphic ideas not only separates some material that might profitably be considered together, but it glosses over some distinctions that quite possibly are important. The fact that only tigers and elephants are thought to have cities where they assume an alternative human form may well point to a distinctive relation between man and these two animals which should be investigated. The same is true of the connection between man and tigers which is indicated by the belief in were-tigers but not in were-lizards or were-trees. There is something special about the system of man-(were-tiger)-tiger and about that of man-tiger-elephant that distinguishes them from the general man-nature system of Skeat's animism. They are probably also distinct from each other. Following Skeat's view, one could only say that the tiger is more anthropomorphic than other things in nature, whereas, by recognizing these relations between the tiger and man as belonging to several separate systems of ideas, one is closer to understanding the full meaning of the tiger.

Skeat's treatment of *sĕmangat* is no less confusing than his notion of anthropomorphic ideas. A large part of the problem appears to be a result of his bias in favour of definition by essence rather than by relations. Instead of following through the idea that *sĕmangat* is the 'common vital principle' of man and nature, he breaks the concept up into a series of souls and tries to determine what objects have souls and what characteristics these souls have in each case. Typical of this is his statement that 'all we can be certain of at present is that a good many trees are supposed by

[1] ibid., p. 190.    [2] ibid., pp. 191–2.    [3] See ibid., p. 192.

them [the Malays] to have souls'.[1] His attribution of a separate
soul to each object or species is, I think, what prompts Levy-
Bruhl to comment that Skeat translates things into animistic
language conceptions that are probably not so definite and clear-
cut in the natives' minds.[2] One result of Skeat's tendency to look
for essences in souls is that he cannot accept contradictory characteristics of the *sĕmangat* of a single thing as being equally real. For
example, he seems to regard the 'thumbling' or manikin conception of the human soul as the real one and to dismiss as mere
metaphor the conception of the soul as a bird.[3] This is not consistent with his citation elsewhere of what might equally be
considered metaphor as evidence of souls or of animistic conceptions about natural objects. The idea of the 'long and flowing
locks' of the wind is a full-fledged animistic conception[4] but,
despite the fact that the human soul is usually addressed as if it
were a fowl[5] and is considered particularly attracted to offerings of
rice,[6] the bird-soul of man is a metaphor. His choice of the manikin
as fact and the bird-soul as metaphor probably derives from his
view that souls are minute replicas of their material embodiment.
But the important thing is not the grounds of his choice but the
fact that he feels compelled to make a choice in the first place. The
contradiction he resolves in this way is of his own creation; it is a
product of his search for unitary essences in concepts that do not
necessarily have them. This example illustrates, in miniature, the
reason Skeat does not successfully bring together the ideas of
*sĕmangat* as a 'common vital principle' and as a series of discrete
'souls'. By his mode of reasoning there is a contradiction, though
it does not exist in Malay thought. The importance of both views
prevents him from choosing between them, relegating one or the
other to an inferior status such as that of metaphor. Thus, he is
forced to hold one view in abeyance while operating with the other.
He speaks of 'souls' throughout his observations and only intro-
duces the notion of an all inclusive vital force in his final summary.
He does not attempt to relate the two because, I suggest, it would
be virtually impossible to do so given his assumptions about
meaning. Clearly, a mode of analysis based on essential definitions
can only hinder understanding of such Malay concepts as *sĕmangat*.

---

[1] ibid., p. 194.    [2] Lévy-Bruhl 1965, p. 33.    [3] Skeat 1900, p. 47.
[4] ibid., p. 44 n.    [5] ibid., p. 47 n.    [6] ibid., p. 76.

Skeat's approach to the meaning of *sĕmangat* not only involves him in problems of internal contradiction, but cuts the concept off from the systems of meaning of which it is part. For example, in his fascination with the fact that souls are addressed as if they had the feelings and desires of human beings, he overlooks the equally important fact that this communication takes place in a manner—through spells and special languages—that is also used in addressing certain demons. One would like to know what 'souls' have in common with these spirits as well as with people.

The source of many of the weaknesses in Skeat's notion of animism is one that is common to many studies that purport to present only the facts, devoid of theory—too little thought about basic concepts. His assumptions, like much of common sense, are not so sensible on close examination. His category of anthropomorphic ideas is merely a homocentric selection of items from a number of different systems of Malay ideas. His preconceptions about the nature of conceptions of the soul lead him to apply a very rigid, monolithic definition to what is really a flexible and complex idea. However, one cannot blame Skeat for not rejecting entirely the most respected anthropological ideas of his time, especially as he professed himself to be only a collector and recorder, not a theoretician. Moreover, in broad outline, Skeat's 'animism' is a helpful guide. It rightly points out that in Malay thought man is an integral part of the natural world. Most important, I think, is Skeat's contention that the conception of *sĕmangat* 'is the central feature of the whole system of Malay magic and folklore, from which all the different branches with their various applications appear to spring'.[1]

## II. CUISINIER'S 'SUMANGAT'

The Malay concept of *sumangat* (*sĕmangat*), as Cuisinier sees it, expresses in specifics the general principles of Oriental and primitive thought: the absence of a distinction between the material and spiritual worlds and an over-all fluidity of thought shown mainly by the ambiguity of concepts.[2] This sets *sumangat* off from Western notions of the soul, which are portrayed as clearly defined and distinct from the body, and groups it with the *khuan* of the Thai and the *wai* and *bia* of the Muong in Viet Nam. Unfortunately,

[1] ibid., p. 579.    [2] Cuisinier 1951, p. 41.

the distinction between the thought of East and West applies less, she admits, to the Malay's *sumangat* than to related notions of other Indonesians.[1] This causes some difficulties in isolating her analysis of the Malay idea from other, more typical Indonesian examples which she repeatedly brings in for comparison. It also creates limits in the extent to which the Malay ideas actually participate in her general conclusions, which correspond, as one would expect, quite closely to her initial assumptions despite the partial anomaly of the Malay case. Still it is worthwhile to follow her discussion of *sumangat* because, for one thing, it addresses itself to problems such as the relation of the common vital principle to individual souls, a problem that is badly handled by Skeat. In any event, my aim is not to criticize, but to extract whatever useful ideas and information I can from Cuisinier's treatment of the subject.

Unlike Skeat, who seems to have found the gulf between souls and Soul an unbridgeable one, Cuisinier concludes that there is no such gulf, that the two are really one. In a sense, then, there is no relation at all because the terms are not separate. Nevertheless, this conclusion does not seem to be shared by the Malays for, as Cuisinier shows, there is such a distinction in their minds. A large part of Cuisinier's discussion is devoted to demonstrating that the only important difference between the ceremony for recalling a missing soul and the one for repairing a damaged soul is ideological: the soul that is appealed to in the former case is conceived as being the particular soul of a particular person, while in the latter it is the store of undifferentiated *sumangat* that is magically utilized in effecting the remedy Nor do the Malays share the idea that *sumangat* is not at least partially separate from its material embodiment. Cuisinier states that the *sumangat* 'peut le quitter [the body], et le quitte notamment pendant le sommeil, pendant un évanouissement, ou s'il est ravi et retenu par quelque maléfice; la séparation n'est dommageable, pour le corps et pour le *sumangat*, que si elle est trop prolongée'.[2] These examples demonstrate, I think, that whereas Cuisinier's conclusions are not very enlightening regarding the Malays, the discussion leading up to them is of considerable interest.

The ceremony for recalling a missing soul (*sambut sumangat*) and that aimed at repairing a damaged one (*membuat sumangat*)

[1] ibid., p. 42.    [2] ibid., p. 206.

are, as I mentioned, almost identical in outward appearance. The charms in both cases appeal to the *sumangat* to enter into the ailing body, to cut short its absence, to restore the vigour, freshness, and peace of its material envelope.[1] In both kinds of charm the *sumangat* is associated with the breath (*ruh*). The offerings are also nearly the same, though there are variations in details such as quantities and modes of presentation. Included among the offerings would usually be some rice, both boiled and parched, some rice flour, some water either pure or perfumed, one or more quid of betel, some money, and some white, untwisted cotton. To this would be added seven red coloured eggs in *sambut sumangat* or, for the repair of the soul, some flowers, cakes, and candles.[2] Cuisinier believes that neither set of offerings is complete because they both fail to include representatives of all three realms of nature—animal, vegetable, and mineral—and of the four elements —earth, water, fire, and air—which she says must be united in the total offering.[3] She supposes that the present collection is a degeneration of a former, fully inclusive array.[4] The reasoning does not seem valid to me. I do not think that the division of nature into animal, vegetable, and mineral realms is an important classification in Malay thought, if it exists at all. Also, the idea of the four elements is prominent in Islamic thought, so it would be more natural for observance of the implied requirements to have become more rigorous, rather than less, as the Malays progressed from paganism toward orthodox Mohammedanism. One point is clear, however: the offerings associated with both kinds of ceremony fall equally short of completeness in terms of Cuisinier's criteria.

There is no significant difference either in the subrite of 'purification' as performed in the two kinds of ceremony. The variations that exist occur according to the option of the *bomor* and do not systematically separate the two types of ceremony.[5] In either type, also, the influence of a malignant spirit may be deemed so serious that the lines of this mysterious power must be ritually broken. This involves a special rite called *melepas* which means to release, untie.[6] *Melepas* consists of a spoken formula and the ritual severing of a knot of coconut leaf fibres.

---

[1] ibid., pp. 222–3, 226–7.        [2] ibid., pp. 219–220.
[3] ibid., pp. 220, 221.            [4] ibid., pp. 220, 251.
[5] ibid., p. 212.                  [6] ibid., p. 213.

It is from these facts that Cuisinier is led to conclude that the basis for the Malay's distinction between *membuat sumangat* and *sambut sumangat* is in the ontological assumptions involved. She says 'le sumangat qu'on invite à réintégrer le corps qu'il a quitté est, en effet, plus individualisé dans l'esprit du bomor qui le rappelle'.[1] Souls are Soul individualized, reduced in scale and attached to objects. It is an operation of the imagination, not a mechanical one. The concept of the individual soul, Cuisinier says,[2] makes it possible to render the all-pervading Soul sensible; it reduces it to human scale. A soul, in other words, is Soul from another point of view.

What then are the characteristics of *sumangat* in its two aspects? As the common vital principle, Cuisinier says, it is material and immaterial at the same time. Though it is an invisible vital force, it draws part of its existence from corporeal elements such as hair, nails, sweat, blood, sperm, saliva, tears; from certain viscera such as the liver and intestines; from the four elements, and above all from wind.[3] These are the centres of Soul material and must be distinguished from things that possess souls, a category that includes nearly everything.[4] Similarly, Soul material divided is not the same as individualized souls. Particles of Soul material are embodied in the offerings in a *membuat sumangat* ceremony; these can be eaten, drunk, breathed or otherwise absorbed by the patient according to the nature of the offering.[5] The particles 'deviennent lui-même en accroissant sa vie'.[6] That is, they are somehow added to the patient's deficient supply of the vital force and thereby bolster up his health. Conversely, a person's store of Soul can be magically diminished by evil spells.

There are natural as well as magical processes of increase, decrease, and transmission of undifferentiated *sumangat*. It may be diminished by sickness, old age, and fatigue and augmented by good health, observance of one's proper station in life, and maintenance of a harmonious relationship with nature.[7] The latter consists of such things as performing agrarian rites, respecting game killed, and refusing to kill needlessly. In some circumstances the Soul substance of a person can be shared with some other person or thing, often with no apparent loss to the original source.

---

[1] ibid., p. 224.    [2] ibid., p. 253.    [3] ibid., p. 202.
[4] ibid., pp. 202, 210.    [5] ibid., pp. 223–4.    [6] ibid., p. 224.
[7] ibid., p. 209.

Such is the case when a mother gives part of her Soul material to her baby.[1] Briefly, then, *sumangat* as the vital principle is both an invisible force and material manifestations; it is affected by certain natural conditions and processes and can be manipulated by magic. It is fragmented as well as unitary, but the fragments are not individualized.

The vital principle differentiated, broken up into distinctive units and attached to objects, is what constitutes souls. All souls are intimately connected to their material embodiments. Cuisinier refers to the soul as making one with the body.[2] She also observes that 'agir sur le *sumangat*, c'est agir sur l'être entier'.[3] While it might be said that undifferentiated *sumangat* animates the body, it is as a soul that it controls it. In human beings, where the soul is so differentiated as to be individualized, this control manifests itself, I would suggest, as a personality. Yet, despite the alleged identity of soul and body, the soul is in some respects independent. As I noted above, Cuisinier points out that the soul can leave the body voluntarily or otherwise, and neither part will necessarily be harmed unless the absence is prolonged. Still, the body without the soul is helpless, as in a swoon or sleep, and extended separation will cause it to become sick and eventually to die. Therefore, the soul, as well as Soul material, must be present for proper functioning of a body and, where the soul is individualized, it is a particular soul that is needed.

A soul, Cuisinier says,[4] has a form yet remains invisible. She adds that perhaps it would be more accurate to say that the soul holds in reserve the form it will take after death. This statement does not, as far as I know, apply to the Malays. All that is necessary to say, however, is that an imaginary concept, such as the soul, may have an image. As to what form the image of the soul takes among the Malays, Cuisinier is not very explicit. She says[5] that the invisible form attributed to the soul is not necessarily that of the body that contains it. Though she does not question the credentials of the manikin-soul as described by Skeat, she argues, contrary to Skeat, that the soul in the form of a bird is probably not merely a metaphor, as this is the commonest belief throughout Indonesia.[6] One point on which she is clear is that the Malays conceive the soul as a multiple unity.[7] It is seen as seven in one

---

[1] ibid., pp. 207, 208.    [2] ibid., pp. 202.    [3] ibid., p. 237.
[4] ibid., p. 203.    [5] ibid., p. 204.    [6] ibid., p. 204.    [7] ibid., p. 205.

and perhaps also as three in one. She says nothing to suggest that the parts have different qualities as do the seven *tondi* of the Batak, nor does she mention the bases on which they are separated and unified.

Before assessing the value of this discussion, I shall turn briefly to a consideration of Cuisinier's general conclusions. She begins by saying that the purpose of the rites for recalling and repairing the soul is to re-establish an equilibrium that has been upset or to establish one not yet attained as in the case of a child retarded in his development.[1] This is achieved by the virtue of offerings, the products of nature, and by the virtue of words uttered in charms.[2] That the equilibrium sought is sometimes the order that should obtain, not merely the previous status quo, suggests that it is, at least in part, a moral one. As Cuisinier says, it is not merely an equilibrium of health, nor even of a single being, because reparation is also necessary to the offender against the equilibrium as well as to the victim of the offence.[3] Thus, the rites go beyond a simple therapy. There are elements in fact of a cult involved, actions of grace performed after a cure is effected or in rites involving a still healthy soul as in the case of the rice-soul ceremony of the Malays.[4] This cannot be centred on a particular soul, Cuisinier says, because a soul is only one part of 'le grand Tout'.[5] 'A travers elle [the soul], à travers son enveloppe corporelle qui ne fait qu'un avec elle-même, c'est au grand Tout que s'addresse l'hommage rendu à l'âme vivante'.[6] This 'grand Tout' seems to consist of *sumangat* in its unitary and differentiated aspects, including their physical forms: Soul materials and the containers of souls.[7] If there is a cult, Cuisinier says, it is not 'un culte des âmes vivantes seulement, mais un culte de la Vie'.[8] But even this is more restricted than must certainly be the case for, as she reminds us in the next paragraph, 'le vivant se trouve restitué à la vie universelle par l'identification de son être au grand Tout où l'organique et l'inorganique sont également vivants'.[9] Perhaps it would be clearer, then, to call this worship of the cosmos unified a 'cult of Existence'.

The unity of all creation is further attested by the fact that 'par les correspondances qu'une ontologie primitive a établies entre

| [1] ibid., p. 247. | [2] ibid., p. 252. | [3] ibid., p. 247. |
| [4] ibid., pp. 247–8. | [5] ibid., p. 248. | [6] ibid., p. 248. |
| [7] ibid., pp. 202, 248, 253–4. | [8] ibid., p. 250. | [9] ibid., p. 250. |

A.A.M.M.—4

les parties du corps et les aspects du monde, l'identification de microcosme au macrocosme est annoncée, et l'allusion faite aux quatre elements, constitutifs du monde et constitutifs de l'homme, la confirme'.[1] The human scale of the individual soul is united with infinity; the abolition of frontiers and boundaries entailed in the 'culte de la Vie' rejects even the distinction between life and death.[2]

It strikes me that this confounding of all forms of matter and energy as well as most of the religions of Southeast Asia undoes all the good of Cuisinier's previous analysis. This grand synthesis submerges all the distinctions that people make in order to cope with the world. It is singularly unenlightening to say that to understand a people's thought and behaviour one must keep in mind the fact that they have a 'cult of Everything'. The idea of the unity of everything in the universe might make a good assumption from which to start an analysis, but it has very little value as a conclusion.

Not only does this conclusion have little explanatory value, it is very unclear to whom it actually applies. It is a result of bringing together a lot of ideas and practices that are in fact held by widely separated groups. For example, in developing the point that there is worship of the vital principle, Cuisinier jumps from Malaya, where no obvious examples of this occur, to Thailand, where they do.[3] The composite of beliefs she describes in service of her hypothesis could just as well be selected on some other basis and used to prove a different point. It is not apparent what any such conclusion has to do with the Malays or any other single people in Southeast Asia.

What I think is most valuable in Cuisinier's discussion is the treatment of *sumangat* as an idea in people's minds that is defined and redefined in different situations according to different needs and conditions. Only in this way can a satisfactory explanation of this complex notion be achieved. To picture it as a thing of any sort necessarily distorts its true nature. No single model from the physical world can accurately represent it. Just as the properties of light can only be explained by use of two seemingly mutually exclusive models—the light ray and the light wave—*sumangat* is not amenable to the most complex physical analogy.

However, I do not agree with the exact terms in which Cuisinier

[1] ibid., p. 251.    [2] ibid., pp. 253–4.    [3] ibid., p. 248.

describes the mental transformations that are involved in the notion of *sumangat*. It is misleading to say that the soul is one with its corporeal embodiment in view of the ability of the former to leave the latter. I think it is equally unreal to say that Soul materials are physical particles of the vital principle. If that were the case, it would be impossible for one such material to be 'more Soul' than another. The vital principle is undifferentiated, homogeneous; a material must be either Soul or not Soul—it cannot be slightly Soul. However, it is a fact that some things are thought to be more the centres of Soul than others. Note the degrees of Soul implied in the statement that 'les produits et les parties du corps, particulièrement les parties génitales, et très particulièrement la tête sont autant de sièges, non de l'âme qui fait un avec le corps, mais des matériaux de l'âme'.[1] Things that are equal to the same thing cannot be unequal to each other.

Putting aside Cuisinier's preconception that Orientals and primitive people confuse the spiritual and material, a more reasonable rendering of the Malay belief would be to say that the vital principle is in things, and it may be present in varying degrees of concentration. This concentration of *sumangat* seems to be independent of the extent to which it is differentiated or individualized. For example, the *sumangat* of the most ordinary human being is thought to be different from that of any other person, while the diffuse spiritual potency of a famous *kramat* may be so generalized that even the name of the buried saint from whom it is supposed to emanate will have been forgotten. I shall elaborate the view that the power of *kramat* is undifferentiated *sumangat* in the following chapter.[2] The mental processes involved in concentration and in differentiation of *sumangat* are entirely different. The former is simply to say that some things contain more of the vital principle than others, though it is present in everything. Differentiation is the process by which *sumangat* is broken up into separate souls, defined more or less distinctly in relation to each other and to other things in the environment. While the soul of a man is completely individualized by a complex process of definition, those of trees are usually considered essentially the same for all the members of a species. The *sumangat* of most minerals is barely

---

[1] ibid., p. 202.
[2] Cf. ibid., pp. 237–8 on the relation of Soul materials to special places such as *kramat*.

differentiated enough to be termed a soul at all. I assume that the characteristics ascribed to a soul in defining it are chosen for some reason, that they are not a random selection. Similarly, I would expect to find some pattern in the things that are said to contain a high concentration of the vital principle which would set them off from less potent materials. Cuisinier describes some characteristics of souls, especially the human soul, but does not attempt to explain why these qualities and not others are ascribed. To say that the soul is pictured as a bird is to connect it with what? To set it off from what? What does it mean? Also, why is it the hair and not the scalp that is a Soul material, or the nails instead of the knees? One would like to know, in other words, why *sumangat* is concentrated and differentiated as it is, not simply that it is done.

As a way of getting at the Malay's meaning of *sumangat*, it seems that Cuisinier's analysis begins at the right point, but proceeds in the wrong direction. She rightly recognizes that the difference between the soul that is recalled and the vital principle is that in the former the *sumangat* is individualized in the Malay mind. By what principles the individualization takes place, she does not say, nor does she try to find out. She seeks to understand *sumangat* by comparing it with superficially similar ideas in other societies instead of with other ideas in the Malay culture. As a result she comes to the conclusion that, in effect, the distinction drawn by the Malays is simply an illusion. I would suggest that this is no more illusory than the concept of *sumangat* itself. As such, the distinction between Soul and souls must be explained and not discarded for a proper understanding of *sumangat* to be achieved. And, as I suggested above, I agree with Skeat that this conception is the central feature of the whole system of Malay magic.

### III. SUFISM

Some of the basic ideas in Sufism are very similar to Cuisinier's general conclusion about the meaning of *sumangat*. The fundamental conception in both sets of ideas is the view that the universe is of one essence which is variously manifest in the multiplicity of things in it. Cuisinier's conclusion that all creation is unified in a 'culte de la Vie' seems almost to be a paraphrase of Sufic pantheism with the mere substitution of the term *sumangat* for Allah. Many of the ideas Cuisinier brings forward as demonstrating this unity of all things, ideas such as that of correspondence between parts of the body and celestial powers, are specifically Sufic notions. But while Sufism has almost certainly influenced the Malay world-view, it is not identical with it. There are many areas of Sufic belief that have had little if any impact on popular Malay thought. The most one can say, I think, is that Sufism has provided, in one aspect, a rough analogy to the concept of *sĕmangat* and that this vague correspondence has guided to some degree the accretion of further aspects of Sufism and of Islam in general to the system of ideas of which *sĕmangat* is the centre. A knowledge of Sufism, then, furnishes an aid to understanding the Malay world-view, but it does not in itself constitute such an understanding.

Sufism began, probably in Persia, as a form of asceticism. Later, renunciation was discarded as a selfish striving to reach heaven. It was replaced by a disinterested love of God, 'quietism'. The idea that Allah was in everything developed into a belief in pantheism. This entailed the notion that beneath the apparent diversity of things was a cosmic unity which was God. Man himself could realize his essential unity with God by casting off the vestiges of his individuality and losing his self-identity. The Sufis supposed that this might best be achieved through love and ecstatic self-abandonment.[1]

Obviously, Sufism borders on heresy from the point of view of the orthodox Muslim. Not only does the belief in pantheism abuse the doctrine of the unity of God, but the abandonment of self in pursuit of religious fulfilment involves a disregard for heaven and hell, love of the Prophet, and many other sacred tenets of orthodox Islam. Consequently, the beliefs and practices of Sufism have generally been carried on only among small groups of mystics and scholars operating in semi-secrecy. Only in the East Indies does it seem to have formed a basic part of both learned speculation and popular belief.[2]

Sufism was probably introduced to Malaya around the middle of the fifteenth century,[3] which means that the beginning of its influence was almost simultaneous with the introduction of Islam. It came from India as did the more orthodox forms of Islam. This Indian Sufism had developed some distinctive features, undoubtedly under the influence of Hinduism and Buddhism, at

---

[1] Nicholson 1928, p. 12.        [2] Winstedt 1925, p. 170.
[3] Gimlette 1929, p. 107.

least in its external form.[1] Among these were the practices of fasting and performing various austerities in order to acquire invulnerability and other magical arts. Also the practice of 'watching the breaths' as a means of worship is probably of Indian origin. Like Brahmanical *mantra*, the secrets and charms of Sufism were esoteric and revealed only to the initiated. The doctrines that a disciple must honour and obey his teacher above all men and that he must pass through several stages of initiation were probably of Hindu origin. Winstedt claims, reasonably enough, that these Indian features facilitated the entry of Sufism into what was then Hindu Malaya.

The basic belief of Indian Sufism was the same as that of the Arabic form: that man is and should be unified with God. This involves, on the one hand, the realization that God is everything, therefore everything is God, and, on the other, the moral precept that one should strive to lose oneself in this sacred unity.

The most vivid demonstration for the Malay pantheist of the one indivisible self of man and its identity with the universe in Allah is the prevalence of things in sets of four. All things in sets of four are equal to each other. The four elements, the four winds, the four righteous Caliphs, the four extremities of man are all unified in their common 'fourness'. The names of Mohammed and Allah, which are both spelled with four letters in Arabic, connect all these in symbolizing the One Being.[2] This identity of sets of four is the basis of many far-fetched analogies that are taken as expressions of and evidence for the all-pervading essence of God. For example, the four Caliphs are supposed to have their seats in the human frame: Abu Bakar in the liver, 'Omar in the spleen, 'Usman in the lungs, and 'Ali in the gall bladder.[3] The variation of sensation in the nostrils as they come and go on the breath was once used as a method of divination.

If all things are in reality unitary, what is the basis of the apparent multiplicity of things in the universe? I think that, like the division of *sĕmangat* into individual souls, the process by which the essence of God becomes manifest in diversity is thought of as a mental operation. For example, in explaining the terms of a pantheistic charm, a Malay Sufi describes the term self as meaning ' "spirit", one of the attributes of God Most High, which parts not from His essence and it becomes an individualized idea and is

[1] Winstedt 1925, p. 167.    [2] ibid., p. 170.    [3] ibid., p. 173.

called man'.[1] A notion that is parallel to Sufic pantheism and possibly derived from it[2] involves the belief that all evil spirits are really one, pervading the whole world, only called by different names according to the environment in which the universal spirit of evil is considered for the moment.[3] I would interpret the statement of one Sufi that 'multiplicity is appearance. Only God exists'[4] to mean that the diversity of things is not a property of the world but of the observer's conception of it.

The practices in which the Sufi indulges in order to attain religious fulfilment seem to be aimed at altering his perceptions to rid himself of this troublesome sensation of diversity. He uses ecstasy and self-induced trances which are intended to eliminate, above all, the sensation of the distinctive identity of the self. To merge one's self with the universe is to achieve a state of sacredness, to become one with God. People who have accomplished this are regarded as saints having supernatural powers.[5] There is little exaggeration in the statement of one presumably successful Sufi: 'There is no God but God. I am God'.[6]

Clearly, Sufic pantheism is, in broad outline, similar to the world-view entailed in the notion of *sěmangat*. In both views there is a single unitary essence that is diffused throughout creation and is more or less individualized in the myriad of things. This individualization in both cases seems to occur by a process of conceptualization on the part of the observer, a definition of things by differentiating the spectrum of sensation. However, there are important differences as well. These point to areas of special interest where the dissimilar ideas come together in Malay thought. It is only fair to point out, however, that the differences I cite would not be recognized as existing by Cuisinier. It is on just these points that I have stated my disagreement with her, and I would contend that she has pictured beliefs about *sěmangat* as being much more like Sufism than they really are.[7]

One major difference, as I see it, is that the undifferentiated

---

[1] ibid., p. 178–9.

[2] The example given by an old man to explain the idea refers to Mecca, so the context of the belief is probably Muslim at any rate.

[3] Winstedt 1925, p. 171.       [4] Winstedt 1922, p. 261.

[5] Winstedt 1925, p. 170.       [6] Winstedt 1922, p. 265.

[7] If I am right, perhaps the reason is that most of her informants were magicians (see Cuisinier 1936, p. 38), people who make it their business to be versed in the most advanced notions about the occult.

principle of Sufism, Allah, is the object of worship, while *sĕmangat* in this form is not (Cuisinier's 'culte de la Vie' to the contrary). This infuses the Sufi system with a sacred element and makes actions with reference to the vital principle matters of morality. While the Malay magician deals with *sĕmangat* in an instrumental way, doing what is necessary to achieve the desired end, he would be compelled as a Sufi to consider what *should* be done with regard to Allah. This difference points to a need for a closer examination of the realm of the sacred as recognized in Malaya. To what extent has the idiom of sanctity merely been transferred from Islam to things whose real distinction derives from the pre-Islamic system of ideas? How far, in other words, are things that are said to be full of Allah treated as if they were full of *sĕmangat*? I think it would be profitable, for instance, to examine the rather unorthodox behaviour that takes place at *kramat*, the so-called sacred places, in this light.

Another basic difference between Sufic pantheism and *sĕmangat* regards the actual form of this universal essence in its differentiated state. Though Sufism has no unified set of beliefs on such points (the idea that there are many layers of meaning in the Koran which can be grasped by the spiritually endowed has, in many areas of belief, led to a variety of interpretations), it seems clear that the Sufi considers things to *be* Allah, while, as I have argued, *sĕmangat* is merely *contained* in things. It seems likely that it is the Westerners in their Sufic mysticism, not the Orientals, who have confused the spiritual and material realms. This particular difference between Sufism and the earlier belief calls for, among other things, a close examination of the meaning of material things, especially ritual objects.

Since Sufism has undoubtedly influenced Malay thought on many matters, it is valuable to keep in mind the connections that exist between it and other Malay beliefs. It is necessary to proceed with special caution in the analysis of areas where incongruities exist.

# IV

## MALAY WORLD-VIEW: A STRUCTURAL DEFINITION OF *SĔMANGAT*

THE foregoing discussion demonstrates that an accurate and adequate description of the Malay world-view must include a full explanation of the meaning of *sĕmangat*. It also shows that the concept of *sĕmangat* cannot be adequately defined in isolation. It will be valuable, therefore, to examine the notion in the context of other Malay ideas and to see what meanings it derives from relations with them. I have suggested that it might be useful to consider the all-pervading vital principle as being subject to two distinct kinds of mental operation. Accordingly, I have divided this chapter into a consideration of the principles by which generalized *sĕmangat* becomes differentiated and Soul becomes souls, and a discussion of the principles by which some things become endowed with a greater concentration of undifferentiated *sĕmangat* than others.

### I. DIFFERENTIATION OF SĔMANGAT

A case can be made for explaining the complexity and contradictions in the concept of the human *sĕmangat* as being due to the fact that most writers have confused into one what are really three distinct types of soul: *sĕmangat, nyâwa, and rôh*. Annandale and Robinson report[1] that the Malay peasants of the Patani States in Thailand hold the three concepts separately, and the characteristics that these peasants divide among the three kinds of soul are the very same that, taken together, are attributed to *sĕmangat* alone by Skeat, Cuisinier, Wilkinson, and others.[2] Giving them separate status, as in Patani, involves a view that the three different vital forces are manifest in man while only two of them appear in animals and just one in the remainder of creation.

---

[1] Annandale and Robinson 1903, p. 95.
[2] Skeat 1900, p. 47; Cuisinier 1951, pp. 199, 203–7; Wilkinson 1906, pp. 48–9.

It is apparent, on the other hand, that many of the Malays themselves combine the three. Annandale and Robinson admit[1] that, even in the same area (Patani), there are many individuals who consider the three to be one. And, unless most of the other writers on the subject are guilty of gross errors in observation, this latter view is probably the more common in the Peninsula. In general, there is considerable overlap in the definitions given the three types of soul. Wilkinson defines *sěmangat* as 'the spirit of physical life; vitality, in contradistinction to the immortal essence or soul (*nyâwa*); the breath of life; health'.[2] He calls *nyâwa* the 'soul, life, spirit'[3] and the *rôh* or *rûh* 'the spirit of life; the breath of life. Often used in Malay as an equivalent of *sěmangat*'.[4] The firm distinction made by Wilkinson between *nyâwa* and the other two is not supported by Cuisinier. She says[5] that *nyâwa* signifies breath and life, that it joins the sense of vital breath with vital principle,[6] and she says further that the vital principle is *sumangat*.[7] Apparently, to take the position that either the separation or combination of the three types of soul is the correct view would be to accuse some Malays, at least, of being mistaken about their own beliefs.

I think it is best to say that *rûh*, *nyâwa*, and *sěmangat* are simply different aspects of the soul of man (which, confusingly I admit, is usually called the *sěmangat*) and that their complete separation is a result of carrying the differentiation of the common vital principle a step further than is ordinarily done. That the characteristics of *rûh*, *nyâwa*, and *sěmangat* seem sometimes to be inconsistent does not mean that the three cannot be aspects of a single thing (the human soul), for, as Bosch has shown,[8] the characteristics of a thing may vary depending on the system in which it is being classified. The distinctive characteristics of the three aspects, therefore, can serve as valuable guides to the systems of ideas of which the human soul is part and in relation to which it is defined. The less distinctly defined souls of the lower forms of creation, naturally enough, do not have all three of the aspects found in the human soul. The sharing or otherwise by things in nature of *rûh*, *nyâwa*, and *sěmangat* with the soul of man is not

---

[1] Annandale and Robinson 1903, p. 95.
[2] Wilkinson 1901, p. 400.     [3] ibid., p. 699.
[4] ibid., p. 347.     [5] Cuisinier 1951, pp. 197–8.
[6] ibid., p. 198.     [7] ibid., p. 199.
[8] Bosch 1960, p. 89 and *passim*.

random and, as I shall show, is a key to one of the important classifications of the world as seen by the Malays.

### Sĕmangat, Free Spirits, and Familiars

Since yet another meaning for the word *sĕmangat* has now been added, I shall specify, before proceeding, the exact sense in which I shall use the term. I use *sĕmangat* only in a specific and highly differentiated sense, as equivalent in these regards to *rôh* and *nyâwa*. The broader category, which includes these three, also sometimes called *sĕmangat*, will be referred to as 'the human soul'. Therefore, I treat *nyâwa*, *rôh*, and *sĕmangat* as specific aspects of the human soul, not as separate kinds of soul. *Sĕmangat* in its undifferentiated state, from which souls and aspects of souls take their existence, will be called 'the vital principle'. Briefly then, I treat *sĕmangat*, *nyâwa*, and *rôh* as aspects of the human soul which, in turn, is a differentiated manifestation of an all-pervading vital principle.

I shall take definitions of *nyâwa*, *rôh*, and *sĕmangat* from the reports of Annandale and Robinson on the Patani Malay peasants. There are several reasons for this. This particular division of the soul is useful because the meanings of the three aspects are quite clearly differentiated in Patani, and the authors describe the concepts very thoroughly. The division has the added value of being a classification actually made by a group of people, not merely the result of abstract analysis. This is not the only possible starting point for the analysis that follows, but I think the fertility of the approach suggests that the distinctions have some general validity in Malay thought. In view of the variations in meaning given *sĕmangat*, *rôh*, and *nyâwa* by different authors, it would be extremely risky to combine their information on those concepts with that supplied by Annandale and Robinson. In any case, nothing would be added since the variations are in how the characteristics are distributed, not in what they are. On the other hand, I shall not restrict my sources in any way in gathering information on related concepts.

*Sĕmangat*, according to the Patani peasants,[1] is the soul that is present in all organized things, guiding and co-ordinating their actions. The boundaries of the thing in which a single *sĕmangat* resides are fairly obvious for man and the higher animals, there

[1] Annandale and Robinson 1903, pp. 95–100.

being one *sĕmangat* per creature. But only the largest of jungle trees are ever said to have an individual *sĕmangat*. Most plants share one among all the members of a species in a limited area. This is clearest with rice for which there is thought to be one *sĕmangat* for all the rice of a given species in a particular field. The domain of mineral souls is very vague, being defined only where a deposit of ore is being exploited. In such a case there is said to be one *sĕmangat* for each mine. The actions that are guided vary, of course, according to the nature of the thing. Some of these, such as the movements of ore deposits, are actions in the orthodox sense, but differ from the actions of animals in being imaginary. Sometimes it is only the act of existence that is guided and co-ordinated as with the house soul which 'preserves the house as an organic whole from dissolution'.[1]

The control of the actions of things is only one aspect of the close interaction between the *sĕmangat* and the body it occupies. Any strength or weakness of the *sĕmangat* is transmitted to the body and vice-versa. They are both weakened by illness, care or worry, and, above all, by fear. Only when the *sĕmangat* is in a weakened condition can a spirit enter the body and cause some disruption.

This dependence of the body on the *sĕmangat* makes it natural that black magic against a person or thing works via the *sĕmangat*. One form of the magic works by extracting the *sĕmangat*, leaving the body out of control. The result of this is not death but madness, the symptoms of which are loss of memory, uncertain speech, and failure to recognize even one's own parents. Madness from loss of the *sĕmangat* may lead to physical illness and eventually death, because the absence of a *sĕmangat* makes the body vulnerable to the entry of a spirit. However, death is a secondary, not a primary, effect of magic which extracts the *sĕmangat*.

Magic may also seek to gain control of a *sĕmangat* without weakening or extracting it. This is the aim of the hunter who would have the *sĕmangat* of his prey lead the more edible corpus into his trap. It is the *sĕmangat* of rice, fruit trees, and tin ore with which one deals magically in an effort to control these things. The true love charm is probably of this type also. As Annandale and Robinson point out,[2] some of what Skeat considered love charms, those working through the abduction of a person's *sĕmangat*,

[1] ibid., p. 100.　　　[2] ibid., pp. 96–7.

would actually result in madness, not in love. It is more likely that they represent the revenge of a shunned suitor than true love charms.[1] The *sĕmangat* of a person makes its appearance at the moment the umbilical cord is severed. A special knife is used which is made of bamboo rather than iron, a material that frightens spirits. The cord is tied off with a thread of black cotton. If either of these observances were omitted, the baby would be affected by fever or delirium. None of the Malays questioned by the authors knew if the *sĕmangat* existed before it appeared in the child; they invariably said it '"became of itself" (*jadi sendĭri*)'.[2] The same is said of the boat soul[3] which 'becomes of itself' when all the planks of the boat have been fitted together. Similarly, 'the *sĕmangat rumah*, or "house soul", comes automatically into existence as the various parts of the walls and roof are fitted together'.[4]

There is some disagreement as to what becomes of the *sĕmangat* after the body dies or dissolves. Annandale reports that several of the people he questioned stated that the *sĕmangat* 'dies with the body, while others appeared to have no definite idea of it apart from the body, and a few said it retained the form of the body as a *hantu* or wandering spirit after dissolution'.[5]

(a) SĔMANGAT AND FREE SPIRITS

This, in brief, is the *sĕmangat*, the one aspect of the human soul that has a counterpart in all other things. What can one deduce about its fundamental meaning from these few facts? To begin with, it comes into existence at the same time as the thing that forms its body gains an independent identity. Until the umbilical cord is cut, the baby has shared in the body of its mother, and the boat or house before assembly was only the sum of its materials. Conversely, most people believe that the *sĕmangat* disappears on disintegration of its body. During their tenure together, disruption results from the *sĕmangat* leaving the body or the intrusion of spirits, and it is the function of the *sĕmangat*, as long as it is healthy,

---

[1] The expression Cuisinier found describing the complex of love charms and rites was *kundang sumangat* (1951, pp. 239–42). This is best translated as control or hypnotic influence over *sĕmangat*, not abduction of it (see Wilkinson 1964, p. 147).
[2] Annandale and Robinson 1903, p. 97.
[3] ibid., p. 81.
[4] ibid., p. 100.    [5] ibid., p. 98.

to maintain the boundaries of the body.[1] It is necessary to combat the forces, such as the belligerent tendency of free spirits to invade things, which tend to break down the boundaries by which the existence of a thing as a discrete entity is established. Thus, 'passive' existence is an act just as are the more obvious activities through which a thing may establish and assert its independent identity. Apparently *sĕmangat* is at once the agent that acts to maintain that identity and a symbol of the thing's existence. It is subject to symbolic attack just as the body may be affected physically, and magic, almost by definition, must act on the *sĕmangat* since it does not act directly on the body. Since the identity and therefore the existence of the thing depends on preserving both the physical components and the symbol of their unity, everything that is defined as a thing is vulnerable on these two planes.

But it is also said that the *sĕmangat*, like a spirit, is afraid of iron. And some people surmise that if it were without a body, for example following the body's death, it would have the form of a wandering *hantu*, a free spirit. It is also apparent that where the boundaries of the *sĕmangat*'s body are drawn so broadly as to take in what in other contexts might be regarded as a number of discrete sub-bodies, what is properly the *sĕmangat* is alternatively called a *hantu*. Such is the case with the *sĕmangat* of tin.[2] Usually each mine is a body for a tin ore *sĕmangat*, but 'sometimes each grain of ore appears to be considered as endowed with a separate entity or individuality'.[3] This fusion and fission of bodies also appears with regard to the trees bearing eagle-wood, camphor, and gutta-percha,[4] and trees in general seem particularly prone to being permanently inhabited by spirits,[5] which is in some contrast to the usual wandering habits of spirits.[6] It seems that when one *sĕmangat* is shared by members of a class in which the members are regarded in some contexts as discrete, the *sĕmangat*, by appearing in all of these members, gives the appearance of flitting from

[1] See e.g., Annandale and Robinson 1904, p. 30.
[2] Annandale and Robinson 1903, p. 99.       [3] Skeat 1900, p. 265.
[4] ibid., pp. 207, 213, 215.
[5] Skeat 1900, pp. 64–5; Blagden 1896, p. 5; Annandale and Robinson 1904, p. 30.
[6] The ideas and symbols connecting trees and nagas, Hindu snake-beings (see Bosch 1960, p. 195), sometimes appear in Malay myths and spells (e.g., Skeat 1900, pp. 3–4).

one to the other. In other words, a simple shift in perspective transforms a *sĕmangat* into a free spirit. Thus, on several points there is a curious similarity between the *sĕmangat* and free spirits (*hantu*) if one disregards for the moment the profound connection of the former with some physical object. It will be valuable to ascertain in exactly what ways the two are similar and what are the important differences between spirits and their body-bound relatives.

The characteristics of the many varieties of free spirits (*hantu* and *jin*) vary extremely,[1] but there are a few common to all forms. Lacking a body, they are often invisible, though it is said that they can be heard, smelled, or even felt.[2] Frequently, however, they do take a visible form, and, while many types have a characteristic appearance, their form can usually be varied at will.[3] They can also change size with equal facility.[4] Thus, to frighten people they can assume any number of terrifying aspects in rapid succession, varying in size from that of an insect to fifteen feet high.[5]

'The majority of spirits are regarded as utterly non-moral',[6] and the most that can be expected of them is that they will mind their own business. Their relations with man generally fall somewhere between mildly mischievous and thoroughly malevolent. To neglect or offend them may prove fatal, but they can usually be kept from interfering in the affairs of men by appropriate offerings and ritual.[7] Annandale believes that spirits 'continually seek for a body, and if they find a man whose soul is weak they drive it out and take its place'.[8] While it is true that spirits sometimes enter bodies, I do not think that they do so in order to take up residence there. Their invasion of a living thing invariably causes sickness and, if they are not exorcised, death. By taking the place of the *sĕmangat*, a spirit would seal its own doom. I think a better explanation is that in some circumstances spirits will enter bodies to devour their soul substance, the vital principle. For

[1] I shall discuss many of these varieties and some of the groupings they form in the following chapter.
[2] Annandale and Robinson 1904, p. 34.
[3] See Annandale and Robinson 1903, p. 81; McHugh 1955, pp. 23–4.
[4] Annandale and Robinson 1904, p. 34.
[5] See McHugh 1955, p. 24; Annandale and Robinson 1904, p. 39.
[6] Annandale and Robinson 1904, p. 35.
[7] McHugh 1955, pp. 24–5.
[8] Annandale and Robinson 1904, p. 35.

example, it is said that the *hantu bungkus*, a bundle of white cloth believed to be a corpse in its shroud, 'unrolls itself, twines itself round his [the victim's] feet, enters his person by means of his big toe, and feasts within on his soul'.[1] Similarly, *Hantu Laut* (Sea Spirits) are believed to live on men, and some fishermen assert that, rather than devouring the flesh, they merely drink up the *sĕmangat*.[2] There is some reason to believe that all spirits are nourished in some way by soul substance. Skeat concludes, after questioning many Malays on the subject, that deities (and I presume spirits also, since he is speaking of sacrifice in general) do not touch 'the solid or material part of the offering, but only the essential part, whether it be "life, savour, essence, quality" or even the "soul"'.[3] Annandale says spirits normally consume the savour (*baku* or *sĕmangat*) of an offering.[4] Just as the soul substance of the offerings in *membuat sĕmangat* can revitalize a weakened *sĕmangat*, the soul substance in offerings to spirits seems to reinforce their existence, or perhaps it provides the fuel for their daily activities. It follows that, if a spirit is neglected or the offerings made to it are insufficient, it may be tempted to enter a human being in search of a 'fix'. Of course, this is most likely to happen when a person's *sĕmangat* is either weakened or absent and can no longer protect the remainder of the soul substance in the body. The eventual death of the person is clearly indicated, as the *nyâwa*, the breath of life, is made up of this soul substance. The relative evil of the various spirits, then, their readiness to attack men, seems to be a function of how great their appetite for soul substance is and how easily they can satisfy it from non-human sources.

Spirits have very low intelligence, and their emotional reactions are simple and basic. They are susceptible to all manner of transparent frauds, be they the ridiculous lies and threats in charms or the substitutes offered for promised gifts. It is important to note that the charms intended to deal with free spirits contain the same combination of lies, threats, pleading, and recitation of names and origins as do charms addressed to *sĕmangat*.[5] While

[1] ibid., p. 22; see also Winstedt 1925, p. 22.
[2] Annandale and Robinson 1903, p. 81.
[3] Skeat 1900, p. 73.
[4] Annandale and Robinson 1904, p. 24.
[5] Skeat 1900, p. 506 n. and *passim*.

the spirits are easily tricked and thereby controlled,[1] they are equally easily insulted, and even a thoughtless remark derogatory to them may bring revenge.[2] Thus, spirits are generally regarded as inferior to man,[3] but are still afforded a respect born of fear. In this respect they are like members of aboriginal tribes with whom they are grouped in some contexts.

The beginnings and ends of free spirits are not very clear. A well known myth has them coming from fragments of God's first failure in the attempt to create man. This was a clay figure that was not reinforced with iron as was the second, successful model and which, consequently, exploded when the Spirit of Life was sent into it.[4] There are many origins ascribed in charms to particular spirits, often a number of different ones in the same charm. Winstedt says that these origins are probably invented by the magician in order to control the spirits[5] and are not, therefore, to be regarded as historical in nature. Some spirits are said to reproduce like (and sometimes with) human beings,[6] and some are continuously being generated, as, for example, the *hantu mati di bunoh*, spirits of murdered men. Though Annandale reports a method by which a spirit can be killed—by being stabbed with a dagger made from the midrib of a *nipa* palm—he says this is probably an Arabic idea.[7] The idea that any of the individualized spirits, such as the Spectre Huntsman, could be killed is unthinkable, and it is probably safe to say that the notion that any spirit is liable to death is very rarely held. It is significant that the simple destruction of a disease-causing spirit is not reported as a possible type of medical treatment.[8] For all practical purposes, I think one can safely say that spirits are immortal.

What light does this information about spirits shed on the meaning of *sĕmangat*? I have pointed out that spirits and *sĕmangat* react similarly to certain physical substances—for example, they both fear iron—and can be controlled by the same kinds of charms.

[1] For example, they are often induced to leave the body of a sick person and enter a raft of offerings which is then set adrift in a river to be carried away by the current (see Skeat 1900, pp. 433–6).

[2] McHugh 1955, p. 25.

[3] In Patani they are always addressed with the familiar rather than the honorific pronoun (Annandale and Robinson 1904, p. 40) and are considered less 'lucky' than man (Annandale and Robinson 1904, p. 34).

[4] Swettenham 1895, pp. 199–200.

[5] Winstedt 1925, p. 32.

[6] Annandale and Robinson 1904, p. 36.

[7] ibid., p. 34.     [8] See Skeat 1900, p. 410.

They both extract the soul material of offerings made to them, and it is likely that both of them somehow incorporate the soul material into themselves. This, along with the confusion of spirits and *sěmangat* in some lower order things (e.g., minerals), suggests that the same vital principle that forms *sěmangat* (undifferentiated *sěmangat*) also makes up spirits, although the process of differentiation or definition is obviously very different.[1]

However, there are important differences between spirits and *sěmangat* which, it will be seen, can all be traced to the freedom of the former from the constraint of a physical body. Spirits can change their size and shape on a whim and transport themselves about with great speed. In *sěmangat*, being normally confined to physical bodies, these abilities are severely limited by the realities of mundane matter. It is meaningless to say that the *sěmangat* can change size or shape while its body remains the same or changes only slowly. Similarly, the *sěmangat*'s movement is limited by the ability of its vehicle to move. Another difference is the fact that the *sěmangat*, being encumbered with a body, cannot pass through the boundaries of physical objects, a simple task for spirits. Also, the duration of a spirit's existence, unlike that of a *sěmangat*, is not clearly limited. Even when, by magic or accident, the *sěmangat* of a living thing becomes detached before death, it seems likely that their intimate interdependence persists and that their inevitable disintegration is simultaneous. At least there is no class of ghosts formed of *sěmangat* driven from their bodies before death. The existence of a *sěmangat* is always limited by its union with a more or less transient physical entity. On all these points the *sěmangat* is confined to clear and predictable actions and characteristics, constrained by the conditions of the physical existence of its body, while the spirit, on the contrary, is free to act in any imaginable manner.

## (b) SĚMANGAT AND FAMILIAR SPIRITS

Free spirits and *sěmangat* are only the poles—the bodiless and the bodied, the free and the constrained—of a classification that

[1] Annandale assumes that in general a 'soul' is 'a spirit permeating an organized body, in which it is innate, which it vivifies, regulates or prevents from dissolution' (1903, p. 93). I have never seen the idea that spirits and *sěmangat* are formed of the same material expressed by a Malay, but the evidence strongly suggests that the connection exists as one of the unspoken assumptions upon which Malay magic is based.

contains intermediate forms. The most obvious of these are the familiar spirits such as the *polong* and *pělěsit*. These should not be confused with the inherited 'familiar spirits' of many magicians which are, properly speaking, free spirits. The most common 'inherited familiar' is the tiger spirit, *hantu bělian*, though a great variety of others appear less frequently.[1] In any case what is inherited, or sometimes acquired, is a special relationship with an independent spirit—an agreement that the spirit will help in expelling other spirits from the sick—not exclusive possession of a particular spirit. *Polong* and *pělěsit*, on the other hand, have an owner for whom they work and with whom they share a body. Yet, unlike the *sěmangat*, they can leave their owner to do his bidding and in doing so behave exactly like free spirits.

There is some confusion as to the relation between *pělěsit* and *polong*. In some places they are regarded as separate kinds of creature and in others as being the same. Skeat describes the *polong* as a tiny manikin and the *pělěsit* as its cricket-like companion; the two cooperate in afflicting a victim.[2] In Trengganu, according to McHugh,[3] they are the same except that the *polong* is attached to men and the *pělěsit* to women. Annandale found that in Patani *polong* was merely a less common name for *pělěsit*, the familiar possessed by women, and another name, *putah rengas*, was applied to the equivalent kept by men.[4] Apparently *pělěsit* and *polong* (or *putah rengas*) share a common position on the scale between *sěmangat* and free spirits and their various definitions represent different ways, functional or sexual, in which that 'rôle' can be divided. However distinctions are drawn, they do not systematically divide *pělěsit* and *polong* on the bodied-bodiless dimension, making one always like a *sěmangat* and the other like a spirit. Therefore, the 'familiar spirit' I shall describe is a composite of the two kinds, since, whatever the division between them, their sum in a general sense is always the same.

A further confusion arises regarding the relation of *polong* and *pělěsit* to certain other spirits. For example, Swettenham states that '*Pôlong* and *Pělsit* are but other names for *Bâjang*'.[5] In many places, however, *bâjang* are a separate kind of spirit, sometimes a familiar and sometimes free.[6] I treat *polong*

---

[1] See Winstedt 1925, pp. 42–5, 98.      [2] Skeat 1900, p. 329.
[3] McHugh, 1955, p. 64.      [4] Annandale and Robinson 1904, p. 42.
[5] Swettenham 1895, p. 197.      [6] e.g., in Kedah; see McHugh 1955, p. 72.

and *pĕlĕsit* as separate from *bâjang* and similar spirits because the former seem always to be familiars—I have seen no cases reported where a *polong* or *pĕlĕsit* was not conjoined with a human 'father' or 'mother', while the others are sometimes familiars and sometimes free spirits. Of course, any division of what is in fact a continuum from *sĕmangat* to free spirits is necessarily an arbitrary one. It is mainly for convenience that I make this division, and I shall go on to the related 'birth demons' immediately following the description of the permanent familiars.

The duration of a familiar's existence seems not to extend beyond the bounds of its owner's life span. Familiars are actually created by their human 'parents',[1] the so-called inherited familiars being, as I have pointed out, really free spirits. Familiars are created by the performance of magical operations on certain special kinds of raw material. The materials used include the tongues of secretly exhumed still-born babies,[2] the blood of murdered men,[3] a person's own blood,[4] the oil of a green coconut,[5] and even, it seems, one's own shadow.[6] I have no explicit information as to whether the familiar lives or dies after its owner's death, but, since I have seen no reference to *pĕlĕsit* or *polong* existing without living owners or to any class of spirits produced from emancipated familiars, I presume that the familiar does not outlive its 'parent'. However, it is reported that during his lifetime an owner may lose control of his familiar as when he is ill or injured,[7] but there is nothing to suggest that, like the *bâjang*,[8] the *pĕlĕsit* and *polong* can become free spirits upon their owner's death.

I have said that the familiar shares the body of its owner. It must be regularly fed on blood from its owner's finger.[9] Significantly, the blood is the part of the mother from which babies are

---

[1] Annandale and Robinson 1904, p. 42.

[2] Skeat 1900, p. 331; Clifford 1897, pp. 230–44; cf. Swettenham 1895, pp. 197–8.

[3] Skeat 1900, pp. 329–30 n.

[4] McHugh 1955, p. 68.      [5] ibid., p. 65.

[6] Swettenham 1895, pp. 197–8.

[7] Annandale and Robinson 1904, pp. 43, 44.

[8] McHugh 1955, p. 72.

[9] McHugh 1955, p. 70; Annandale and Robinson 1904, p. 43; Skeat 1900, pp. 329, 330. Sometimes it is the middle finger that is specified (Annandale and Robinson 1904, p. 43); this is the finger called the '*hantu*' finger' because supposedly when the angel Azrael reached forth to take the heart of Earth from which God would mould man, the Earth-spirit caught hold of this finger, stretching it until it became longer than the rest (Skeat 1900, p. 20).

thought to develop. During the early months of pregnancy 'the foetus is still regarded as part of its mother's blood'.[1] This is so up until the sixth month when the baby receives a *nyâwa* (life breath) and 'becomes a person' (*jadi orang*).[2] Before the sixth month the baby seems to be considered a part of the father also as the latter is subject to a large number of prohibitions (the foremost being against taking the life of any creature), the violation of which would injure the unborn child.[3] Possibly the use of the terms 'father' and 'mother' for the owners of familiars alludes to this early stage of parenthood during which the offspring is a part of the parent's body.

Familiars show several similarities to and connections with *sĕmangat*. The characteristic appearance of the *polong* is that of a manikin, a description that Skeat admits 'tallies curiously with the Malay definition of the soul'.[4] The cricket or grasshopper form of the *pĕlĕsit*, while not a usual manifestation of the human *sĕmangat*, is a common form for 'souls' to take. For example, the rice-soul can appear as a grasshopper, and the house soul is said in Negri Sembilan to appear as a cricket.[5] The absence of the familiar on a mission of destruction leaves the owner lying 'as if asleep, face downwards, with his or her mouth making a noise "like a cat licking up water"'.[6] A weakening of the familiar results in illness for its master, and the latter feels whatever the *bomor* does to the familiar when it is inside a victim.[7] It may even be that in some cases the familiar is part of the human soul converted to a more useful form. Swettenham describes how a *pĕlĕsit* can be made from one's shadow,[8] and the shadow is generally thought to be a manifestation of some aspect of man's soul.[9]

Familiars, despite resemblances to the *sĕmangat* (especially in their close connection to their owner's body), operate in many ways like free spirits. A familiar can fly freely about searching for the victim designated by its master.[10] When the correct person is found, it enters his body and causes illness by feeding on the

[1] Annandale and Robinson 1904, p. 65.
[2] Annandale and Robinson 1903, pp. 93–4.
[3] ibid., p. 94; cf. Skeat 1900, pp. 348–50.
[4] Skeat 1900, p. 329.
[5] Winstedt 1925, pp. 72, 73.        [6] McHugh 1955, p. 72.
[7] Cf. Wavell 1958, p. 102; Annandale and Robinson 1904, p. 44.
[8] Swettenham 1895, pp. 197–8.
[9] Skeat 1900, pp. 50 n., 575 n.; Cuisinier 1951, p. 203.
[10] Skeat 1900, p. 330.

soul substance therein, a necessary part of the familiar's diet.[1] The *bomor* attempts to exorcise it, as he would an ordinary spirit, though the special nature of the familiar permits him some special techniques. This usually entails forcing the familiar, through the mouth of the patient, to reveal who its 'father' or 'mother' is, whereupon an attempt is made to compel the owner to recall it.[2] Besides eating the owner's blood and the souls of his enemies, familiars are given regular offerings of a more conventional kind by their owners to keep them healthy and obedient. These are usually of rice[3] or eggs[4] and sometimes even pork,[5] which suggests that *pĕlĕsits*, at least, are most unorthodox Mohammedans. There is an obvious connection with the belief in Negri Sembilan that putting a bone from a jungle pig into a well may cause a *pĕlĕsit* to devour its owner,[6] but the exact meaning of this is not clear in the report. Possibly a charm is recited wherein the depositor of the bone, who becomes the familiar's master by virtue of the offering, orders the familiar to attack its former 'parent'.

I shall summarize briefly. Familiars are intimately involved in the bodies of their 'parents', the most important connection being their dependence on infusions of the owner's blood. Consequently, they are restricted in range of travel and in longevity and are vulnerable to physical pressure applied to their material halves. Still, they can leave their owners for a time and behave to all appearances as free spirits.

## (c) SĔMANGAT AND BIRTH DEMONS

A class of spirits that is closely related to the familiars is that of 'birth demons' or 'vampires'. This includes the *bâjang, langsuir, pontianak,* and *penanggalan,* terrifying demons which specialize in attacking women and children at childbirth.[7] The *bâjang* takes the form of a pole-cat and 'is well-known for causing mild fevers and convulsions in children and for making people quarrel'.[8] The *bâjang* is the male equivalent of the *langsuir,*[9] which appears as an owl or a beautiful woman and develops from women who die in

---

[1] Annandale and Robinson 1904, p. 43.

[2] See Skeat 1900, p. 331; Annandale and Robinson 1904, p. 44; Swettenham 1895, p. 195.

[3] Skeat 1900, p. 330.      [4] McHugh 1955, p. 70.

[5] Cuisinier 1936, p. 28.      [6] McHugh 1955, p. 66.

[7] Skeat 1900, p. 320.      [8] McHugh 1955, p. 72.

[9] Clifford and Swettenham 1896: Malay-English Dictionary, s.v. *bajang.*

childbirth or soon after.[1] *Pontianak* are also owl-shaped, and are transformations of still-born children.[2] The *penanggalan* is a bodiless head with trailing entrails which flies about at night, glowing in the dark.[3]

I treat these spirits as being between familiars and free spirits because they are sometimes one and sometimes the other. For example, in Kedah some people believe that the *bâjang* may be a familiar, but becomes a free spirit upon its owner's death.[4] The *penanggalan* is regarded in some parts of the country as a familiar and in others as a vampire.[5] A *langsuir* supposedly can be tamed if one can catch her, cut short her nails and her long hair, and stuff them into the hole in her neck by which she sucks children's blood.[6] Naturally, even the Malays sometimes confuse these spirits in their familiar phase with the full-time familiars. Skeat notes that one of his informants considered the *bâjang* to be the man's equivalent of the woman's *pĕlĕsit*.[7] Swettenham was led to believe that *bâjang* and *langsuir* were simply familiars[8] and that *polong* and *pĕlĕsit* were but other names for *bajang*.[9] Still, there is little doubt that these spirits, with the possible exception of the *bâjang*, are primarily free of human ownership. Certainly their preference for attacking babies cannot be related to the usual function of the familiar, which is to act as an instrument of its owner's malice toward his enemies.

The existence of birth demons is not tied to the life of any single person. Even as familiars, they are independent to the extent that they may be handed down to someone[10] or, as I noted above, may go free upon their owner's death. Like the familiars, they may break loose from the owner's control during his lifetime if they are not properly cared for or if the owner becomes weakened.[11] I cannot tell from the published information whether this is more likely to happen with birth demons than with familiars or not.

Even in their free state, birth demons have an attachment to bodies in general that is comparable to that of a familiar for its owner's body in particular and has no counterpart in the relation of free spirits to bodies. This is the need to ingest blood, a trait

---

[1] Skeat 1900, p. 325.    [2] ibid., p. 327.    [3] McHugh 1955, p. 82.
[4] ibid., p. 72.    [5] ibid., p. 64.
[6] Cf. Annandale and Robinson 1904, p. 23; Skeat 1900, p. 326.
[7] Skeat 1900, p. 321.    [8] Swettenham 1895, p. 194.    [9] ibid., p. 197.
[10] Winstedt 1925, p. 21; Swettenham 1895, p. 196.
[11] e.g., McHugh 1955, p. 72.

which accounts for their frequently being characterized as vampires.[1] All members of this class attack people, usually but not always babies and women having babies, mainly to suck their blood.[2] Whereas the familiar and the person from whom it receives blood are in a symbiotic relationship, there are no reciprocal benefits for the object of a vampire's attentions. The close connection of the vampires with parasitic figs,[3] plants which eventually kill their host, expresses by clear analogy the relationship of the vampire to its victim and to living bodies in general.

Thus, on the scale from *sĕmangat* to free spirit, the birth demon is quite close to the free spirits. The difference is that free spirits may obtain their required soul substance from any organized body, while birth demons have a generalized dependence on living bodies containing blood, and this sometimes even becomes particularized as they lapse, out of convenience or coercion, into the rôle of a familiar. The freedom of action of birth demons, therefore, is slightly more restricted than that of the free spirits.

There is, however, a complicating feature of the birth demon's relationship with the world of material bodies. There are indications that these demons incorporate all or part of their dead original body into their being. Elaborate precautions are taken to demobilize the corpses of women and infants who die in childbirth. For example, to prevent the unfortunate woman from becoming a *langsuir* 'a quantity of glass beads are put in the mouth of the corpse, a hen's egg is put under each arm-pit, and needles are placed in the palms of the hands', so she 'cannot open her mouth to shriek (*ngilai*) or wave her arms as wings, or open and shut her hands to assist her flight'.[4] The attack of the vampires is surprisingly physical, at least when they are in their independent physical state. For example, the *pontianak* may 'drive her long claws into the body of the expectant mother, killing her and the

---

[1] It is interesting to note that the picture of a *bâjang* printed in *Malay Magic* (Skeat 1900, opposite p. 321), copied from an anti-*bajang* charm in which the outlines of the figure were composed of words from the Koran, looks somewhat like a leech with wings.

[2] Skeat 1900, pp. 326, 327; McHugh 1955, pp. 72, 123.

[3] McHugh 1955, pp. 44, 46; Annandale and Robinson 1904, p. 23. Coincidentally, the very same 'strangling fig' is the tree that Bosch concludes (1960, pp. 70, 75) is the basic model for the celestial tree (mainly because of its habit of growing downward, toward the ground, from a seed deposited by birds high in a previously established tree).

[4] Maxwell, quoted in Skeat 1900, p. 325.

unborn child'.[1] Birth demons also kill by sucking the blood but do not often, it seems, cause illness by invading the body as do familiars and free spirits, though this sometimes happens. Furthermore, birth demons are especially susceptible to physical defences. The best deterrent for the *penanggalan*, for instance, is a barrier of thorns or bent nails which she fears will catch hold of her trailing intestines.[2]

This dual relation of birth demons to bodies results, I think, from the involvement of these creatures in two distinct but related systems of ideas. As vampires, they occupy a clear and logical position between familiars and free spirits in the system of ideas that relates physical bodies to vital essences. Yet their association with birth and death, both in origin and in preoccupation, cannot be explained in terms of these ideas. I shall show below that they derive their meaning as birth spirits, including the retention of traces of a body, from their position in the system of ideas by which life and death are distinguished and connected.

Before going on to consider the *nyâwa* or 'life-breath', I shall attempt to put the foregoing discussion into more general terms. Until now I have treated *sĕmangat* and the various kinds of spirit as if they were things. However, my initial premise was that the *sĕmangat* was just one of several forms the vital principle takes upon being differentiated in man. What is the basis of this differentiation? It seems that the vital principle permeates the whole of the physical world, and its division into *sĕmangat* is an integral part of the division of matter into significant discrete 'things'. On the conceptual plane, the *sĕmangat* contributes to the object's identity, preventing it from being merged into another concept, and this is expressed in physical terms as the function of the *sĕmangat* to guide the actions and preserve the boundaries of the body. The *sĕmangat* is both a symbol and a force preserving the integrity of the material thing to which it is attached. Each *sĕmangat* is naturally differentiated and defined to the same degree as its body. A single *sĕmangat* will be attached to each 'thing' whether the significant unit is the individual organism, as for men and animals, or the field, as for rice. Where the body is clearly bounded the *sĕmangat* will be so also, and a vaguely bounded entity, such as a mine of ore, will have an ill-defined *sĕmangat*. The *sĕmangat*, in other words, 'fits' its body as a vital reflection of it

[1] Winstedt 1925, p. 18.  [2] McHugh 1955, p. 82.

and shares, therefore, many of its particular abilities and limitations.

I have shown that there is good reason to regard spirits as derived from the same vital principle as *sĕmangat*, and their close relation to *sĕmangat*, as opposed to the other aspects of the human soul, suggests that the principles of the differentiation of spirits may be similar to that of *sĕmangat*. But if this is so, what could be the equivalent for spirits of bodies for *sĕmangat*? I think the answer is the units into which the Malay divides his experience of the non-material environment. He conceptualizes this realm of experience just as he does his perception of the physical world, and spirits, like *sĕmangat*, symbolize the entities so created. And as *sĕmangat* control their bodies, so spirits are regarded as the cause of the experience they represent. This is not to say that all non-material concepts have spirits attached, but many of those dealing with the more powerful, immediate, and uncontrollable forces that impinge on man are symbolized in this way. Such forces are principally those of nature, especially disease, but are sometimes the powers of men as expressed, for example, in the state spirits which protect the royal family and their political realm.[1] Often the concepts into which the experience of these forces is broken have no other names than those of the spirits that personify them. For example, the diagnosis of disease is simply the discovery of what spirit is plaguing a person; the spirits are the categories of disease. Many times the spirits represent the fears into which the Malay divides his experience of hostile nature; the list of such spirits is a catalogue of the 'things' that he fears. These range from wild beast tracks (*hantu denei*) to getting lost in the jungle (*hantu puteri*). Not all of the power in the non-material environment is threatening, nor are all spirits considered dangerous, at least not to the same degree. But on the whole the forces of nature (and of man) have negative values for the Malay, and the nature of the spirits reflects this bias.

The differentiation of spirits and that of *sĕmangat* differ, then, in the kinds of concept to which the vital principle is adapted. Material bodies are the most constraining of concepts, being by their nature subject to classification into a large number of rigid and unchanging categories. Bodies, and therefore their resident *sĕmangat*, cannot readily change shape, size, colour, texture, and

[1] Swettenham 1895, pp. 155–156; cf. Skeat 1900, p. 40.

location as can the units of invisible force that spirits symbolize. It is the low level of definition of the concepts represented by spirits that gives the spirits their power to break through the boundaries of more highly defined categories such as bodies. Spirits, being only slightly differentiated from the mass of the vital principle, retain much of the power it derives from its infinite flexibility.[1] As the vital principle is attached to more and more clear and rigid concepts, tending more and more towards complete conjunction with a physical body, it loses this potential and becomes more predictable and controllable. It may be that the repetitions of names, descriptions, and origins of spirits in spells is to define them clearly. The extreme expression of this procedure, and the most effective, is the rite in which a spirit is drawn into a physical body, such as a lime, which can be physically disposed of. A similar method is used by the Ndembu when they symbolically describe the forces of disease, making the hidden clear and visible, thereby reducing their power.[2]

### Nyâwa, Badi, and Ghosts

The nyâwa, according to the Patani Malays[3] is the breath of life; it is almost, but not quite, a physical thing. According to many people it is the part of man that goes to heaven (surga) or hell (jehannam) after death. It enters the human foetus, as I noted above, 'at the end of the sixth month of pregnancy, at which date the child "becomes a person" (jadi orang), having previously been "part of its mother's blood" (saparoh darah hibu)'.[4] The removal of the nyâwa is synonomous with death. ᐧ

The nyâwa, then, is the aspect of the human soul that distinguishes the 'living' from the 'dead' and, in its wider distribution, distinguishes man and the higher animals from the 'non-living' rest of creation. Though the exclusion of plants and probably the non-breathing lower animals from the realm of the living is not exactly in line with the ideas of modern biology, the distinction is clear and close enough to the Western idea to warrant using the terms life and death. At death the nyâwa leaves the body and the earth, and, since the sěmangat is probably extinguished at that time, the body disintegrates. Nothing could be simpler: the presence of nyâwa is life, its absence non-life.

[1] Cf. Douglas 1966, p. 94.    [2] See Turner 1967, pp. 303–304.
[3] Annandale and Robinson 1903, pp. 93–4.    [4] ibid., pp. 93–4.

While this clear distinction holds for natural deaths, there is a large class of deaths for which a much more complex situation exists. This is the case with things that 'die of being killed' (*mati di bunoh*),[1] instances of violent or otherwise unusual death. People who die such deaths are appealed to for magical powers, may become ghosts or, in some cases, birth demons, may have parts of their bodies converted into charms or familiar spirits, have their bodies disposed of in various extraordinary ways, and in general are regarded with a great deal of fear and awe.

The key to this complex of ideas is the *badi*, a very important yet mysterious thing that remains with the body in cases of violent death. *Badi* has been variously defined by different writers; the concept seems to vary from place to place and to be rather ambiguous in any given location. Skeat calls it the 'evil principle which, according to the view of Malay medicine-men, attends (like an evil angel) everything that has life', and he reminds us that many inert objects are animate from the Malay point of view.[2] He translates the word as 'mischief'.[3] Von de Wall calls *badi* 'the enchanting or destroying influence which issues from anything', 'the contagious principle of morbid matter'.[4] Wilkinson defines it as 'a nervous fit; sudden and inexplicable fits of trembling, attributed by Malays to supernatural agency; the sense of being haunted; the infection of a disease; panic fear; the ill-luck of a place', and he notes that *membuang badi* means 'to drive away the evil influences which haunt a spot'.[5] Annandale acknowledges the term's vague meaning in the Federated Malay States, but says that, in Patani, *badi* are definite bad spirits rather than evil influences.[6] The incongruity of these definitions reveals the need for a careful reconsideration of the concept of *badi*, and I suggest that a true understanding of its meaning can best be reached by first ascertaining its position in the broad system of ideas of which *sĕmangat* and spirits are part.

It is important in the beginning to determine what things do and what do not have *badi* associated with them. Skeat says *badi* attend all things that have 'life', but, since he includes in this category seemingly inert objects, the concept of life to which he refers is obviously broader than that associated with the possession

---

[1] See ibid., p. 101.
[2] Skeat 1900, p. 427.
[3] ibid., p. 428 and *passim*.
[4] Quoted in Skeat 1900, p. 427.
[5] Wilkinson 1901, p. 78.
[6] Annandale 1903, p. 100.

of a *nyâwa*. He states specifically that *badi* reside in earth, anthills, wood, water, stone, elephants, and rhinoceroses, taking his information from a charm to expel the *badi* from the carcase of a dead elephant or rhinoceros.[1] But immediately following, he cites examples from a deer-charm in which the *badi* in the carcase are requested to return to their places of origin—to the monitor lizard, heart of timber, and the yellow glow of sunset—as if these were the same thing as places of residence.[2] He adds that in another deer-charm the *badi* are asked to return to clouds and hollows of the hills from whence they came as offspring of the *Jin Ibn Ujan*.[3] I think there is a fundamental misconception involved in Skeat's mixing the animals whose carcases are attended by *badi* at death with the places of origin of *badi* and saying that these are all things in which *badi* reside. Even in the first charm mentioned (for elephants and rhinoceroses) the *badi* of various things are asked to return to them as to a point of original departure (*pulang*),[4] not simply to a dwelling place other than the infected carcase. However, the animal's body is referred to in the same way as these other things (*Badi gajah pulang ka gajah*), but Skeat admits elsewhere[5] that 'this particular line should probably come at the end of the charm instead of the middle'. Such uncertainty leaves some doubt about the accuracy of Skeat's transcription on this point, and the weight of the evidence indicates that the bodies from which *badi* must be expelled and their alleged places of origin are not confused. There is no reason to separate the attribution of many origins to *badi* (singular or plural) in a charm from the same practice as used on spirits. And it would not be sensible to say that the forest, for example, where certain spirits live, is like the fragments of the first great failure to create man, one of the many supposed origins of spirits. Leaving out the 'residences' of *badi* that are almost certainly origins, the things to which *badi* are attached (at least on the occasion of their violent death) are breathing animals alone, possessors of *nyâwa*.

Annandale, however, rather than finding *badi* distributed to things outside this class, reports that the Patani Malays regard *badi* as being absent from many things that have *nyâwa*. He says 'no domesticated animal possesses a *badi*, even though its wild congener may do so'[6] and, of wild animals, the squirrels (including

[1] Skeat 1900, p. 428.    [2] ibid., pp. 428–9.    [3] ibid., p. 429.
[4] See ibid., p. 603.    [5] ibid., p. 156 n.    [6] Annandale 1903, p. 101.

gibbons, which are classed as squirrels) and birds other than the quail, jungle fowl, stork, and vulture do not have *badi*.[1] I think these are exceptions, for one reason or another, to a general rule that things with *nyâwa* have *badi*. The 'exceptions' seem to be things that are not normally killed or are killed in a special ritualized way that is closer to the harvesting of crops than to murder. Taking the latter first, it should be noted that domestic animals (not including pets, as cats are definitely said to have *badi*—see Skeat 1900, pp. 191, 398) are only slaughtered in the orthodox Muslim manner; this involves cutting the throat and—significantly, as I shall show—draining the blood in a controlled way.[2] Such treatment may take the violence and unexpectedness out of the death, compared with normal cases of *mati di bunoh*. As for the wild animals without *badi*, perhaps they are ones so infrequently killed that their *badi* is simply of no consequence. There seems to be a gradation in the strength of *badi* that varies directly with the frequency with which various wild animals are killed in hunting. For example, the deer and the jungle fowl are the two commonest objects of the chase,[3] and their *badi* are thought to be extremely strong.[4] On the other hand, the *badi* of wild pig, monkeys, and monitor lizards is considered very weak.[5] These animals are probably seldom killed—for food anyway, which is when the expulsion of *badi* is most critical.[6] Pork is forbidden as human food and the flesh of the others is not, as far as I know, very highly regarded, though information on such things is scanty. If this interpretation of the gradation in *badi* strength is correct, it would follow that animals that are not hunted at all would have *badi* so weak as to be negligible. Squirrels and the smaller birds, along with rodents and other small animals not mentioned by Annandale as having *badi*, are probably only killed to prevent them destroying crops and the like and are not actively pursued or prepared for eating.[7]

The *badi* of animals never or seldom hunted, not being dealt with ritually, may simply fail to achieve the status of the 'definite spirits' which Annandale came to expect in Patani; they would

---

[1] ibid., p. 102.    [2] Winstedt 1925, p. 108.
[3] Annandale and Robinson 1903, p. 103.
[4] Annandale and Robinson 1903, p. 102; Skeat 1900, pp. 132, 177–178.
[5] Annandale and Robinson 1903, pp. 102-103
[6] See ibid., p. 103.    [7] See Winstedt 1911, p. 25.

remain like *badi* in the Federated States, indefinite evil influences. There is, however, a complication regarding the relative strengths of *badi* in various animals. Those creatures with the strongest *badi* of all are never hunted but, on the contrary, are scrupulously avoided. These are vultures, wild dogs, white crocodiles, and certain cobras with white rings around their necks.[1] These are probably all considered supernatural creatures for one reason or another. The latter two are *kramat* ('sacred') animals,[2] wild dogs are believed to be members of the pack of the Spectre Huntsman,[3] and vultures, being given the bodies of murdered men to eat,[4] are possibly thought to retain some of the *badi* surrounding such corpses. It may be that the attribution of powerful *badi* to these things means that they cannot be killed or that to do so would bring death to the slayer. Annandale says 'the *badi* of the vulture is so strong that no man may strike the bird'.[5] All this, of course, is merely speculation in view of the lack of complete information about the meanings of various animals for the Malays, but I have thought it important to mention the fact of variation in the strength of *badi* even if I cannot fully explain it. To return to the original point, while it cannot be said with any certainty that all things with *nyâwa* also have *badi*, it is safe to say that man and most of the important wild animals with which he comes in contact do have *badi* and that objects without *nyâwa* almost certainly do not possess *badi* though they may be regarded as origins of them.

The *badi* seems to be an independent entity that remains in place of the *nyâwa* in cases of violent or unusual death. It is not a transformation of a partially released *nyâwa* for 'although the *badi* of a murdered Mohammedan remains by his bones, this does not prevent him from enjoying the delights of Paradise',[6] and, as I pointed out, the *nyâwa* is the part that goes to heaven or hell. Nor is it modified *sěmangat* since the bodies of still-born babies very likely have *badi*, as I shall explain, though such babies have died before the umbilical cord was cut. The *badi* is never confused with the *sěmangat* or *nyâwa*,[7] and there is evidence that it co-exists with them, in a rather dormant state, during life. Annandale

---

[1] Annandale and Robinson 1903, p. 102.
[2] Annandale and Robinson 1903, p. 102; 1904, p. 29.
[3] Skeat 1900, p. 183 n.    [4] Annandale and Robinson 1903, p. 101.
[5] Annandale 1903, p. 102.
[6] Annandale and Robinson 1904, p. 23.
[7] Annandale and Robinson 1903, p. 100.

says the *badi* is present in the blood and originates from it.[1] It will sometimes issue from a person's teeth when they are filed for the first time.[2] Cats,[3] Negritos,[4] and several types of snake[5] are specifically stated to have active *badi* prior to death. I think the shadow is the physical embodiment of a living creature's *badi*. It is prohibited to let one's shadow fall on the newly erected centre-post of a house or the hole in which it is placed,[6] on rice being reaped,[7] or on one's superior or his shadow.[8] It is said that the shadow of a poisoner will be lacking its head,[9] as if part of it were incorporated in the potion, and it appears that a person's shadow can be sent on missions of black magic by beating it with a cane and telling it to go take control of another's soul.[10] The magic of waxen images works through *badi*,[11] and it is likely that a person's *badi*, like the shadow, is sent out to do the prescribed damage, manipulations of the wax figure serving as an example of what is expected.[12] The connection of blood and shadow is strikingly established by the belief that a certain kind of snail can suck the blood of a grazing animal through its shadow, with no physical contact at all.[13] The evidence of the connection of the shadow with the *badi*, though circumstantial, is convincing, I think, and this will be even more clear when I have explained the connection between the *badi* and familiars which permits one's shadow to be converted into a *pĕlĕsit*. In any case, the *badi* most likely exists in the living man or beast, and, in cases of *mati di bunoh*, it alone is left in attendance when the *nyâwa* flies to heaven or hell and the *sĕmangat* disintegrates.

'To die of being killed' is to die in any 'violent, sudden or unusual way (as by murder, accident, cholera or smallpox)'.[14] Probably the most common cases of this are men being murdered or animals killed in the hunt (when blood is often spilled), and women and children dying in childbirth, an occurrence that is usually if not always assumed to be caused by a birth demon's

---

[1] Annandale 1903, p. 101. The Temiar, Senoi people, have a concept similar to *badi* which is called caʔāy, 'the odour of blood' (Geoffrey Benjamin, personal communication).

[2] Skeat 1900, p. 356 n.     [3] ibid., pp. 191, 398.

[4] Annandale and Robinson 1903, p. 101.

[5] Annandale and Robinson 1904, p. 29.     [6] Skeat 1900, p. 143.

[7] ibid., pp. 244, 245, 248.     [8] Cuisinier 1951, p. 203.

[9] Gimlette 1929, p. 16.     [10] Skeat 1900, p. 575.

[11] ibid., pp. 430–431.     [12] Cf. Wilkinson 1906, pp. 72–3.

[13] Skeat 1900, p. 306.     [14] Annandale and Robinson 1904, pp. 77, 80.

attack. Malays do not seem to regard most deaths as unnatural as do, for example, the Azande.[1] Apparently, when death occurs at a normal speed in understandable conditions, even if caused by a spirit, there is time for the body and the whole of its soul to make a complete and permanent transition from the living to the dead state. Usually, after various funeral ceremonies are performed and the corpse is convinced that it is dead, the body is laid to rest and its connections with the world of the living are ended.[2] Sometimes it is said that the *rûh*, which will be considered below, returns to its old dwelling place each night for seven days after death before it disappears for good,[3] but this brief lingering does not lessen the finality of the eventual separation of living and dead. The occurrence of a violent death, however, is entirely different, as the corpse and the accompanying *badi* are then of great significance to the living for some time, probably until the body has decayed away.

The *badi* is involved in an intimate relationship with the corpse to which it is attached. The *badi* always remains by the body: 'if the body be removed, the *badi* goes with it'.[4] The *badi* appears to lose its power when separated from the material carcase. Hence, it can be rendered harmless by merely being cast out of the corpse. This is done with animals; the carcase is brushed with a black cloth, tree branch, or leaf brush, and a charm is recited ordering the *badi* to leave, often to return to its origin.[5] The process is in most ways like the casting out of an evil spirit from a sick person. I have seen no formula for casting out the *badi* of murdered men or other human victims of violent ends; I assume that it cannot be done. In any case, the common strategy for nullifying the power of such people is to isolate, immobilize, or destroy the body. Of course, it would be exceedingly dangerous to destroy the body oneself, but it is always possible to arrange for it to be done by natural agencies. For example, in Jalor and Patani the corpse of a murdered man was formerly 'cast forth to be eaten by vultures and dogs'.[6] Now, most commonly, it would be buried in the jungle or some waste place, or, if in a cemetery, in the part furthest from human habitation.[7] I have described above the special precautions

---

[1] Evans-Pritchard 1937, pp. 26, 38.
[2] See Skeat 1900, pp. 397–408.     [3] McHugh 1955, p. 91.
[4] Annandale and Robinson 1903, p. 101.
[5] See Skeat 1900, pp. 155–6, 177–8, 428–30.
[6] Annandale and Robinson 1903, p. 101.
[7] Annandale and Robinson 1903, p. 101; 1904, p. 80.

taken to render impotent the body of a mother or child dead in childbirth. The danger here, I think, is that the *badi* will reanimate the body as a vampire. A *badi* may even activate a body other than its own, for example, the corpse of a person whose death was natural. Skeat points out that 'cats must be very carefully prevented from rubbing up against a corpse, for it is said that on one occasion when this was neglected, the *badi* or Evil Principle which resides in the cat's body entered the corpse, which thus became endowed with unnatural life and stood up upon its feet'.[1] Though it is unusual for a *badi* to bring the body back to 'life', it is probably the *badi* in the blood of a murdered man that makes this material so potent that it can be converted into love and gambling charms[2] or into a *polong*.[3] Similarly, the power of a still-born infant's tongue to become a *pělěsit*[4] probably derives from the presence of a *badi* in or on it. Thus, *badi* depend on bodies in some mysterious way for their power, but they also give back to those bodies a potency not found in the remains of the victims of normal deaths.

The *badi* is free to leave the corpse, however, and to act in many ways like a spirit. It is generally invisible, though it resembles the person from whom it is derived.[5] It can enter bodies at will, 'devouring the *sěmangat*, or as it is sometimes said, the "liver" (*hati*), of those who approach'.[6] Skeat says the *badi* will 'possess' anyone who accidentally comes in contact with it and cause him to become sick.[7] In Patani, the *badi* of animals are thought to cause a kind of madness wherein the actions and even the appearance of the afflicted may come to resemble those of the animal from which the *badi* came.[8] They may also cause blindness.[9] A *badi* is cast out of the patient by means similar to those used for spirits[10] and which also resemble the methods for removing the *badi* from the original corpse. These include charms of the usual type and offerings, substitutes, cleansings, and brushings all designed to get the invader out and powerless, so it can be disposed of. In the hierarchy of spirits, *badi* occupy a rather low position: they are sometimes called the slaves of the great spirits (*hamba hantu raya*).[11]

[1] Skeat 1900, p. 191.   [2] See Gimlette 1929, p. 9.
[3] Skeat 1900, p. 329 n.   [4] ibid., p. 331.
[5] Annandale and Robinson 1903, p. 101.   [6] ibid., p. 101.
[7] Skeat 1900, p. 429.   [8] Annandale and Robinson 1903, p. 102.
[9] Winstedt 1925, p. 26.   [10] See Skeat 1900, pp. 429–33.
[11] Annandale and Robinson 1903, p. 104.

The concept of *badi*, then, represents the extension of life into non-life in clear violation of the usual 'all or nothing' boundary derived from possession or lack of a *nyáwa*. It is also, I suggest, involved in the earliest transition from non-life to life. For the first six months of pregnancy, the foetus is thought to be 'part of the mother's blood', and it is not unreasonable to infer that the first differentiated aspect of the baby's soul substance is the *badi*, developing out of the *badi* in the mother's blood just as the body develops from the blood itself. The prohibition on the father's killing anything during this early stage of the baby's development is probably to prevent the interference of any alien *badi* in this initial formation of the child.[1] By the time the *nyáwa* enters, in the sixth month, the *badi* has done its work, bringing order out of the formless, a body from the primordial fluid. It performs almost exactly the opposite function in conducting a body back into chaos when its sudden demise has prevented society from making adequate social and emotional preparation.[2] The *badi* takes the place of a funeral,[3] but it also takes the matter out of human hands; it represents a loss of control at the crucial boundary between life and death and between existence and non-existence. The marginal and uncontrolled nature of the *badi* is probably at the root of its exceedingly nasty character. I shall explain this in proper detail when the complete system of ideas is sketched out, when I can bring together the concept of *badi* with the familiars and birth demons on the one hand and were-tigers on the other.

There is still to be explained the matter of ghosts, spirits that seem to come from the dead. If the *nyáwa* goes to heaven or hell and the *sĕmangat* and *badi*, in most cases, disappear at death, what is it that could stay behind as a ghost? Part of the answer is very likely that the *badi* of murdered men eventually become detached from the corpses, probably when these have disintegrated, and take up an existence as independent spirits. The ghosts of murdered men (*hantu orang mati di bunoh*) are believed to be particu-

---

[1] The affliction of the child resulting from the father's killing something has the same symptoms as the attack of an animal's *badi* as described above (see Annandale and Robinson 1903, p. 102). For example, the baby may have a physical deformity resembling, or may himself unconsciously imitate, the animal that was killed (Skeat 1900, pp. 349–50).

[2] See e.g., Winstedt 1925, p. 143.

[3] The body of a murdered man is usually buried 'hastily in the jungle' (Annandale and Robinson 1903:101) and, though sometimes the outlines of a funeral are performed, the loss of real control is evident (see Winstedt 1925, p. 146).

larly powerful and malicious.[1] They are also a source of magical power for those courageous enough to contact them in the prescribed manner.[2] And besides the unspecialized *hantu orang mati di bunoh*, there are the *hantu dagok*, also derived from murdered men, which take the form of peculiarly shaped clouds.[3] I have no explicit support for my assertion that these ghosts are the *badi* gone free, but it would be unlikely that chance alone would single out the class of murdered men, which almost uniquely among men retain their *badi* at death, as producing a prominent class of ghosts. There is one type of ghost—the *jimbalang orang*—that almost certainly develops from human *badi*. These take the form of men with red caps, leaning on sticks and eating earth.[4] They originate from dead men, probably murdered ones since they appear in waste places, and are also called *hantu orang*, a name sometimes given to the *badi* of men.[5] *Jimbalang* in general, which are basically earth spirits,[6] are similar to *badi* in general.[7] Maxwell characterizes them as 'evil influences',[8] and they are said to be servants of *jin*[9] which is nearly the same as *badi* being the 'slaves of the great spirits', given the virtual identity in meaning of the terms 'spirit' and 'jin'.

Another type or class of ghost is the common graveyard variety. This is probably one type of ghost whose several different aspects have different names. Wilkinson[10] considers the *hantu bungkus* (the bundle or package ghost), the *hantu golek* (the rolling ghost), and the *hantu kochong* (a shrouded ghost) simply to represent different characteristics of the *hantu bangkit* (*bangkit* = rising up), '"a sheeted" ghost; the ghost of a man wearing his grave clothes'. The *hantu bangkit* is also the same as the *hantu kubor*,[11] *kubor* being derived from the Sanscrit for tomb. This graveyard ghost is the one that lurks near cemeteries in the form of a bundle of rags and may enter a hapless passer-by to devour his soul.[12] There is no firm

---

[1] Wilkinson 1901, p. 690; McHugh 1955, p. 90.
[2] See Skeat 1900, pp. 60–1.
[3] Wilkinson 1901, p. 690; McHugh 1955, p. 124.
[4] Annandale and Robinson 1904, p. 21.    [5] ibid., p. 21.
[6] Winstedt 1925, p. 27; Wilkinson 1964, p. 107; cf. Annandale and Robinson 1904, p. 21.
[7] Possibly *jimbalang* are ghosts developed from *badi* of all murdered men and animals.
[8] Maxwell 1906, p. 9.    [9] Cuisinier 1936, p. 33.
[10] Wilkinson 1901, p. 690.    [11] McHugh 1955, p. 90.
[12] See Annandale and Robinson 1904, pp. 21–2.

evidence that this ghost develops from *badi* or murdered men. Still, there may be some suggestion of such a connection in the beliefs that the *hantu bungkus* is 'somehow to be related to the *hantu* of women dying in childbirth',[1] and that its proper form is that of a cat,[2] a creature, as I mentioned above, with a particularly strong *badi*. But another possibility is that the graveyard ghost comes from the *rôh*, the third aspect of the human soul, which I shall describe shortly. There is a striking similarity between the behaviour of the *rôh* after death—it 'returns at night from the grave and eats and sleeps in the house'[3]—and that of the *hantu bungkus* which returns 'to revisit its old home or haunts'.[4]

Whichever aspect of the living person's soul develops into a ghost, in crossing completely the boundary from life to death it becomes assimilated to the world of spirits. Though ghosts are defined with some reference to their connection with dead human beings, there is nothing in their basic nature or behaviour to set them off from the other *hantu*. Ghosts are without bodies so they can change their form or become invisible at will.[5] It appears that soul substance freed from a body by the process of death is in every important way like the soul substance that was never conjoined with a body. The distinction between life and death, in other words, expresses diachronically the relation between matter and vital principle that is expressed synchronically by the contrast between spirits and *sěmangat*.

The cultural concepts in terms of which ghosts are differentiated from the mass of the vital principle are probably conventional fears surrounding death. The *hantu orang mati di bunoh* seem to symbolize the fear of death itself, especially sudden and violent death, and the *hantu bangkit* may represent the fear of people or of particular enemies as it persists even after their deaths.

Before leaving the subject of ghosts, it is necessary to mention *kramat* men and animals, the class of beings most often called ghosts in the literature. These are the so-called sacred creatures often found around or in 'sacred' places. It is only important at this point to note that these things are not really dead, and there exists an elaborate fiction to this effect. A Malay told Winstedt

---

[1] McHugh 1955, p. 90.      [2] Annandale and Robinson 1904, p. 21.
[3] McHugh 1955, p. 91.
[4] Wilkinson 1901, p. 103; see also Annandale and Robinson 1904, p. 22.
[5] See McHugh 1955, p. 90.

that 'a kramat never dies, not really',[1] and Annandale reports that *kramat* animals 'do not really die, though their bodies may appear to do so'.[2] They are deliberately retained in the class of the living despite all appearances for reasons I shall explain. They are better described not as ghosts, but as immortals or at least as beings whose grip on life is especially tenacious.

## Rôh, Animals, and Were-Tigers

The Patani Malays describe the *rôh*[3] as that which goes out of man when he sleeps. They generally agree that it is peculiar to man, distinguishing him from beasts. It is the most individualized aspect of the human soul. If a person's face is painted while he is asleep, his *rôh* may not recognize him, and he will not be able to awaken. The *rôh* may also go out of the body when one takes a long drink of water and perhaps when one yawns or sneezes.

The major importance of the *rôh*, I think, is that it sets man off from all the rest of creation. It is essentially the spirit of life that passed from God to Adam at his creation and is handed down in turn to each new member of the human race.[4] It seems that the portion accruing to each person becomes distinctive and is involved in establishing his individual identity. It is possible, as I noted above, that this individualized particle of the eternal *rôh* may persist after a person's death as a ghost, but the evidence on this is unclear. In any case, the fundamental distinction is not among *rôh*, but between things with a *rôh* and those without. Above all, possession of a *rôh* establishes one's identity as a human being.

It follows that a person is most likely to turn into something else when the *rôh* is absent. Without the *rôh*, a man is reduced to the level of animals, possessing only body, *sĕmangat*, and *nyâwa*, and his identity as a human is not assured. People would be especially vulnerable to changing into animals when asleep, shocked, drinking water, and perhaps when sneezing or yawning though the loss of the *rôh* at this time is only a surmise on Annandale's·part.[5]

Annandale reports that 'Malays are always unwilling to awake a sleeping person, lest his *rôh* should not have time to come back

---

[1] Winstedt 1954, p. 66.     [2] Annandale and Robinson 1904, p. 21.
[3] Annandale and Robinson 1903, pp. 94–5.
[4] See Cuisinier 1951, p. 198.
[5] Annandale and Robinson 1903, p. 95.

to him',[1] but he does not say what the consequence of awakening someone abruptly would be. It is significant that the most flagrant violations of the man-animal boundary—the were-tigers—are men who become transformed at night when they would be expected to be asleep.[2] Perhaps some men, through a kind of congenital weakness in their identity, become tigers simply by going to sleep, losing their *rôh* and their last hold on their humanity. The tendency to become were-tigers seems to be loosely hereditary; the Malays believe that it is confined to natives of the state of Korinchi in Sumatra.[3] This view implies that the ability to become a were-tiger is rather an affliction than a product of a man's evil volition. Clifford describes a family who later proved to be were-tigers as 'quiet, well-behaved people' who were 'regular in their attendance at the mosque'[4] and adds that the head of the family treated his newly wedded wife kindly and with courtesy, despite her shortcomings, which pleased her very much until she realized he spent his nights as a were-tiger.[5] That people who lose their identities in sleep should become tigers rather than some other animal is probably due to the convergence of several ideas. For one thing, the tiger is the most dangerous of creatures, the embodiment of danger on the earthly plane. The act of violating the boundary between man and beast is a very threatening one, for reasons I shall soon explain, and demands a malevolent symbol: the production of a were-rabbit would not adequately express the magnitude of the threat to order contained in this transformation. Also, the tiger is equivalent to man in a sense, having a position among the animals of the jungle that is analogous to that of man in relation to domestic animals, each being the 'king of beasts' in his own realm. The were-tiger, then, is a transformation of the human body that very likely takes place in sleep when the *rôh* is absent.

There is evidence that the *rôh* may also depart the body when a person is shocked or frightened suddenly. *Panggil rôh*, the summoning of the *rôh*, is 'the name given to a number of formulae for recalling one's composure when faint with the shock of sudden excitement'.[6] It is interesting that nearly all the legendary meta-

---

[1] Annandale and Robinson 1904, p. 95.
[2] Swettenham 1895, pp. 200, 201; Clifford 1897, p. 68.
[3] Skeat 1900, p. 160.      [4] Clifford 1897, p. 66.
[5] ibid., p. 68.      [6] Wilkinson 1901, p. 347.

morphoses of people into animals take place in periods of suddenly heightened emotion. Skeat records cases of people becoming various birds and animals when startled or surprised,[1] frightened,[2] in a rage,[3] and in a fit of frustration.[4] Perhaps significantly, one of the few cases cited where a man becomes something other than an animal is when a man in a fight is transformed into a tree at the moment he dies,[5] when he would be expected to lose his *nyâwa* as well as his *rôh*. This is the only case I have read where death is involved in the metamorphosis. Such transformations as these appear to happen only in the legendary past when, perhaps, the boundaries of the world were not so firmly fixed as now. But it is still important that they took place at just those times when one would expect the *rôh* to be absent or at least loosened.

I have read of no examples of a person's changing species when drinking water, sneezing, or yawning. I can, however, as a matter of interest, suggest a possible basis for the belief that the *rôh* may flee in the course of drinking. Under certain conditions a reflection of a person's face may be seen in the water; this might be taken to be the *rôh* since the reflection, like the *rôh*, is distinctive for each individual. Skeat mentions a 'reflection-soul',[6] but never explains what it is.

The *rôh* is differentiated in conjunction with the differences among individuals. The soul substance of lower species is not differentiated to this degree because the differences among individual members of a species are not very significant. But in the anonymity of sleep or in reversion to a basic emotional mode of behaviour, man loses his individuality and his *rôh* and is reduced almost to the level of the beasts. In ancient times and under special conditions today, a person in this condition might slip over the boundary between man and the animals.

## Sĕmangat, Nyâwa, and Rôh

I have found it convenient to describe the elements of this system of Malay ideas as if they were parts of three sets of ideas radiating from a focus in the soul of man. In fact, the various other elements in the three sets are probably just as closely related to each other as are the three aspects of the human soul. With this outline of the basic components of the system in mind, it is now

---

[1] Skeat 1900, pp. 130, 187.
[2] ibid., pp. 158–9, 185–6.
[3] ibid., pp. 122, 123, 201.
[4] ibid., p. 126.
[5] ibid., p. 205.
[6] ibid., p. 50 n.

possible to examine the cross-cutting relationships and to re-establish the unity that was dissected for purposes of analysis.

Some writers, struck by the differences between the Malay world-view and our own, have made some rather strange statements about the Malay outlook. For example, Annandale says that 'Patani Malays make no fundamental distinction between men and animals, or, indeed, between animals and highly organized in-animate objects'.[1] It would probably be rather shocking to a European to hear a Malay say that we do not distinguish men from dogs in that we class them both as mammals. Of course, we do separate men from dogs by some criteria, but group them together by others. The Malays do the same, but with a different set of criteria. The three aspects of the human soul, taken together, form the basis of a classification that both unites man with and separates him from the rest of creation in an orderly way. Posses-sion of *sĕmangat* groups together all things, including man, that are set off as significant material entities from the Malay point of view. These are distinguished from 'non-bodies' on the one hand —the grain of rice or cup of water, and from non-material 'things' on the other—spirits, for example. The *nyâwa* involves man in a class with most animals, set off against the lower animals, plants, and minerals as well as the non-bodies and non-material things. The *rôh* distinguishes man still farther from the rest of the world, even separating him from the higher animals; it expresses the uniqueness of man despite this involvement with the rest of creation. The *sĕmangat*, *nyâwa*, and *rôh* represent successive stages in the differentiation of the soul material of man; these permit an orderly view of the universe despite the participation of man in an all pervading vital principle or even in a 'culte de la vie' as Cuisi-nier says. What is united at one level is separated at the next, so the Malays are able to express the differences among men and the unity of the cosmos in terms of a single system of ideas based on *sĕmangat*, the vital principle.

It must be remembered, however, that the most common use of the term *sĕmangat* is for the entire soul of whatever creature is being considered. For man this would include all three of the aspects described above, for animals only the *rôh* and the *sĕmangat* in the narrow sense, and for other things the latter alone. Thus, some of the contradictions in the qualities attributed to the

[1] Annandale and Robinson 1904, p. 45.

*sĕmangat* (soul) of man probably derive from reference being made to different aspects of that soul. For example, the image of the *sĕmangat* as a bird probably refers to the *rôh*. Skeat points out that the expression used when a person is astonished or surprised is *kur sĕmangat*, *kur* being the word used to call fowls.[1] I have pointed out that the specific aspect of the soul that is feared to depart at such times is the *rôh*. It seems perfectly appropriate that the part of man's *sĕmangat* that is believed to fly from the body is thought of as a bird; it is a metaphor, as Skeat says.[2] On the other hand, the aspect of the *sĕmangat* that has to do with the bounds and integrity of the body, the *sĕmangat* narrowly defined, might be expected to take the form of that body—in other words, to have the image of a manikin. The *nyâwa* is represented by the physical breath, and this also is taken in some situations to be a manifestation of the *sĕmangat*, the soul of man.[3] Thus, the *sĕmangat* as bird, manikin, and breath refers to the same divisions of the soul as are indicated by Patani Malays in the terms *rôh*, *sĕmangat*, and *nyâwa*. While these three aspects are sometimes merged in one concept—*sĕmangat* as the total soul—each of their attributes will still be present.

### Spirits, Ghosts, and Animals

The differences between man and the rest of creation, then, are not of an 'all or nothing' sort, but are arranged in a graded series. Man shares much with animals, even wild ones, and can exert some control over them. Even plants and minerals with no breath of life can be dealt with in a direct, physical way. Ghosts are like free spirits, but they are slightly closer to man than the perpetually free spirits for having gone through a phase of having a body. Free spirits themselves are still more like man than the completely undefined—the vital principle and formless matter. The things that are set off from man by lack of one or more of the aspects of his soul form a large and heterogeneous group. Still, they are all equivalent in that their exclusion as a set is what defines man.

The division between man and non-man is a most important one. One Malay classification of the world is very interesting in that it groups Negritos with spirits and animals.[4] The Negritos

---

[1] Skeat 1900, p. 47 n.      [2] ibid., p. 47.
[3] Cuisinier 1951, p. 203.      [4] Annandale and Robinson 1903, pp. 8, 101.

seem to be on the boundary between man and non-man. Though the Malays regard Negritos as *orang* (persons),[1] they are not thought to be subject to spirits, 'being akin to them'.[2] I noted previously that Negritos are regarded with fear and awe mixed with contempt. Malays are afraid in approaching their camps and ascribe to them, therefore, active *badi*.[3] Negritos are usually believed to be the best magicians,[4] and relics from their bodies are thought to have magical powers.[5] As might be expected, these permanent dwellers on the boundary between men and beasts seem especially close to those beings that habitually transgress it— the were-tigers. Skeat records the belief in Kelantan that the local Semang (Negrito) medicine men are able to become were-tigers.[6] Clifford tells of a similar belief in Pahang.[7] This is significant because normally only Korinchi Malays are accorded that power. I have no information about the state of the *rôh* in Negritos, but it could be that Negritos, being pagans, are out of the mainstream of the transmission of this basically Moslem force. Apparently the contempt for Negritos that is involved in their being classed with spirits and animals is derived largely from their unorthodox religious beliefs.[8]

## Familiars, Vampires, Badi, and Were-Tigers

Familiars, birth demons, and *badi* are closely connected in a number of ways. For example, birth demons and familiars often originate in things that would be expected to be infested with *badi*. The *langsuir* and *pontianak* come from mothers and babies who 'die of being killed', presumably by birth demons, in the process of childbirth. Familiars may be created from dead babies' tongues, the blood of murdered men, and one's own shadow, which is, I contend, an aspect of the *badi* during life. They can also come from a person's own blood, which contains the *badi*, or from the oil of a green coconut. There is often a connection made in Indonesia between coconuts and human heads: a possible inference is that the oil represents blood. The bulk of the evidence suggests that the *badi* is the differentiation of the vital principle that

[1] Annandale and Robinson 1904, p. 34.
[2] Annandale and Robinson 1903, p. 101.      [3] ibid., p. 101.
[4] ibid., p. 21; Blagden 1896, p. 12.
[5] Annandale and Robinson 1903, p. 101.
[6] Quoted in Annandale and Robinson 1904, p. 29 n.
[7] Clifford 1897, p. 202.      [8] See Annandale and Robinson 1903, p. 9.

animates birth demons and familiars, and with the vampires there is even some retention of the original body that the *badi* inhabited.

Birth demons, if not also familiars, participate in the domain of *badi*, the transitions between life and non-life. They originate from death in birth, and their preoccupation is to recreate the event.

Familiars, vampires, and *badi* share an intimate connection with blood: the first two depend on it, and the last arise from it. The nature of blood provides a clue to the basis of the connection between these three types of being. Blood is part of a large number of organized bodies, but it is in itself formless. It is intermediate between organized physical bodies which contain *sĕmangat* and undifferentiated matter whose essences are free. The great potential of blood for being ordered, by contrast with other components of the human body, is probably the basis of the belief that babies develop from the blood.[1]

Familiars, vampires, and *badi* are intermediate between complete dependence on organized bodies and freedom from nearly all constraining categories. The life-death dimension and the progression from *sĕmangat* to free spirits represent the diachronic and synchronic aspects respectively of this basic continuum. The freeing of a ghost by the disintegration of a body reproduces the degrees of freedom represented statically by the positions of *sĕmangat*, familiars, birth demons, and free spirits in relation to bodies. The connections among *badi*, familiars, and vampires arise from their sharing a position on a single basic continuum in Malay magical thought.

Were-tigers and Negritos share a position intermediate between man and the beasts. The former fluctuates back and forth while the latter does not, but the poles of the were-tiger's fluctuation are the same as those used to define the constant nature of the Negrito. Were-tigers and Negritos are considered similar, being feared as semi-natural creatures of the forest, and are even identified by some in the belief that Negrito magicians are were-tigers.[2]

One striking feature of Negritos and were-tigers is that they habitually occupy or transgress the boundary between two major categories in the Malay classification of the world, namely, those of man and non-man. A close look at vampires, *badi*, and familiars

---

[1] See Douglas 1966, p. 94.
[2] Annandale and Robinson 1904, p. 29 n.

reveals that their intermediate position is also a marginal one; they are between the major categories of free spirits (including ghosts) and spirits bound up in bodies. Seen in this light, some of the confusing aspects of the three are somewhat clearer.

The ambiguity and contradictions in the definition of *badi* can be partially accounted for by the fact that they do not fall clearly within the categories of spirit or of *sĕmangat*. This may also be behind the unusual variation in the division of the familiar rôle and the oscillation of birth demons, in popular thought, between the characteristics of familiars and those of free spirits.

While the origins of vampires and familiars are usually parts of bodies that are infested with *badi*, the origins ascribed to *badi* themselves are diverse. Those most commonly mentioned, according to Skeat, are three drops of Adam's blood, a monitor lizard, the 'Heart of Timber', the yellow glow of sunset, and the Jin Ibn Ujan or Ibnu Jan.[1] I cannot say why *badi* should have come from Adam,[2] but it should be clear from the previous discussion why, if he were considered the source, the *badi* would have developed from his blood. The monitor lizard seems to represent an intermediate state between crocodile and the tiger. It is a common belief that the mother crocodile watches her babies hatching and eats whichever ones turn toward land rather than their proper habitat. If one escapes her, however, and reaches the jungle, it will turn into a tiger.[3] But Skeat adds 'there is perhaps more point in the Selangor tradition, according to which the little runaways turn, not into tigers, but into "iguanas" (Monitor Lizards)'.[4] If these two beliefs are related, and they almost certainly are, monitor lizards must be regarded as intermediate between tigers and crocodiles. The symbolism of the 'Heart of Timber' is not completely clear to me, though it is certainly important. I shall show subsequently how it can be regarded as the key to the rites of brushing out *badi* with tree branches or leaf brushes. The yellow glow of sunset refers to the hour that is neither perfect day nor night.[5] Skeat says the expression 'Jin Ibu Ujan' may refer to 'Jan' who is said by some Arabian authorities

---

[1] Skeat 1900, p. 428.

[2] There seems to be some tendency in Malay myths to treat the first failure to create man in the manner of nagas (see e.g., Skeat 1900, p. 95), Indian snake-beings from whose bodily components come many of the things in the world (see Skeat 1900, p. 4).

[3] Skeat 1900, pp. 286, 289.    [4] ibid., p. 289.    [5] ibid., p. 90.

to be the Father of the Genii.[1] This probably reflects the fact that *badi* are similar to *jin* and are sometimes conceived to be *jin* or *hantu*. Thus, of the five main origins of *badi*, at least three—the blood, monitor lizard, and sunset—seem clearly to express their intermediate and marginal nature.

Negritos and were-tigers, then, are structurally equivalent to vampires, *badi*, and familiars, all being on the boundaries between major categories, even though the two complexes of ideas are quite different in substance. Van Gennep shows that the transitions between socially important categories in time and space can be expected to have common features despite great differences in the nature of the categories. People in transitional zones are sacred.[2] Specifically, this means that they will have great power, since they are outside society's control,[3] but will also be in danger, because they are beyond its protection.[4] Mary Douglas shows that there is power and danger in the interstices between categories in general. The power is derived from the potential of the unclassified to be ordered in a number of ways.[5] But disorder is dangerous to the existing order as it challenges the distinctions out of which order is created.[6] Douglas further contends that ambiguous phenomena that cannot be clearly classified will be considered unclean.[7] It will be valuable to see how far these characteristics apply to those elements of Malay thought that have been shown to be, in a sense, anomalous to their classification of the world. There are similarities and even concrete connections between all of these things. Since they cannot be explained in terms of cultural content, they may well be based in the structural equivalence of the concepts.

Vampires, familiars, *badi*, were-tigers, and Negritos are all definitely dangerous. They appear to be more malicious in most cases than the classes of things they fall between. For example, most spirits 'are regarded as utterly non-moral; they are certainly not good, they are only "vicious" (*jahat*) in self-defence',[8] and Skeat remarks that 'the Genii *may* do good'.[9] By contrast, the whole *raison d'être* of birth demons is to attack people, and familiars are kept mainly to inflict harm on one's enemies. There is great variation among bodied things, but in general they are far

[1] ibid., p. 95 n.    [2] Van Gennep 1960, p. 114.
[3] ibid., p. 114.    [4] ibid., p. ix.
[5] Douglas 1966, p. 94.    [6] ibid., p. 40; see also Leach 1964, pp. 23, 34.
[7] Douglas 1966, p. 40.    [8] Annandale and Robinson 1904, p. 35.
[9] Skeat 1900, p. 94.

less noxious than the demons of the intermediate zone. *Badi* never do good,[1] but whether ghosts are any more gentle I cannot say. Living creatures as a group certainly do not approach *badi* in nastiness. Still, I think the *badi* may do some secret good work in the privacy of the womb. Some animals, especially tigers, are extremely dangerous in their normal form, but were-tigers are even more so; they take an unnatural delight in killing human beings.[2] Even habitual man-eaters do not rival these in ferocity. Interestingly enough, the were-tiger in the story recorded by Clifford was believed to suck more blood than eat flesh, and this was said to prove he was a were-tiger, not an ordinary one.[3] Human beings, on the other hand, are the gentlest of creatures, at least somewhat more kindly than were-tigers. The other thing falling between man and the animals—the Negrito—is considered dangerous in the only way he could be, given his pathetic physical and political state. He is feared as a magician and an associate of the spirits, and, significantly, is thought to have active *badi*.[4]

The power of these intermediate things, unlike their viciousness, does not always seem to exceed the things they lie between. It seems a fairly simple matter to protect someone from birth demons —usually a barrier of thorns or simple snares will do[5]—and familiars can be forced to reveal their owner, allowing him to be dealt with. But free spirits are often quite hard to handle, and Malay *bomor* seem to lose a lot of their patients. Similarly, *badi* are fairly simply made powerless, at least those attached to dead animals, but ghosts enjoy all the freedom and resources of the free spirits. Were-tigers are more in line with expectations, being at least as powerful as their animal counterparts, and Negritos are thought to have great magical power.[6] But the relative weakness of *badi*, familiars, and vampires must be explained. I think Douglas's basic contention that the power lies with the unstructured holds good. It is just that in these particular classifications, with one end in concrete bodies and the other in the invisible realm, the lack of structure does not fall between the major categories, but inside one of them. As clear as the boundaries of the class of spirits and ghosts are, the actual members of the class are rather poorly defined. Internally, there is flux. Things change shape, size,

---

[1] ibid., p. 94.    [2] See Clifford 1897, p. 196–210.    [3] ibid., p. 202.
[4] Annandale and Robinson 1903, p. 101.    [5] Skeat 1900, p. 334.
[6] Blagden 1896, p. 12; Annandale and Robinson 1903, p. 21.

location, and all other conventional indices of identity quite haphazardly, and, as I explained above, I think this infinite flexibility of spirits, their potential to be structured and restructured, is the key to their power and freedom from control. Vampires, *badi*, and familiars are more constrained, owing to their association with physical bodies. However ambiguous or variable they may be as a class, relative to the class of spirits, as individual entities they are never as free as spirits and are not, therefore, as formidable.

Whether these boundary concepts are considered unclean or not is open to debate. There is some question whether there is a well developed notion of impurity in Malay thought. The problem is whether what is usually reported as ritual cleansing is not better seen as protection rites[1] or facilitation of transition. The washing of corpses, mothers, and babies and the practice of roasting recent mothers[2] may be seen as cleansing impurity. Skeat calls the forty-four days of isolation of the mother a period of uncleanness,[3] but it could just as well be termed a period of vulnerability or transition. I have no evidence that birth demons, *badi*, were-tigers, or Negritos are believed to be unclean (except perhaps the latter in a physical sense). There is the unusual practice of offering pork to a *pĕlĕsit*, but this may be done for free spirits as well under extreme circumstances.[4] Impurity does not seem to be an attribute of these particular marginal creatures. Fuller evidence might reveal its presence, but it is just as likely that it does not exist; ideas of impurity may simply be a common cultural elaboration of the basic qualities of marginal phenomena: power and danger.

This rough outline of the manifold relations of the human soul in its various aspects to a number of other Malay concepts should serve as a guide to the meanings of the forms into which the vital principle is differentiated. But differentiation is not the only mental operation performed on *sĕmangat*, the vital principle; I shall turn now to a consideration of the concentration of *sĕmangat*.

## II. CONCENTRATION OF SĔMANGAT

In this section I shall examine the conditions under which one thing is said to have more of the vital principle than another com-

---

[1] Cf. Van Gennep 1960, p. 45.    [2] See Skeat 1900, pp. 342–343.
[3] ibid., p. 343.    [4] Winstedt 1961b, p. 22.

parable thing and seek out the principles by which this deter-
mination is made. I use the term concentration to indicate the
amount of *sěmangat* contained by a unit of matter: the more
*sěmangat*, the higher the concentration. Since the detailed differentiation of the vital principle is not of major concern here, I shall
revert to the use of the term *sěmangat* for the vital principle.
Whenever I use the term in its narrower sense, I shall try to make
this clear.

Changes over time in the 'strength' or 'hardness' of a body's
soul probably reflect changes in the concentration of *sěmangat* in
that body, since all aspects of the soul draw their existence from
the vital principle. The vigour of a living body and the existence
of any body depend on the strength of the *nyâwa* and *sěmangat*
(in the narrow sense), so changes in the concentration of vital
principle would naturally affect the health and integrity of a body.
A loss of *sěmangat* may be due to magic (for example, when part
of the soul is abducted), or to natural causes such as weariness,
worry, or fear.[1] This leads to a lessening of the breath of life, and
the weakened *sěmangat* (in the narrow sense) may not be able to
prevent the invasion of spirits. In either case the result may well be
illness. To combat this, ceremonies can be performed to increase
the supply of *sěmangat*. *Membuat sěmangat* rites, for example, work
by transferring the *sěmangat* of offerings to the patient.[2] A con-
tinued adequate level of *sěmangat* can be maintained by harmony
in a person's relations with nature and with the obligations of his
social rank.[3] This will be reflected in continuing good health. In
Malay theory, then, changes in the concentration of *sěmangat* will
lead to changes in the condition of the body. The mental connection
of the observer is probably made the other way around: the
condition of the body is taken as the index of the concentration of
*sěmangat*.

It is not so clear why some parts of bodies have an innately
higher concentration of *sěmangat* than other parts. According to
Annandale, though the *sěmangat* (in the narrow sense) permeates
the whole body, including parts that are physiologically dead such
as hair and finger nails, its 'special abode' is the head and the liver.[4]

---

[1] See Cuisinier 1951, p. 209; Annandale and Robinson 1903, p. 96; 1904,
p. 30.
[2] Cuisinier 1951, pp. 211–28.     [3] ibid., p. 209.
[4] Annandale 1903, p. 97.

A.A.M.M.—7

Skeat says certain portions of the human frame are invested with sanctity: the head, hair, teeth, ears, nails, eyebrows, and saliva.[1] Cuisinier calls the blood, sperm, hair, nails, sweat, saliva, tears, liver, and intestines 'soul materials'.[2] I assume the *sĕmangat* of animals is concentrated along these same general lines. Rice, whose body is the field, seems to have a concentration of *sĕmangat* in the rice soul (*sĕmangat padi*) which is in a freak ear of one kind or another.[3] This ear, along with six others, is reaped with special ceremony, being treated all the time as a new-born baby. Especially large trees are sometimes said to have individual souls,[4] but usually one is shared among a group of trees. I think this too indicates a concentration of *sĕmangat* in some parts of a body, in this case the diffuse body constituted by a group of trees.

What pattern is here, if any at all? I think, in the first place, that some of the parts of the human body listed as being especially potent or associated with the soul derive this distinction not from an unusual concentration of *sĕmangat*, but from their position in relation to the margins of the body. Being invested with only a normal proportion of a person's soul, they still have the distinction of being removable from the body. Thus they must be treated with special precautions lest they fall into the hands of someone who would work evil magic on the original owner through them. This is a common notion throughout the world (Frazer's 'contagious magic') though the ideologies behind it vary. It is well known among the Malays who sometimes incorporate such materials into wax images which they then torture or destroy.[5] While some marginal parts (saliva, sperm, sweat, tears) become detached from the body naturally, others are cut off, further complicating the basis of their importance. Hair and nails are cut regularly, the teeth are filed off, and the ears are pierced though nothing is removed. Blood undoubtedly accompanies the ear-piercing, and *badi* may issue forth when the teeth are filed for the first time.[6] These particular body parts not only leave the body with their store of *sĕmangat*, but leave behind ruptures in the body's boundaries. Thus, the *sĕmangat* of such things as hair, fingernails, teeth, eyebrows, saliva, blood, sperm, sweat, and tears may not

---

[1] Skeat 1900, pp. 43, 46.
[3] Shaw 1911, p. 23.
[5] Skeat 1900, pp. 45, 569–73.
[6] ibid., p. 356 n.

[2] Cuisinier 1951, pp. 201–2.
[4] Annandale and Robinson 1903, p. 98.

be of disproportionate concentration, but would still be of special significance.

There remain the head, liver, and intestines of the human body which are comparable, I think, to the freak ear of rice and the outsized tree. These are not marginal to their bodies, but solidly within them. They are clearly basic to the body, and yet they are not typical of its parts, but stand out as figure on ground. The head is the most distinctive of the body's appendages, and the liver stands out among the internal organs in its large size and dark colour. The intestines are probably singled out for their strange form which especially recommends them as the lower half of the *penanggalan.* The ear containing the rice soul is determined specifically by its standing out from the other ears in the field,[1] and only the largest trees or deformed ones are supposed to have individual souls.

The most distinctive parts of bodies, the ones containing a high concentration of *sěmangat*, have what might be called an intense vital potency, the power to infuse all aspects of a soul with new vitality. These parts are a kind of storehouse of *sěmangat* for their own body, and this store can be transferred to other bodies as well. Cuisinier says that these, and marginal parts, are especially suited to being given as offerings to nourish a weakened soul.[2] The relationship between concentration of *sěmangat*, level of vitality, and the distinctiveness of body parts seems to hold whether the bodies are diffuse or compact and well defined.

Since the concentration of *sěmangat* in a particular body some-times changes, it is likely that the various members of a class of similar things will differ somewhat at any given time in the 'strength' of their souls. The pattern of differences would be temporary, of course, changing as the concentration varied in the particular members of the class. It is possible that there also exist permanent differences in the amount of *sěmangat* contained by the members of a category. Direct evidence of this is scarce, but a logical case can be made for it, and it fits the known facts. The value of the exercise is that it gives further information about the properties of concentrated *sěmangat* and furnishes extra data from which to extract the general principles by which the concentration of *sěmangat* is determined.

The fact that the highest concentration of *sěmangat* lies in the

[1] Shaw 1911, p. 23.　　　[2] Cuisinier 1951, p. 202.

distinctive parts of a body suggests that the members of a class of things that stand out from the rest should contain the most *sĕmangat*. It is often noted that the Malays attribute unusual powers to unusual objects. Coconuts without the normal three 'eyes' are supposed to protect one from bullets as are the rarely found internodes of bamboo that are solid rather than hollow.[1] Mineral concretions found inside plant and animal bodies (bezoar stones) are believed to make powerful medicines and protective charms.[2] Skeat says the ugliest dogs are regarded as the most formidable, 'the so-called good points being for the most part a mere list of deformities'.[3] Persons with deformities have similar unnatural powers. Persons with black birthmarks covering part of the face are sometimes believed capable of causing changes in the weather and of killing by a curse.[4]

Often unusual things are regarded as *kramat*, a term usually translated as sacred.[5] These are sometimes the distinctive parts of diffuse bodies such as strangely shaped rocks or unusually large or deformed trees.[6] *Kramat* may also be unusual members of a class of things. Graves found deep in the jungle with headstones extremely far apart constitute a common type of *kramat*.[7] Albino animals such as tigers, elephants, and crocodiles are often associated with *kramat* places and are themselves called *kramat*.[8] Also very large animals or those with a misformed leg or tusk (for elephants) are frequently considered *kramat*.[9] Manufactured objects may be *kramat*, for example, knives with peculiar flaws in the blade.[10] Even some living human beings are *kramat*: people who are distinguished by a physical defect such as a black tongue or a hairy uvula[11] or by special religious learning.[12] *Kramat* are closely connected with fasting places where religious penance is practiced; these are usually 'either solitary hills or places which

[1] Skeat 1900, p. 195.    [2] ibid., pp. 195–7, 274–6.
[3] ibid., p. 182.    [4] Annandale and Robinson 1903, pp. 82–3.
[5] Winstedt 1924; Blagden, in Skeat 1900, pp. 673–4. Possibly the term *kramat* comes from the Arabic *karāmaāt*, miracle worked by a saint (Wehr 1961, p. 822). This is the plural of *karāma* which means nobility, honour, respect, esteem, etc. (ibid., p. 822).
[6] Skeat 1900, p. 63; Annandale and Robinson 1904, p. 30; Winstedt 1954, pp. 66, 67; McHugh 1955, pp. 43–4.
[7] Skeat 1900, pp. 65–70.
[8] Winstedt 1924, pp. 268, 271–2; Annandale and Robinson 1904, p. 29.
[9] Skeat 1900, pp. 68, 70–1.
[10] Annandale and Robinson 1904, pp. 32–3.
[11] Winstedt 1954, p. 67.    [12] Annandale and Robinson 1904, p. 24.

present some great natural peculiarity; even remarkable trees and rocks being . . . pressed into the service of this Malay "natural religion"'.[1] Clearly, the things designated as *kramat* are those that stand out within a class of things whether the class be the parts of a single body or the members of a class of discrete bodies. Things that are *kramat* have supernatural power.[2] They can influence events, and people can forecast the future from them, presumably because the *kramat* will reveal by signs the direction that influence will take.[3] People make offerings, usually incense,[4] or sacrifice an animal, often a white chicken, goat, or even buffalo,[5] in hopes of influencing the power of the *kramat* to their own ends. Usually people desire to help the sick, find some stolen property, foresee a future event, or in some way improve their fortunes.[6] The power of a *kramat* is essentially amoral; it serves the wicked as well as the good. Some *kramats* are called 'accursed' or 'evil'. These include certain snakes of especially large size or having unusual markings, said to have *badi* souls,[7] and the white buffalo whose flesh is believed to cause sickness, but which is still the most acceptable offering to the spirits.[8] It is assumed that *kramat* will have a great influence on events whether this fits the wishes of a petitioner or not; they may intervene even when not called on, and even a favourable occurrence may not be the one asked for.[9] Obviously the terms 'miracle working' and 'sacred' have the wrong connotations as descriptions of *kramat*. It is best seen, I think, as simply an intense version of the supernatural power that attaches to all unusual things. Its influence over things and events is considered so strong that accurate predictions can be made by gauging that influence. Still, it is only quantitatively different from the formidable ugly dog or the man disfigured by a large birthmark who can change the weather and kill by a curse.

The designation of things as *kramat* seems to follow the same principle as that used for ascribing concentrated *sěmangat* to certain parts of bodies. In a few cases there is actual overlap;

[1] Skeat 1900, p. 71.   [2] Wilkinson 1964, p. 132.
[3] Annandale and Robinson 1904, p. 24; Cuisinier 1936, p. 32.
[4] Skeat 1900, p. 67.
[5] Winstedt 1924, p. 274; Annandale and Robinson 1904, p. 32.
[6] See Winstedt 1924, p. 271; Annandale and Robinson 1904, p. 31; Skeat 1900, p. 67.
[7] Annandale and Robinson 1904, p. 29.
[8] ibid., p. 30; Skeat 1900, pp. 189–90.
[9] Cuisinier 1936, p. 32.

large or deformed trees, for example, are the part of a forest with individual souls, and they are the ones most likely to be called *kramat*. Still, this is no proof that *kramat* power is due to highly concentrated *sěmangat*. Annandale reports that people become *kramat* 'by study and a strong soul (*sěmangat kuat*)'.[1] This is suggestive, but hardly conclusive. There is a way in which evidence can be brought to bear on this question. One would expect that a high concentration of *sěmangat* in a body would increase the ability of the various aspects of the soul to perform their functions. The reinforced *nyâwa* of a living *kramat* should intensify life, and a stronger *sěmangat* (in the narrow sense) could protect the body better than a normal one. If *kramat* is an expression of a very high concentration of *sěmangat*, *kramat* that have once been alive should be more resistant to death than their normal counterparts; in other words, *kramat* should approach immortality.

The evidence tends to bear this out. There seems to be a gradation in the matter of mortality that corresponds closely to the gradation of supernatural power from the most revered *kramat* down to the white cock which makes an especially good sacrifice. *Kramat* people are said never to die though they may appear to; they go on living invisibly and may appear to men in dreams and in the forest.[2] The *kramat* animals of the wilds—mainly crocodiles, tigers, and elephants—are sometimes said to be invulnerable[3] or immortal,[4] yet people are enjoined not to harm them.[5] Even so, they are sometimes killed, though it is usually very difficult to do it, and their death may cause the good fortune of the neighbourhood to depart.[6] White buffaloes are agreed to be *kramat*, but they are killed regularly in sacrifice to spirits and to more powerful *kramat*.[7] White monkeys can also be killed, though they are regarded as *kramat*, and their bones are coveted as powerful good luck charms.[8] It seems only a small step from this to the deformed dog which is regarded as formidable, but which will eventually die as all dogs do.[9] The evidence seems to support the

---

[1] Annandale and Robinson 1904, pp. 24–5.
[2] Winstedt 1954, pp. 66–7; Annandale and Robinson 1904, pp. 21, 25.
[3] Skeat 1900, pp. 153, 163.
[4] Annandale and Robinson 1904, p. 29.
[5] Skeat 1900, p. 68; Wilkinson 1964, p. 132.
[6] Skeat 1900, p. 153; Zainul Abidin bin Ahmad 1922a, pp. 36, 38.
[7] Annandale and Robinson 1904, p. 30.       [8] ibid., p. 30.
[9] See Skeat 1900, p. 182.

proposition that the state of *kramat* is a high concentration of *sĕmangat*, if resistance to death is a valid measure of that concentration. It follows that things that have died can no longer be *kramat*. The act of dying releases most, if not all, of the body's *sĕmangat*—that composing the *nyâwa* and *sĕmangat*, and probably also the *rôh* of human beings. I have read nothing indicating whether *kramat* that are subject to death, such as white buffalo, are considered *kramat* after being killed. I think they would not be. Their special value as sacrifices probably lies in the large supply of *sĕmangat* that is released, for the nourishment of the spirits, at their death. Those things that have continuing *kramat* power are usually not subject to sudden death, being mainly trees and rocks. Graves and 'living shrines' present problems for this scheme of ideas; it is resolved by saying that the persons in *kramat* graves are not really dead and that 'living shrines' do not really die though they may appear to do so. This fiction of eternal life is exactly what is required if *kramat* is the power of concentrated *sĕmangat*, but it goes exactly against the interpretation of *kramat* put forward by Blagden[1] and Cuisinier[2] that it is a system of ancestor worship, unless it is assumed that some ancestors are not really dead. This is clearly not the intention of those two writers.

It is quite certain, I think, that *kramat* is a condition based on a high concentration of *sĕmangat*, and the evidence of *kramat* confirms the principle glimpsed earlier that concentrated *sĕmangat* is attributed to things that stand out from the set of comparable things. As one would expect, concentrated *sĕmangat* improves the functioning of a body's soul, but somewhat less obvious is the fact that something possessing concentrated *sĕmangat* has supernatural influence over things and events. The extent of this power varies with the level of concentration. A healthy soul is thought to give good luck (*tuah*) as well as good physical health.[3] At the other end of the scale are well-known *kramat* which are believed to have almost complete control over events. The exact nature of the influence emanating from centres of concentrated *sĕmangat* is not perfectly clear to me. I have never seen an account of an indigenous explanation of the working of *kramat* power. Undoubtedly, the basis of the power is the fact that all things are maintained

---

[1] Skeat 1900, pp. 673–4.    [2] Cuisinier 1936, pp. 32–3.
[3] Annandale and Robinson 1903, pp. 80–1.

and controlled by souls composed of the all-pervading *sĕmangat*. Special concentrations of *sĕmangat* somehow act as centres of control over the widespread differentiations of the vital principle which, in sum, directly control the course of events.

Though my major concern has been with the principles according to which *sĕmangat* is concentrated and the properties that accompany this concentration, it is important to describe briefly the lines of its differentiation in the concentrated state. Obviously, the *sĕmangat* of a grave *kramat* is in the form of the soul of a human being, an outstanding individual who has overcome death. These fall roughly into the following categories: great medicine men of legend, Mohammadan saints, recently 'dead' living shrines,[1] and founders of villages.[2] I think the one chosen and the name given him are matters of accidental circumstance. It is the power of the unusual grave, not the person alleged to be in it that is important. Skeat says, 'even where there is some evidence of the existence of a grave, the name of the departed saint is usually the one fact that is remembered, and often even that is forgotten'.[3]

It is relevant in this connection to note that the outstanding qualities and powers attributed to sultans are just what would be expected for a low-grade *kramat*. It is widely believed 'that the Sultan by his personal influence or good luck can bring or ward off pestilence and bad harvests'.[4] He is supposed to exercise his supernatural influence 'by the passive fact of his existence and not by the performance of ritual'.[5] One of the things especially reserved for the sultan are albino buffaloes,[6] the domesticated equivalent of the *kramat* animals of jungle and water, and sultans are said to have white blood.[7] The distinction that makes the sultan *kramat* lies in the office and not in the man himself. There is nothing to suggest that the person who becomes sultan has any special powers before he takes office; it is said that he is 'vested with majesty (*daulat*) at his installation'.[8] He also loses his special powers when he leaves office, (i.e., dies), and they become attached to his successor. There is no pretence to cover up the fact that a sultan can die, but his name is changed at death to 'the late Sultan'[9] as if to emphasize that the dead person is not the sultan.

---

[1] Annandale and Robinson 1904, pp. 24–5.  [2] Skeat 1900, p. 62.
[3] ibid., p. 63–4.    [4] Gullick 1958, p. 47.
[5] ibid., p. 54.    [6] ibid., p. 46.
[7] Skeat 1900, p. 37.    [8] Gullick 1958, p. 45.  [9] ibid., p. 46.

Many *kramat* are not people or graves, and the stationary (non-animal) ones are called *kramat jin*[1] or *kramat hantu*.[2] The differentiation of *kramat*-level *sĕmangat* into a *jin* or spirit seems to occur whenever the *kramat* is a peculiar feature of the physical environment. These are usually outstanding parts of diffuse or scattered bodies—unusual trees or rocks—and I have shown how the souls (*sĕmangat* in the narrow sense) of such things are often called spirits because of their seeming detachment from any particular part of the body. The *sĕmangat* of *kramat* animals probably forms either the soul of the animal or the soul of a human 'living shrine' who has met his so-called death. If an unusual animal appears soon after a 'living shrine' departs, the animal is thought to be the new form of that person.[3] If no such 'death' has occurred, the animal will most likely be taken as *kramat* in its own right, possibly as a guardian of a stationary *kramat* if one is near by. Lesser *kramat* animals, such as white buffaloes, are probably thought simply to have strong souls of the appropriate kind. Similarly, the concentrated *sĕmangat* of material objects that are called *kramat*, for example, the solid joints of bamboo, would be differentiated into nothing other than a particularly strong *sĕmangat* in the narrow sense.

I have suggested that the degree of concentration of *sĕmangat* correlates with power: both the power to exist and the power to influence natural events. A high concentration is usually found in those parts of a body that stand out from the rest as figure on ground and in similarly outstanding members of classes of things having separate bodies.

[1] Skeat 1900, p. 62.     [2] Annandale and Robinson 1904, p. 24.
[3] See Zainul Abidin bin Ahmad 1922a, pp. 36–9.

# V

## SIGNIFICANT DIVISIONS OF THE
## MALAY WORLD

THE preceding chapter describes the relational meaning attached to *sĕmangat* by virtue of its central position in a system of related concepts. The system is, in a sense, a classification of some of the forces and beings in the Malay world. Besides revealing the outlines of a segment of the Malay world-view, the description of the classification uncovered one of the fundamental features of Malay magical thought: the distinction between body and essence. If analysis of one portion of the Malay pantheon can yield this dual result, to work out the basic classification of the pantheon as a whole could lead to an understanding of the wider order in Malay ideas and of the basic principles of classification that underlie that order. Since the examination of the creatures that are intimately connected with bodies is fairly complete, I shall begin by seeking out the order in conceptions of free spirits (including all divinities not tied to bodies), a subject that has been touched on only lightly. It should then be possible to find the fundamental classification that includes both free spirits and their body-bound relatives. If the basic principles of organization embodied in this classification are not peculiar to the pantheon alone, their discovery should give some insight into the order of the Malay world as a whole. A clear conception of the world-view is necessary as the proper context in which to view the magical practices of the Malays.

The main problem in uncovering the fundamental categories of the Malay pantheon is that the beliefs lend themselves, in their great richness and variety, to many alternative modes of classification. The first task is to sort out the distinctions that are not important from those that are. The former includes distinctions that are not widely recognized, ones that are verbalized but not used, those that apply only to a narrow segment of the whole, and ones that do not exist at all in the minds of the people, but rather represent the interests and biases of the writers. These, of course, are not mutually exclusive categories, and some distinctions can be eliminated for more than one reason. The syncretic process by which the Malay pantheon has developed lies behind several types of misleading distinction. One of these is the kind in which several words of different origin are applied to things which, in the Malay context, are treated as the same. The distinction between *hantu* and *jin* is, I think, an example of this. In properties, distribution, and behaviour, *hantu* and *jin* differ less as categories than the members of each category differ from each other. Both are usually invisible, but can assume visible forms and change them at will. Both can invade a person's body causing illness or 'possess' a shaman and, as a 'control spirit', help evict a malevolent spirit.[1] They are both contacted through charms and persuaded by offerings and deceit. Both pervade the world, often existing side by side. The connection is sometimes so close that *jin* and *hantu* appear to be the alternative names for the same spirit, the one used depending, perhaps, on the Muslim orthodoxy of the speaker. Earth spirits, for example, are sometimes *hantu tanah* and sometimes *jinn itam* (black *jinn*).[2] Usually, however, individual *jin* are distinguished from individual *hantu*, but the differences between the two as types (e.g., one of Annandale's informants said *jin* were more powerful than *hantu*[3]) are insufficient to warrant their being considered significantly different categories.

Another kind of problem arises when distinctions within a body of imported beliefs are retained in spells and mystical texts, but do not become important in popular thought. In other words, the distinctions persist in the private and secret symbolisms of ritual specialists, but do not become cultural in the sense of being widely shared. A good example of this is the belief that *jin* are divided into internal and external varieties.[4] There are supposedly a large number of internal *jin* in man controlling his senses, bodily processes, and even his will.[5] Internal *jin* usually protect the health of the person, but sometimes they turn on him causing mild illness, and, more seriously, they may cooperate with external *jin* in creating a deadly malady.[6] Only with the cooperation of the internal *jin* are external *jin* able to enter a person's body. Exactly

---

[1] Gimlette 1929, pp. 87–91 and *passim*.
[2] Annandale and Robinson 1904, pp. 36, 38.     [3] ibid., p. 37.
[4] See Gimlette 1929, pp. 27–9, 33, 36.
[5] ibid., p. 28.     [6] ibid., pp. 28, 33, 36.

how the latter enlist this cooperation is not explained. The classification of *jin* into external and internal, however important it may be in Arabia or Moslem India, has had almost no impact on Malay ideas and practices. The idea is not compatible with the notion of *sĕmangat*, and the basic importance of that concept can hardly be overstressed.

One of the classifications that is wholly alien to Malay thought is also based in the syncretic development of the Malay pantheon. This is the grouping of entities on the basis of cultural origin as exemplified by the work of R. O. Winstedt. He separates the influences of Brahmanism and Islam (mainly Sufism) from each other and from the substratum of Indonesian animism.[1] The wealth of historical information, especially in the most recent edition of *Shaman, Saiva, and Sufi* (supertitled *The Malay Magician* [1961]), obliterates almost all sense of cohesion in the material. His tracing of the origins of beliefs is very interesting, but it gives no clues as to how those beliefs are organized in the Malay context.

Even this is not so far removed from the people's thought as Skeat's division of the pantheon into two categories: 'gods' and 'spirits, demons, ghosts'.[2] The former includes the important Hindu divinities in their various forms (Siva, Brahma, Vishnu, Sri, Kala, etc.), major indigenous spirits such as the Spectre Huntsman, and the Indonesian *mambang* which dwell, among other places, in the sun and moon.[3] The latter class includes *jin, badi,* angels, prophets, sheikhs, *hantu,* ghosts, pixies, elves, and birth demons.[4] The artificiality of this division is demonstrated by the extension of connections and some of the subclasses themselves across the boundary. For instance, he calls *jin* an 'extensive class of quite subordinate divinities',[5] but admits that one of them, the Black King of the Genii (Sang Gala Raja or Sa-Raja Jin), rises to the level of the great Hindu divinities and is sometimes confounded with Kala, the destructive side of Siva.[6] The inappropriateness of his descriptive framework seems to prevent him from working out the full implications of his most brilliant insights. He notes the intriguing fact that avatars of Siva are associated with the jungle and with the sea and that the most dangerous form—Kala—rules over the intermediate zone between them.[7] He further suggests

---

[1] See Winstedt 1925, 1954, 1961a, 1961b.
[2] Skeat 1900, pp. 83–106.   [3] ibid., pp. 83–93.   [4] ibid., pp. 93–106.
[5] ibid., p. 93.   [6] ibid., p. 93.   [7] ibid., p. 90.

that the expression 'Grandsire Long-Claws' may refer to the manifestation of Siva on land with the 'personality of the Tiger, just as the Crocodile-spirit appears to represent Shiva by water'.[1] At that point, sadly, he ends this line of inquiry, possibly because his investigations have led him out of the category of 'gods' into the inferior realm of animals and spirits. Skeat claims no analytic value for his arrangement of the material, and, indeed, it has none. His contribution is made in spite of the classification, not because of it.

Many more distinctions could be mentioned which should be discarded because of their limited usefulness in exposing the basic principles on which the Malay world-view is based. It would be found, for example, that the distinction between good and bad spirits, while real enough, only applies to a minute fragment of the whole body of spirits. Only the white *jin* are moral—they are always good. They reside in the hearts of all Mohammadans preventing them from being wicked.[2] The great majority of *jin* are amoral.[3]

There is no single classification of spirits by colour, and the several that exist are either unconnected or contradict each other. The moral white *jin* are possibly set off against the mass of amoral *jin* which may be called black.[4] This might parallel the division into *Jin* Islam and *Jin* Kafir (infidel *jin*).[5] *Jin* Kafir are sometimes equated with earth spirits which are also termed black spirits (*Jinn Itam*).[6] But the broader classification in which earth spirits are black contrasts them with the white spirits of the sea,[7] which are in no sense moral.[8] This classification also includes red demons of the air and yellow *jin* from fire.[9] This whole scheme of colour categories is contradicted in the tradition that the spirits originated when Cain and Abel bit their thumbs and the blood that spurted to the earth became the white spirits (*Jin Puteh*).[10] It is clear that distinctions of good and bad, faithful and infidel, black and white must have a place in the fundamental order of the Malay pantheon, but they are not the basis of that order.

The process of eliminating non-essential distinctions and

[1] ibid., p. 91.    [2] Annandale and Robinson 1904, pp. 37–8.
[3] ibid., p. 35.    [4] See Skeat 1900, pp. 94–6.
[5] See ibid., p. 96 and n.    [6] Annandale and Robinson 1904, p. 38.
[7] Gimlette 1929, p. 32.    [8] See Annandale and Robinson 1903, p. 81.
[9] Gimlette 1929, p. 32.
[10] Gimlette 1929, p. 27; see also Skeat 1900, p. 95.

classifications is far from complete, but it has reached the point of diminishing returns. With the possibilities narrowed and some pitfalls exposed, it is best to proceed to a positive formulation that can then be examined in the light of the evidence.

The association of avatars of Siva with land and sea is all the more remarkable, Skeat says, because Hindu mythology 'knows next to nothing of the sea, and any such attempt as this to define the respective boundaries of sea and land is almost certain to be due to the influence of Malay ideas'.[1] The basic distinction is probably between water (river and sea) and jungle, if the association with crocodile and tiger is made correctly. Jungle is also set off from the earth; Annandale points out that one classification of spirits in Patani separates spirits of the jungle (*Hantu Raya*— Great Spirits) from spirits of the earth (*Hantu Tanah* or *Jimbalang Bumi*).[2] McHugh suggests that the Malays originally lived surrounded by jungle with the sea or a river at their door, hence 'the oldest *hantu*, they say, are those which dominate the land, the jungle, or the water'.[3] I shall attempt to show that a division among earth, water, and jungle is the basic one embodied in the classifications of free spirits. I suggest further that a fourth quasi-geographical realm intrudes into those three, namely, the abode of man, represented in the total classification by familiars and, to some extent, the birth demons.

Not all supernatural beings reside in these four regions, however, much less form patterns exemplifying the divisions between them. Among those excluded are the *mambang* of the sun and moon, the angels, and the sheikhs at the four corners of the world. At first glance, these might seem to be the celestial beings in a division of the supernatural proposed by Gimlette which separates earthly and celestial beings. But his celestial beings (*jin*, *pĕri*, *dewa*, *mambang*, pixies, elves, and all inferior divinities of the clouds)[4] include many classes that have members residing on earth. And, while there are indications of a simple up-down symbolism, it seems to relate to the ranking of any spirits,[5] rather than to indicate a systematic distinction between heaven and earth. I think it is misguided to regard those beings not localized on the earth

[1] Skeat 1900, p. 90.
[2] Annandale and Robinson 1904, p. 37.
[3] McHugh 1955, p. 24; see also Skeat 1900, p. 281.
[4] Gimlette 1929, p. 29.          [5] See e.g. Skeat 1900, pp. 232, 512.

as necessarily residing in the heavens. Nothing is explained by doing so, and there is little to suggest that a heavenly realm exists in the same sense as the four mentioned above. I suggest that those beings not associated with jungle, waters, earth, or villages are not localized at all, but are organized to express important abstract distinctions, for example, those in time and space.

## 1. JUNGLE-WATER DIVISION

The basic divisions of the world are not between geographical regions but between types of region, categories defined as distinctive kinds of environment. The jungle-water division is not simply a division between land and sea; the penetration of rivers into the land leads to a rather more complex situation. In most basic ways spirits of river and sea are alike. They both cause boats to run aground, people to drown, etc.[1] Sacrifices at river mouths may be directed to sea and river spirits indiscriminately.[2] Still, some of the meanings of the sea and the legends and beliefs associated with them—the navel of the seas (*Pusat tasek*) in which the comings and goings of a giant crab cause the tides,[3] and the legendary lands across the sea to which spirit boats are commanded to go (sometimes identified as Celebes)[4]—are probably only vaguely associated with rivers. Relative to the sea in this grander sense, it might be said that rivers are regarded as merely part of the jungle and of the habitation of man. Most commonly in this perspective, however, rivers are seen as mediators between man's dwellings and the sea. A very common way to rid a person or village of disease, and also to get rid of noxious spirits of the jungle, is to construct a spirit boat, entice the spirits aboard with offerings, and set it adrift in the river instructing it to carry the offenders out to sea.[5] Sometimes the crocodile-spirit and the God of Midcurrents are identified as forwarding agents.[6] The boundary between jungle or village and water shifts with changes in perspective, but even when rivers seem, by default, to be included within the terrestrial divisions, for example, during a sacrifice to the sea spirits, the distinction between land and water environments is maintained and sometimes even emphasized.[7]

[1] McHugh 1955, p. 53.  [2] See ibid., p. 54.
[3] Skeat 1900, p. 7.  [4] ibid., p. 434.
[5] See ibid., pp. 235, 413, 414, 433–6.  [6] ibid., pp. 88 n, 435.
[7] See e.g. ibid., p. 418.

The classification of Siva's avatars mentioned above is slightly more complex than it appears at first sight. Skeat elaborates thus: 'The supreme god of the State Chamber (*balei*) is Batara Guru, on the edge of the primeval forest (*di-gigi rimba*) it is Batara Kala, and in the heart of the forest (*di hati rimba*) it is 'Toh Panjang Kuku, or "Grandsire Long-Claws." Similarly, "Grandsire Long-Claws" is lord of the shore down to high-water mark; between that and low-water mark Raja Kala is supreme, and Batara Guru di Laut (Shiva of the Ocean) from low-water mark out to the open sea'.[1] This is somewhat confusing if it is assumed that all of these associations occur at the same time and place. It seems to imply that 'Toh Panjang Kuku is lord of the deep forest and of a strip of the shore extending some indeterminate distance inland, perhaps to the state chamber or to just the edge of the forest. The situation is clear if it is said that Kala will always preside over the boundaries between categories and that the realm of man, symbolized by the State Chamber, may or may not be included in the reckoning. Including man's abode, the sequence of deities from sea to jungle would be: Batara Guru di Laut, Kala, Batara Guru, Kala, 'Toh Panjang Kuku. The association of 'Toh Panjang Kuku with the shore probably applies away from the villages, where the jungle is only separated from the water by the narrow strip between the high and low water marks. There, a three-fold classification applies, distinguishing Batara Guru di Laut from 'Toh Panjang Kuku with Kala between them. This second classification and the simple division between jungle and water indicated by it are of major concern at the moment.

There is no clear reason to suppose that the strip of shore that is alternately land and water holds any more real danger than the open sea, though the advance of the tides may pose some threat to unwary souls hunting crabs among the mangrove roots. Nevertheless, disproportionate danger is implied in the association of the most sinister form of Siva—Kala—with this region. This is probably another manifestation of the danger Malays attach to the boundaries between important categories. If this is correct, the distribution of Siva's avatars in this way serves to emphasize the significance of the division between jungle and water environments.

'Toh Panjang Kuku ('Grandsire Long-Claws') seems sometimes

[1] ibid., p. 91 n.

to be identified with the Spectre Huntsman, a powerful demon of the forest.[1] Skeat suggests that this manifestation of Siva as a tiger might well be seen in juxtaposition to Sambu, the crocodile spirit, which is another form of Siva.[2] At the level of supernatural animals, the forms of Siva again conform to a jungle-water division. I have pointed out in the previous chapter that the monitor lizard, which is called an origin of *badi* and whose intrusion into a house is considered a particularly bad omen,[3] is quite clearly regarded as being a transitional form between crocodile and tiger (see p. 83 above). The tiger and crocodile sometimes seem to represent the forest and the water in fables also. In one story the crocodile and tiger intrigue to catch Mousedeer; if on land the victim goes to Tiger, if in the water to Crocodile. Mousedeer, finding himself trapped, dances along the edge of the bank. Tiger springs and misses, falling into the water where he is devoured by Crocodile.[4] Mousedeer's use of the boundary to undo his foes is probably not purely accidental, as he is found elsewhere causing, to his advantage, a fight between the Wild Bull of the Clearing and the Wild Bull of the Young Bush on the boundary between their domains.[5] The position of the crocodile in the classification is not absolute, however, but variable. Being associated mainly with fresh water, it is subject to the same shifts in position as rivers are. In one frame of reference the rivers mediate between villages and the sea, so it is not unexpected that the crocodile-spirit is identified as one of the agents that may forward spirit boats to their destination.[6]

Sometimes there are said to be four *mambang* (Indonesian divinities) associated with the sea and shore, but Winstedt points out[7] that on linguistic grounds the credentials of one of them, the *mambang* of banks or beaches, are suspect. He suggests that a fourth *mambang* was probably added when these divinities came to be linked with the four archangels. Probably the basic grouping includes only a *mambang* of the bays, one of the headlands, and the fiercest, the *mambang* of the tideways and currents.[8] I think the last is the Mambang Tali Harus (Winstedt does not give the Malay name) misinterpreted by Skeat as 'The god of mid-

---

[1] ibid., p. 91.    [2] ibid., p. 89 n; also Winstedt 1961a, p. 34.
[3] Skeat 1900, p. 535.
[4] Wilkinson 1907, p. 46; see also Skeat 1901, pp. 22, 24.
[5] Skeat 1901, p. 30.    [6] Skeat 1900, p. 435.
[7] Winstedt 1925, p. 6.    [8] ibid., pp. 5–6.

currents (the Malay Neptune)'.[1] Skeat persists in seeing the
Mambang Tali Harus as a god of the deep,[2] but I think the weight
of the evidence indicates that he is one of the class of beings
intermediate between sea and land and that his specific association
is with the tidal currents or tiderip, alternately penetrating into
the land via rivers and going out again to the sea. The term *tali
harus* alone means the 'line of scum where tides meet, tiderip'.[3]
Skeat says the expression applied to the Mambang Tali Harus is
'*yang bĕrulang ka.pusat tasek*'.[4] This could be translated roughly:
'who (goes) repeatedly to centre of ocean'.[5] The term *bĕrulang*,
repeatedly, makes no sense as a description of the 'Malay
Neptune', but it fits a deity of the tides. Furthermore, Skeat says
'"the god of mid-currents" is requested to forward a message to
Dato 'Rimpun 'Alam, which appears to be merely another name
for Batara Guru, the reason given for the preferment of this request
being that he is in the habit of "visiting the Heart of the Seas"
in which 'Toh Rimpun 'Alam dwells"'.[6] Elsewhere he notes that
spirit boats are 'taken down to the sea or river and set adrift,
invariably at the ebb tide, which is supposed to carry the boat (and
the spirits with it) "to another country"'.[7] The *mambang* of
bays, headlands, and tideways appear to form another threefold
classification expressing the relationship between the land (which
is largely jungle) and the water.

Some lesser spirits are also aligned with the division between
land and water. There are ghost princesses in both realms who
lure people to their destruction.[8] And a charm connected with
launching spirit boats includes the following information: 'Sa-
rĕkong is the name of the (spirit of the) Bay, Sa-rĕking the name
of the (spirit of the) Cape, Si 'Abas, their child, is the rocky islet'.[9]
The last term combines land and sea and constitutes, therefore,
another kind of mediation between the realms, not a communi-
cator but a child of the two parents. This would imply that land
and sea are related as male to female; I have no evidence to suggest
which category is which sex, but perhaps it does not matter.
Colours associated with the two realms indicate that they are
related as white to black, but the specific association may be

[1] Skeat 1900, p. 85.   [2] e.g. ibid., p. 91n.
[3] Wilkinson 1964, p. 92.   [4] Skeat 1900, p. 92 n.
[5] See Wilkinson 1964, pp. 113, 216, 301, 307.
[6] Skeat 1900, p. 88 n.   [7] ibid., p. 434.
[8] McHugh 1955, p. 41.   [9] Skeat 1900, p. 435–6.

either way. Winstedt cites a tradition that green *jin* came from a leaf that soared into the (green) sky, black *jin* from a leaf that fell at the gate of the forest, and white *jin* from a leaf that fell into the sea.[1] But there is a white angel in charge of the jungle[2] and, of the *mambang* described above, that of the bay is black and that of the headlands white.[3] Either way the symbolic qualities are assigned, the distinction between land (jungle) and sea (water) is indicated and defined as a kind of opposition.

In many ways the spirits of jungle and water are treated by men as separate but equivalent. Offerings to both may be made in the same ceremony. Similar offerings may be given to the two types,[4] or unequal ones as when the Spectre Huntsman is given a raw egg and the sea-spirit a cooked one.[5] Skeat describes one ceremony in which three similar trays of offerings were used.[6] The first was taken into the jungle, hung from a mangrove branch, and dedicated to the land spirits (*orang darat*).[7] The second was suspended from a wooden tripod erected for the purpose in the centre of a shoal about half-way between the fishing-stakes and the fishermen's hut.[8] The third tray, which was probably the most important as it contained the goat's head, was suspended from a pole projecting from the seaward end of the fishing-stakes.[9] Skeat does not specify the spirits for whom the last two trays are intended, but it is probably safe to say that the last is for some spirit or deity of the sea. I think the second tray is for the earth spirits, but direct evidence is lacking. Besides being propitiated in similar ways, spirits of jungle and sea are held at bay by related methods. Blagden says charms are hung at the borders of villages to keep wild spirits out,[10] and it is reported that white flags are hung on fish traps on the Johore River to keep away spirits that might frighten the fish.[11] And being both outside the realm of man, the sea and the jungle are equally satisfactory places in which to dispose of the *badi*-infected limes left from the cleansing of a victim of *badi* attack.[12]

In these many ways the fundamental division between jungle and water is expressed. The elaboration of mediators or com-

[1] Winstedt 1925, p. 32.  
[2] Skeat 1900, p. 98.  
[3] Winstedt 1925, p. 6.  
[4] Djamour 1959, pp. 90–1.  
[5] Skeat 1900, p. 418.  
[6] ibid., pp. 310–13.  
[7] ibid., p. 312.  
[8] ibid., p. 313.  
[9] ibid., pp. 313–14.  
[10] Blagden 1896, p. 4.  
[11] G.C. 1885, p. 53.  
[12] Skeat 1900, pp. 431–2.

municators between the primary categories in the various classifications is probably connected with the variable and ambiguous nature of the boundary between the two realms.

## II. EARTH-JUNGLE DIVISION

The division between earth and jungle is more clear-cut than that between jungle and water. Spirits of earth and jungle are said to be akin,[1] but they are distinguished in many ways. Earth spirits, by the nature of their position and environment, are of almost continuous concern to man. They reside directly under the villages and fields and must, therefore, be considered when planting crops, mining, digging wells and foundations, and even when a play is performed, presumably because the noise might disturb the spirits below.[2] While the *Hantu Raya* (great spirits) usually stay in the jungle unless summoned by medicine men,[3] earth spirits (*Hantu Tanah* or *Jimbalang Bumi*) may intrude in man's life at almost any time. I think that one of the reasons Malays usually build their houses on stilts is to give themselves some small buffer between themselves and spirits of the earth.

The division between earth and jungle spirits is made especially clear in Patani and Kelantan.[4] Both are used in magic but in slightly different capacities. Earth spirits seem to be one of the guardians of magical traditions, having some vague association with the ghosts of departed magicians.[5] Earth spirits are also called Black Jins and Infidel Jins, and they are especially prominent in evil magic; this is most clear when charms are buried and earth spirits are actually invoked to work some mischief.[6] The *Hantu Raya* of the jungle are used for more noble purposes, namely, for curing. The best known of such spirit helpers is the *hantu bĕlian*, the tiger spirit, which serves most respected *pawang*.[7] Other jungle spirits can be used, and even the Spectre Huntsman can be raised by some magicians to help drive out disease-causing

---

[1] McHugh 1955, p. 48.

[2] See Skeat 1900, pp. 143–4, 229, 238, 244 n., 269, 506; Blagden 1896, pp. 8–12; McHugh 1955, p. 49.

[3] Annandale and Robinson 1904, p. 39.

[4] See Annandale and Robinson 1904, pp. 37–40.

[5] Cuisinier 1936, p. 11.　　　[6] e.g. Skeat 1900, pp. 572–3.

[7] See e.g. Swettenham 1895, pp. 153–9; Skeat 1900, pp. 436–44; Cuisinier 1936, pp. 38–40; cf. Wilkinson 1932, p. 128.

spirits.[1] A really well equipped magician will have the assistance of spirits of both types. In Patani a man supposedly can contract, by offering sacrifices, for the services of six spirits at a time. These compose three pairs, each with a member from the earth and one from the forest.[2] They are fed regularly; the pole on which the offerings are placed is divided, and the portion for the earth spirits is placed low down and that for the *Hantu Raya* on top.[3] A similar division of the sacrifice occurs when a newly cleared plot of land is prepared for planting, i.e., when both jungle and earth spirits must be propitiated. Some of the rice soul, a rod of iron, a smooth stone, and three quids of betel are placed at the base of a special dibble which has been embedded in the ground, and seven portions each of sweet rice, sugar cane, banana, and jungle fruit are hung from a shrub that is tied upon the dibble.[4] McHugh reports that earth spirits are thought, in Perak, to dwell in trees among other places,[5] and probably one of the reasons trees are believed to be especially infested with spirits[6] is that their branches and foliage are in the jungle realm and their trunks and roots penetrate into the earth; they are part of both categories and probably house two kinds of spirit. Also, as mentioned in the previous chapter, the ambiguous position of trees on the scale from individual bodies to shared bodies makes even the souls of trees seem to be spirits.

The most important prophet for the Malays is, of course, Mohammad. He often occurs in charms but in the same formal and stylized way as Allah does. Of more immediate concern are the various prophets who rule natural phenomena; they are invoked at nearly every turn. Most important are Solomon, who rules both the animals and spirits of the jungle,[7] 'the Prophet Tap (Tĕtap or Kĕtap), "lord of the earth"; the prophet Khailir (Khaithir or Khizr), "lord of water"; the prophet Noah, "lord of trees"; and the prophet Elias, "planter of trees"'.[8] Skeat also mentions 'the prophet David, celebrated for the beauty of his voice; and the prophet Joseph, celebrated for the beauty of his countenance'.[9] I have never read of these two being invoked or propitiated as are

[1] Gimlette 1929, p. 40.   [2] Annandale and Robinson 1904, p. 41.
[3] ibid., p. 41.
[4] Winstedt 1961a, p. 46.   [5] McHugh 1955, p. 51.
[6] See e.g. Blagden 1896, p. 5; Annandale and Robinson 1904, p. 30.
[7] Skeat 1900, pp. 99, 133–9, 266; Gimlette 1929, p. 26.
[8] Skeat 1900, p. 99.   [9] ibid., p. 99.

the prophets associated with nature, and I suspect that their importance is purely literary and legendary. It may be noted that of the five prophets of most everyday concern, one is associated with each of the three major divisions of the environment and two with trees. I should like to reiterate that the disproportionate representation of trees probably derives not from their practical value so much as the fact that they participate in two if not all three of the fundamental natural realms. Not only do trees rise out of the soil into the jungle, but several kinds, such as the ubiquitous mangrove trees, penetrate through the water in the process.

Colour associations seem to relate earth and jungle, like jungle and water, as black to white. This is far from certain, however, as black and white creatures of the same sort are not juxtaposed as they are for jungle and water. There is a white angel in charge of the jungle[1] which is probably the same as the white sheikh, wizard, or king of the virgin jungle cited in charms.[2] The earth, on the other hand, is almost always associated with black. The *jin* of the earth are black,[3] they are given black offerings,[4] and the coat of a mining *pawang*, but only the *pawang*'s coat, is black.[5] At one mining ceremony of a type that seems to deal with both earth and jungle spirits (both are disturbed when a mine is constructed), the offerings must include both white and black fowls in equal proportions.[6]

Mines are carved out of the jungle and out of the earth, so the possibility of confusing the two realms must be faced. Some of the prohibitions observed in mines can well be interpreted in terms of the necessity to keep the activities proper to earth and jungle separated. These include the prohibition on killing any sort of living creature in the mine and on bringing the skin of any beast into it,[7] activities that might be confused with hunting, and the prohibition on chopping trees for wooden aquaducts within the precincts of the mine, and even on cutting or hacking the wooden posts of the smelting house.[8] The latter constitute or might be confounded with logging.

The many similarities between earth and the jungle suggest that

[1] ibid., p. 98.        [2] ibid., pp. 268, 269.
[3] Annandale and Robinson 1904, p. 38; Gimlette 1929, p. 32; Skeat 1900, p. 506.
[4] Skeat 1900, pp. 232, 237.        [5] ibid., p. 257.
[6] ibid., p. 270.        [7] ibid., p. 269.        [8] ibid., p. 258.

they are comparable categories. The multitude of specific contrasts contained in the various classifications of supernatural beings insure, however, that they are not confused.

## III. EARTH-WATER DIVISION

The division between spirits of earth and water is not emphasized as much as the divisions between spirits of jungle and water and between those of jungle and earth. This may be due, in part, to the fact that the physical intersection of earth and water realms is not emphasized, which in turn seems to reflect some ambiguity in Malay thought as to exactly where the environments of water and earth meet. Though water is used in the mines to separate the heavy ore from worthless lighter minerals and in the fields to water the crops, there is no certain evidence that symbolic statements of the relations between the two realms (e.g., double sacrifice) are made in these contexts. Perhaps it is water as a substance that is used in these cases, and, while it certainly derives some meaning from the natural realm it represents, it takes on other meaning from its relations within a set of substances having practical and symbolic value for the Malays. It may be that the importance of the earth spirits in mines and fields simply overshadows the importance of those of water. This seems to be the case in wells, for example, where earth spirits dwell, but the presence of water spirits is not reported.[1] At the seashore, where all three realms meet, the division between jungle and water seems to predominate.[2] However, it is sometimes difficult to interpret what is described as an opposition between land and sea deities, since land might equally well mean jungle, earth, or the habitation of man.

One case where the division of spirits is quite clear is the sacrifice at the fishing-stakes mentioned above (p. 105). Of the three trays of offerings prepared, the first is hung from a tree in the forest, the last on the fishing-stakes, and the second hung from a wooden tripod erected on a shoal about half-way between the fishing-stakes and the fishermen's hut.[3] The success of fishing-stakes depends on the earth, which holds them in place, as well as the water, which brings the fish. Skeat reports that spirits are

[1] See McHugh 1955, p. 51.    [2] See e.g. Wavell 1964, pp. 163-4.
[3] Skeat 1900, p. 313.

invoked when the first stake is planted, and, if their response is favourable, 'it will enter the ground readily, as if pulled from below'.[1] It is apparent that the spirits invoked are earth spirits, and it is not unreasonable to expect that they would be considered in a major ceremony to insure the efficacy of the fishing-stakes.

Double sacrifices—to representatives of earth and water—are reported by Winstedt, but he does not specify exactly where or to what purpose the ceremonies are performed. In upper Perak an albino buffalo without blemish is sacrificed when the grain in the rice fields is beginning to swell.[2] The shaman invokes 'the ancestral spirits, genies, and goblins, owners of the earth and water of the district' and asks them 'to cherish all from danger and hurt'.[3] This seems to be a general protection rite for the inhabitants of the area designed to placate two important categories of spirits, those of earth and water. The protection rites on the first day of a wedding ceremony include offerings of yellow rice, rice-paste, betel, candles, and cigarettes to 'all the spirits of earth and water'.[4] Part of this ceremony takes place on the river bank where some of the offerings are arranged on the ground, some are scattered, presumably partially in the water, and others mixed with the water in which the groom is bathed.[5]

The supernatural representatives of earth and water are fairly often dealt with together. Cuisinier describes a love charm in which the woman working it invokes a spirit of earth, and one of water.[6] Malay babies are ceremonially introduced to 'Mother Earth and Father Water' forty-four days after birth.[7] Mother Earth (*Ibu-ku Bumi*) and Father Water (*Bapa-ku Ayer*) are also mentioned in a charm used when the ground is cleared for a mine.[8] The Prophet 'Tap, lord of the earth, and the Prophet Khizr, lord of water, are frequently invoked together in charms, usually along with other prophets (*nabi*) and other beings of general importance.[9] The four-elements idea of disease contrasts the dry disorders of the earth, associated with black *jin*, with the damp chills of water, connected with white ghosts.[10] These are associated with the dry heat of fire (yellow *jin*) and the hot moistness of air (red demons).[11] In general earth is black to the whiteness of water, though many

---

[1] ibid., p. 315.   [2] Winstedt 1961a, pp. 66–7.   [3] ibid., p. 66.
[4] ibid., p. 117.   [5] ibid., p. 117.   [6] Cuisinier 1951, p. 240.
[7] Winstedt 1961a, pp. 38, 109–10.   [8] Skeat 1900, p. 619.
[9] See e.g. ibid., pp. 315–16.   [10] Gimlette 1929, p. 32.
[11] ibid., p. 32.

exceptions exist; for example, the heart of earth from which Adam was created was white.[1] This probably arises from another system of ideas in which whiteness is an attribute of divinities and royalty.

The equivalence of earth and water environments is attested by the fact that some of the taboos observed in both places, both verbal and behavioural, are the same. Sarongs, umbrellas, and shoes or boots may not be worn in mines or at fishing-stakes.[2] A number of special words are substituted for the ordinary terms for such objects of general concern as tin sand, metallic tin, and centipedes in mines,[3] and for fish, crocodiles, and the seaward compartment of the stakes at the fishing-stakes.[4] In the one example reported in which the same object is specified, the term used is the same. In both environments the snake is called *akar hidup*, living creeper.[5] And yet, there are ways in which earth and sea seem to be consciously distinguished. For example, bathing in the mine is not allowed and 'a man must not work in the mine with only his bathing-cloth around his body. He must wear trousers'.[6] On the other hand, it is forbidden to bathe (at the fishing-stakes, at least) without wearing a bathing-cloth.[7] Although the realms of earth and water are not frequently juxtaposed, when they are considered together, they are treated as equivalent but distinct divisions of the world.

## IV. HABITATION OF MAN

The fourth major division of the physical environment—the habitation of man—is not of the same sort as the other three. It intrudes into the realms of earth, water, and jungle in such a way that even its most permanent parts, the dwellings of the *kampong*, must be protected and re-won from time to time. The village must be protected from the spirits and animals outside, and yet their aid must be enlisted in order to maintain life, be it by hunting, fishing, or agriculture.

The Malays have no single, simple division between culture and nature; the habitation of man is not a homogeneous realm set off clearly and absolutely from the three realms of nature. Man's

---

[1] Skeat 1900, p. 21.  [2] ibid., pp. 256 n, 263, 265, 314, 315.
[3] ibid., pp. 254–5.  [4] ibid., p. 315.  [5] ibid., pp. 255 n, 315.
[6] ibid., p. 264.  [7] ibid., p. 315.

habitation intrudes into nature in several degrees, corresponding to the degrees of control he has and the permanency of his occupation. I think at least four stages of intrusion are distinguished: the house, the village (*kampong*), semi-permanent outposts such as mines, and the temporary intrusion of hunting expeditions and the like. The exact position of the boundaries of the *kampong* is not perfectly clear. The term admits some variation of meaning in Malay. Gullick says 'the word *kampong* is used for a homestead as well as for a village made up of several homesteads'.[1] I shall use the term village to mean all the dwellings at a site, but not the padi fields associated with them. I treat the latter as outside the village, being comparable to mines and fishing-stakes. This may be justified by the fact that the fields are usually some distance from the dwellings,[2] but this is no guarantee that the Malays see it this way or that writers of English exclude the fields when they write 'village'. Fortunately, the investigation does not rest on a definition of the exact geographical position of village boundaries. The aim is to get at the abstract nature of those boundaries and to compare them with other boundaries in the habitation of man.

The house has the most clearly defined boundaries and is most insulated from wild spirits. It is set back physically from the water and jungle and elevated above the ground. It can be further protected magically by hanging various herbs, charms, and spirit traps around it.[3] These defences are erected mainly against familiars and vampires, as wild spirits can usually be intercepted at the village boundary. The only spirit that would normally be found inside a house is a familiar owned by one of the household.[4] Familiars seem generally innocuous to their owners and others in the owner's household, but they will attack members of other households.[5] The characteristic behaviour of familiars emphasizes the separation of the houses of a village. The occasional familiar spirit is the only exception to the general rule that the proper state of affairs is the exclusion of spirits from the house. The Malays, unlike many other non-European peoples (e.g., the Kachin), do not have household spirits or a shrine into which spirits are invited for offerings. Even the intrusion into the house of animals

---

[1] Gullick 1958, p. 32.  [2] See e.g. ibid., p. 28.
[3] See e.g. Skeat 1900, pp. 322 n, 328–9 n, 334.  [4] See ibid., p. 329.
[5] This is similar to the Sir Ghost of the Manus which protects the members of its former household, but is to other households merely a malicious ghost (Fortune n.d, p. 11).

that do not normally reside there is considered bad luck.[1] Interestingly, the most dreaded visitors of this sort are iguanas, tortoises, and snakes,[2] all of which inhabit or violate the division between land and sea.

The spirits that are most disturbed when a house is built are those of jungle and earth, especially the latter. After divination has established that the spirits of a place are amenable to a house being built there, the site is cleared and the boundaries symbolically defined by the pegging of dead sticks at the four corners.[3] When a propitious time arrives, a hole is dug for the centre-post. When the hole is finished, an offering of hard woods, nuts, and iron or copper objects is deposited in it. Then a fowl, goat, or buffalo is killed and the blood, feet, and head put in the hole as an offering to the earth demon (*puaka*).[4] The centre-post is erected on top of these. It appears that the jungle spirits are summarily cleared out, but the earth spirits are treated a little more carefully. The flesh and blood given to the latter are undoubtedly an offering in the traditional sense, but the wood, nuts, and metals, as I shall show in the next chapter, are most likely intended to seal the boundary between the earth and the new house. One charm used at the ceremony for erecting the centre-poles asks the earth demon to retire 'to the depths of the Ocean, to the peace of the primeval forest'.[5]

The boundaries of the village can be defined and protected by methods similar to those used with houses. The Malays seem resigned to the existence of familiars and birth demons within the village, if not inside the houses, but they do make an effort to keep wild spirits out. Blagden reports that charms are hung at the borders of the villages to keep the 'wild spirits in their proper place, viz., the jungle, and to prevent them taking up their abode in the villages'.[6] When spirits do get in and attack the village as such, i.e., more than one household, there may be a village-wide ceremony of expulsion. When an epidemic occurs, for example, the villagers may prepare a spirit boat to take away the spirits of disease.[7]

The rites needed in establishing a village are probably no more than the sum of the rites performed in the building of its houses. I have no evidence of any further ceremonies.

[1] Skeat 1900, p. 534.　　[2] ibid., p. 535.　　[3] ibid., p. 142.　　[4] ibid., p. 144.
[5] ibid., p. 145.　　[6] Blagden 1896, p. 4.　　[7] Skeat 1900, p. 235.

The boundaries of the outposts of civilization, fields, mines, and fishing-stakes, are quite clear and may be emphasized symbolically,[1] but, unlike those of house and village, they cannot be fixed and sealed. Water must continue to flow through the fishing-stakes, new ore is continuously extracted from mines, and the jungle is regularly pushed back from fallow fields and the soil broken anew. Spirits can be pushed back, but never expelled permanently from these outposts. Consequently, the Malays are forced to establish a cooperative relationship with some spirits of earth, water, and forest.

One method used is the making of offerings to the spirits. For tin mines there is a special *pawang* who makes offerings to the local spirits when a mine is opened[2] and to the spirits in the mine regularly thereafter.[3] In addition, he may make special prayers if the ore appears to be leaving the mine.[4] I have already described the sacrifice at the fishing-stakes. Another version of this, perhaps a desperation measure, involves the offering of an alcoholic drink —arrack—to the gods of the sea.[5] I cannot say for certain how often such ceremonies are held, but it is probably at some regular interval. The growth of padi depends on the spirits of the soil, and a number of rites are performed to ensure their goodwill. The Prophet 'Tap is asked to care for the padi seed until it sprouts,[6] and he is consoled with offerings of sugar cane, rice, and rice-paste when the first padi is cut.[7] Also, a stone, an egg, a cockle-shell, a candle nut, and a big iron nail are placed at the base of the first sheaf cut[8] to keep him in the ground, I think, even if he is not satisfied. A mock combat (*puar*) which is performed every three or four years to drive evil spirits out of the fields[9] sometimes ends with the burial of flesh from a buffalo to placate the earth spirits remaining.[10] Blagden describes a further ceremony of infrequent occurence that is performed at an altar in the middle of the padi fields.[11] A large variety of offerings is made, some placed on the altar (there is a ladder up to it for the convenience of the *hantu*), some on the ground, and some buried below. A large iron nail is also placed in the hole beneath the altar.

---

[1] See e.g. ibid., p. 247.　　[2] ibid., pp. 256-7.　　[3] ibid., p. 256 n.

[4] ibid., p. 256 n.　　[5] Winstedt 1961b, pp. 22-3.　　[6] Skeat 1900, p. 229.

[7] ibid., pp. 239, 240.　　[8] ibid., p. 240.　　[9] Blagden 1896, p. 7.

[10] Winstedt 1961b, p. 23.　　[11] Blagden 1896, pp. 7-11.

A number of special behavioural and linguistic prohibitions are observed in the outposts of civilization. They seem designed mainly to avoid arousing the spirits whose domains are being exploited. There are several facets of the strategy employed to this end. To avoid drawing the spirits' attention to the intrusion, special words are used for the creatures whose form the spirits may take and for the product that is sought. For the same reason, certain typical symbols of civilization are prohibited in mines and at fishing-stakes. Also, to avoid angering the spirits, things that are harmful to them are forbidden, and their names may not be mentioned in the spirits' vicinity.

Malays will not use the proper name of the tiger when they suspect one is around for fear of attracting its unwelcome attention.[1] Probably for the same reason, they use special words for some of the animals that habitually inhabit the spheres in which man's outposts are located. These include snakes and centipedes in mines[2] and snakes and crocodiles at the fishing-stakes.[3] These seem to be regarded as forms that the lords and spirits of those realms often take. Skeat mentions a charm in which lizards and centipedes are begged to bring the tin-ore to the mine.[4] The crocodile, as I pointed out, is the manifestation of Siva in the water. Snakes are almost always regarded as supernatural by the Malays,[5] probably because they occur in all three natural spheres and show no hesitation in crossing the boundaries. This special position of snakes in Malay thought probably accounts for the persistence of earlier ideas about supernatural snakes from both Indonesian and Indian sources. There are significant bodies of lore surrounding the lucky snake Sakatimuna, which Newbold thinks is a Menangkabau idea,[6] and the Indian nagas. Sometimes the two notions are merged as when Sakatimuna is identified as the serpent that broke apart, the pieces forming the major classes of *jin*.[7] The mysterious attributes of these snakes and the great creative potential of nagas in particular are quite in keeping with what one would expect of creatures that are anomalous to a people's fundamental classification of the world. Snakes are found

[1] Clifford 1897, p. 201.   [2] Skeat 1900, p. 255.
[3] ibid., p. 315.   [4] ibid., p. 266.
[5] See Annandale and Robinson 1904, p. 29; Skeat 1900, pp. 302–5, 426.
[6] Quoted in Skeat 1900, p. 3 n.
[7] ibid., pp. 3–4, 95.

in mines and around fishing-stakes, and it would be foolhardy not to treat them as deities.

The special words applied to tin sand and metallic tin in mines,[1] to fish at the fishing-stakes,[2] and to the freak ears of rice that are said to contain the rice-soul[3] are probably used to avoid warning the spirits of each sphere of the products man wishes to extract. This might anger the spirits and cause them to withhold the goods.

The prohibition on wearing shoes or sarongs and on carrying umbrellas in mines and at fishing-stakes may exist because these too strongly recall civilization to be ignored by the spirits. The proscription on taking cats, elephants, and water-buffalo into mines and on using their common names there[4] may be based on similar ideas: cats are close companions of men and even live with them; elephants and buffalo work for men and assist them in agriculture, which is a definite irritation to earth spirits.

Such things as limes, being dangerous to spirits, are forbidden in mines and may not be mentioned.[5] Probably for similar reasons iron tools and weapons are avoided when possible[6] or are kept covered up.[7] The first ears of rice are cut by a magician 'hiding in his palm a tiny blade, whose handle is carved in the shape of a bird for disguise'.[8] This is usually interpreted as an attempt not to frighten the 'rice-soul',[9] but it must be remembered that until the padi is cut it is still in the care of the earth spirits and probably is animated by them. It would be just as accurate to say that the sight of the blade would frighten and offend the Prophet 'Tap and his associates. It is they who are propitiated and, as an added precaution, confined to the earth when the rice soul is separated from its original matrix.[10]

Whenever an outpost of civilization is established or substantially expanded, an effort is made to clear out as many spirits as possible and to propitiate those left. For example, mining *pawang* have charms to 'clear evil spirits away from the ground before commencing the work of excavation' and others to 'propitiate the local spirits and induce the tin-ore to show itself'.[11] Rites are performed even when a road is cut through the forest to exorcise

[1] See ibid., p. 255.    [2] See ibid., p. 315.    [3] See ibid., p. 248.
[4] ibid., p. 254.    [5] ibid., pp. 254–5.
[6] See e.g. Maxwell 1885, p. 20 n.
[7] Skeat 1900, p. 259.    [8] Winstedt 1961a, p. 50.
[9] See e.g. Wilkinson 1906, p. 50.    [10] See Skeat 1900, pp. 238–42.
[11] ibid., p. 267.

and placate the spirits.[1] But only superfluous spirits are ousted by these ceremonies, and it is recognized that the expulsion cannot be permanent. Some spirits must necessarily be allowed to remain, for they act as the *sĕmangat* of the diffuse body man would exploit. The growing rice is animated by earth spirits, fish are controlled by spirits of the sea, and tin ore is governed by the *sĕmangat* of the mine. Man's aim is to gain and maintain the cooperation of the spirits in the outposts of civilization despite regularly extracting their products.

Temporary excursions into the natural spheres are launched for such purposes as hunting, fishing, seeking camphor wood, and simply travelling. Under these circumstances it is impossible to erect boundaries and expel the spirits from within them. Charms may be used, however, to shore up the last line of defence—the human body.[2] In general the balance of power is in favour of the spirits; therefore, the intruders attempt to solicit their cooperation or at least to ensure that they do not interfere. Offerings are usually made before an expedition embarks and are repeated regularly during the excursion. For example, the eagle-wood *pawang* burns incense at the edge of the forest and prays to the Divinity of Eagle-wood to guide him. When he finds a likely-looking tree he sets up a shelter, inquires into the spirit's needs, and offers the required sacrifices.[3] Camphor hunters 'always throw a portion of their food out into the jungle before eating, as an offering to the *bisan* [camphor spirit]'.[4] Charms may be recited without offerings at various stages in an expedition. The deer *pawang* will employ charms to ask for a tree from which to suspend his snares, to ask for deer and have them come out to meet the dogs, to turn back the deer that have escaped, to urge on the dogs or make them bark, and for many other purposes.[5] The charms are usually addressed to the spirits who are the 'herdsmen' of the deer.[6] Special vocabularies are usually employed on such expeditions for approximately the same reasons they are used in mines and at fishing-stakes.[7] The special language of fishermen in Patani, for example, replaces all words that would reveal the

[1] ibid., p. 149.    [2] See e.g. ibid., p. 274.
[3] ibid., pp. 207, 210–11.  [4] ibid., p. 213.
[5] ibid., pp. 173–4.    [6] See ibid., pp. 173, 175, 176.
[7] Winstedt suggests that the *pantuns* (half-verse, half-riddle) exchanged by workers in the padi fields in Negri Sembilan are the remnants of a 'taboo' language (1961a, p. 55), but this is far from certain.

terrestrial origin of the fishermen, and it also avoids reference to the sea spirits themselves. No beast, reptile (especially snake), or Buddhist monk may be mentioned by name at sea. Fish, surprisingly, can be spoken of and so can birds with the exception of domestic fowls and vultures—the only birds, presumably, that would be unfamiliar to the sea spirits.[1] Interestingly, the language used by camphor hunters contains a high proportion of words from aboriginal languages[2] which are more appropriate to the forest, apparently, and do not alarm the spirits as much as Malay words do.

The realm of man, then, is divided, and the amount of human control, permanence of man's occupation, and the strength of boundaries diminishes from house to village to fields and beyond. The association of familiar spirits with houses, birth demons with villages, and free spirits with areas outside reflects the successive diminution of man's control over those spirits. This classification exactly parallels the classification of spirits by degrees of freedom from bodies. The correspondence suggests that the inmost division of the human domain, the most secure and controlled, is the individual body whose proper spirit is the sěmangat. A number of similarities exist between bodies and the divisions of man's realm; these strongly imply that they are the same kind of thing and part of a single classification. For both, boundaries are established and defended against invading spirits. Even some of the same materials can be used to reinforce the boundaries of the two. A piece of iron is placed in the basket containing the rice-baby[3] to protect it and seal in the soul, and an iron nail is placed at the foot of the sheaf from which the rice-baby was cut[4] to keep the earth spirits in the ground and prevent them from following the rice-baby into the sphere of man. When a spirit gets inside a body, it may be expelled by the same kind of rite as is used to evict a spirit from a house or village. For example, a spirit boat may be prepared to rid an individual of an ailment or to rid a village of an epidemic. The analogy between the body and the house, village, and outposts of civilization is far-reaching and important for the interpretation of Malay magical practices.

It may be wondered how the three divisions of nature fit into

[1] See Annandale and Robinson 1903, pp. 84–7.

[2] Skeat 1900, pp. 212, 213, 214.

[3] ibid., p. 237; Winstedt 1961a, p. 51.      [4] Skeat 1900, p. 240.

this scheme. I think that the categories earth, water, and jungle are the 'bodies' of free spirits. A natural realm is vaguely constraining to its spirits, and they, as a group, serve their domain as a sĕmangat serves its more condensed body. They control the body's parts, the ore and fish and animals, and protect it from outside invasion, in this case not by spirits, but by men. There is also some suggestion that the natural spheres are seen as analogous to the domain of man, but with other creatures playing the dominant role. The cities deep in the jungle where tiger or elephant spirits go about in human form, living as human beings, can be understood in this light. I have found no similar situation reported for the realms of water and earth, but suspect that such ideas exist in some form. The Land Dayaks of Sarawak think that cities exist beneath some rivers and that they are ruled by nagas.[1] These alternate between the form of men and the form of dragons, probably modelled on crocodiles. There are also cities under the earth ruled by the same creatures,[2] this time, I suspect, with the snake-like side of their identity to the fore. I have seen no such beliefs recorded for the Malays, but there are numerous folk-tales involving enormous riches originating somewhere beneath the waters of deep rivers.[3] The analogy between tigers and crocodiles in Malay ideas suggests that a crocodile city, like that of the Land Dayaks, might be the source of this wealth.

## V. NON-PHYSICAL DIVISIONS

A number of spirits and deities are not localized. Their classifications express, most importantly, divisions of society, time, and space.

### Social Divisions

Spirits are often ranked, and sometimes this ranking almost amounts to a class system. The 'Black King of the Genii (Sang Gala Raja, or Sa-Raja Jin) . . . appears at times a manifestation of Shiva Batara Guru, who is confounded with the destructive side of Shiva, i.e. Kala'.[4] While Siva rules all *jin*, the prophets Solomon, 'Tap, and Khizr are lords of their respective regions and, I think, the immediate superiors of the spirits of each realm. Solomon is

---

[1] See Geddes 1961, p. 99.      [2] ibid., pp. 117–18, 125.
[3] See e.g. Skeat 1900, pp. 563–6.      [4] ibid., p. 93.

sometimes called the 'king of the Genii', but this seems to refer specifically to the *jin* of the forest which are directly important to hunters and trappers.[1] Major spirits, such as the tiger-spirit, have subjects,[2] and *jimbalang* are considered the servants of *jin*.[3] Some unfortunate spirits are even more depressed than that: the *badi* of wild beasts are called the slaves (*hamba*) of the great spirits controlling deer, etc.[4]

These social and 'political' distinctions among *jin* parallel those among men. Gullick describes traditional Malay society (between the time of the Malacca Sultanate and the abolition of slavery by the British) as including sultans of the states, chiefs of districts, headmen of villages, freemen, debt-bondsmen, and slaves or con-cubines.[5] The first two form a ruling class which is set off by endogamy from the subject class; this division is a fundamental feature of the Malay social and political systems.[6]

A division of spirits into ruling and subject classes is not clearly marked, but the superior-inferior relationship is noted frequently. The relative division between ruler and ruled at all levels is, I think, a basic feature of the Malay outlook and is of crucial importance in the operation of magic. Up-down symbolism, which usually distinguishes earth spirits from other kinds, sometimes reflects the division between superior and inferior, both for men and for spirits.[7]

## Time Divisions

One classification of *mambang* includes the white *mambang* in the sun, the black *mambang* in the moon and the yellow *mambang* of the yellow sunset-glow.[8] The last is very dangerous, especially to children, and sunset is the hour when all evil-spirits have most power.[9] The division indicated is undoubtedly the one between night and day, a rather important distinction in some kinds of magic. The concentration of danger at sunset, rather than sunrise, is probably derived from the former's being marginal between night and day and also between successive days. 'The religious day commences at sunset, like that of the Arabs and Hebrews'.[10]

Malay weeks last seven days beginning on Friday, the Moham-

[1] See ibid., p. 99.     [2] See Winstedt 1961a, p. 70.
[3] Cuisinier 1936, p. 33.     [4] Annandale and Robinson 1904, p. 40.
[5] Gullick 1958, pp. 21–2, 97–105.     [6] ibid., pp. 21–2, 65.
[7] See e.g. ibid., pp. 110–11; Skeat 1900, pp. 37–8, 417–18.
[8] Skeat 1900, p. 92.     [9] ibid., pp. 15, 92.     [10] ibid., p. 554.

medan Sabbath.[1] Friday, like sunset, marks the transition between one cycle and the next, and it is also fraught with danger, being the day when spirits are most active; thus, people take special precautions then.[2]

Months are figured in a number of ways.[3] The Arabian month, alternating between thirty and twenty-nine days, the Persian month of thirty days, and that of Rum with thirty-one days are all used. The lunar month, however, remains the most important for agriculture[4] and seems so also for magical purposes. The critical part of the month is the full moon. The night of the full moon is when one may gain magical powers at the graves of murdered men,[5] and the three nights centring on the full moon are when a pĕlĕsit can be created from one's own shadow[6] or a soul 'abducted' by a certain method.[7] One ceremony to acquire invulnerability is performed at the full moon and can be repeated for the two following full moons if the first attempt fails.[8] In some places the pawang forbids people to work in the rice-fields on the 14th and 15th days of the lunar month.[9] If the heightened power of spirits at the transition from one time cycle to the next holds in the case of the lunar month, the special significance of the full moon may be the result of a view that months begin and end at that time.

Both the solar year of 365 days and the lunar year of 354 are recognized by the Malays.[10] Neither is of special magical significance as far as I know.

Time, then, seems to be seen as the passing of events, and it is measured by the recurrence of similar events. Natural cycles provide several of the significant units of time. When man controls the sequence of events, as in magical ceremonies, he usually groups them into series of 'three' and, less frequently, 'seven'. When units of time or numbers of repetitions are specified in the ceremonies described by Skeat in Malay Magic (1900), the number given is 'three' in one hundred and three cases and 'seven' in thirty-nine cases. In only forty-two instances is any other number specified.

[1] ibid., p. 554.
[2] Annandale and Robinson 1903, p. 81; 1904, p. 30.
[3] Skeat 1900, pp. 553–4.  [4] ibid., p. 554.
[5] ibid., p. 60.  [6] Swettenham 1895, p. 197.
[7] Skeat 1900, p. 576.  [8] ibid., e.g. pp. 522–3.
[9] ibid., p. 58.  [10] ibid., p. 553.

## Space Divisions

Four mythical sheikhs are penned in the four corners of the world surrounded by ring-fences of white iron.[1] These may have replaced pre-Moslem gods residing in the same positions. One Peninsular charm refers to 'the four children of Siva who live at the corners of the world'.[2] The number and arrangement of the sheikhs suggests that their basic significance is to indicate that the world, to the Malays, is a quadrilateral. Many lesser demarcations of space are defined as quadrilaterals, sometimes with strong suggestions that the area indicated is a diminished copy of the world. When a likely site for a house is found, some ground is cleared and a rectangle of sticks laid in the centre. Soil is dug up inside the frame and the lords of the spot are addressed as follows:

> Ho, children of Mĕntri Guru,
> Who dwell in the Four Corners of the World,
> I crave this plot as a boon[3]

If the omens are good, the four corners of the main building are pegged out with dead sticks and the area cleared. Then the ceremony for erecting the central house-post is begun.[4] The shed that forms the Malay theatre is square.[5] The *pawang* defines the space needed for the performance by moving from within the enclosure 'four paces in each direction of the four corners of the universe' and asks the spirits within that area not to be disturbed.[6] Before rice-seed is sown in a field, a rectangular frame of poles is placed in the middle of the clearing and four small plants (banana tree, lemon grass, sugar cane, and saffron) planted at the corners. The time to plant is divined by watching for omens affecting the frame and the coconut shell full of water that is placed in the centre.[7] Before the rice-soul is cut, knots are tied in rice leaves at each of the four corners of the field and a ceremony performed to confine noxious spirits to the boundaries of the field thus defined.[8] Even the temporary clearing in the jungle made by the pigeon hunter is rectangular; railings are placed around it, and the space contained is called King Solomon's Palace-yard.[9]

[1] ibid., p. 100.
[2] Winstedt 1925, p. 6; see also Skeat 1900, p. 100 n.
[3] Skeat 1900, p. 142.    [4] ibid., pp. 142–3.
[5] ibid., p. 504.    [6] ibid., p. 507.
[7] ibid., p. 229.    [8] ibid., p. 247.    [9] ibid., p. 133.

Certain basic items of magical equipment are also quadrangular. Altars, offering trays (*anchak*), and the platforms erected in the houses of bride and groom are usually approximately square.[1] The Malays, like ourselves, recognize four cardinal directions; these sometimes serve to orient fixed quadrilaterals. The world itself is thought to be situated with its corners toward the four cardinal points. According to a Malay charm-book, the pillar of the Ka'bah (a cubical building in the centre of the mosque at Mecca), which is the navel of the earth, has growth comparable to a tree, its four branches extending 'north, south, east, and west, where they are called the Four Corners of the World'.[2] The sides of a square altar used for propitiating earth spirits in rice-fields are said to 'face accurately towards the four cardinal points'.[3] Graves in Trengganu are oriented on a north-south axis with the corpse's head to the north and the face turned west toward Mecca. Living people make a point of sleeping in the reverse position: with the head toward the south.[4] Houses are usually oriented with reference to the four directions at least to the extent that people avoid having the door face south, since this would bring bad luck.[5]

Despite the frequent recognition of the cardinal directions in situating quadrilaterals, it would be a mistake, I think, to give the directions primacy over the shape. The names for directions vary from place to place and are sometimes connected with concrete facts of geography. For example, in parts of Kelantan the term for north includes the word *hilir*, down-stream, and south is called *hulu bani*, 'up-stream people'.[6] This would not apply in other parts of the peninsula where the main rivers run east and west. Furthermore, Rentse implies that only ritual specialists are much concerned with the four directions and what they should be called,[7] and I have been told that people usually use the terms for up-stream and down-stream to orient themselves.[8]

The fundamental distinction that is being made with regard to space seems to be between bounded and unbounded space, and the quadrilateral is, for the Malays, the bounded space *par*

[1] ibid., pp. 231, 369, 414.
[2] ibid., p. 3, 3 n; cf. Chelhod 1964, pp. 537–45.
[3] Blagden, quoted in Skeat 1900, p. 231.
[4] Humphreys 1926, pp. 133–4; cf. Hamilton 1922, p. 385.
[5] Skeat 1900, p. 141 n.        [6] See Rentse 1933b, p. 252.
[7] ibid., p. 252.        [8] William Wilder, personal communication.

*excellence.* Occasionally enclosures are circular as, for example, cock-fighting pits,[1] but usually, I think, circles are contrasted to quadrilaterals as unbounded to bounded space. The contrast between terrestrial and heavenly space is expressed in the legend that the creator made 'the Earth of the width of a tray and the Heavens of the width of an umbrella, which are the universe of the Magician'.[2] Winstedt interprets this to mean that the universe was created in miniature,[3] but I suggest that shape, not size, is the important factor. The circular umbrella of the heavens is unlimited, but the earth was created by being defined as a quadrilateral like an offering tray.

The number usually associated with bounded terrestrial space, naturally enough, is four, indicating four corners. However, even numbers are generally regarded as unlucky;[4] thus, four is sometimes transformed into a more auspicious number—five—by emphasizing the four corners and the centre. This is done regularly with the portions of offerings placed on offering trays. Still, four points are enough to define an area by the Malay reckoning, and the number persists with reference to territory despite its potentially unfavourable connotations.

[1] See Skeat 1900, p. 476.  [2] ibid., p. 3.
[3] Winstedt 1961a, p. 10.  [4] See e.g., Skeat 1900, p. 437.

# VI

## THE OPERATION OF MAGIC

UNDOUBTEDLY, the information given in the two preceding
chapters, insofar as it is correct, forms part of the *ilmu* the
magician must acquire. But for the magician a knowledge
of essences, both spirits and souls, and of the basic divisions of the
world only defines the problem: how to gain control of these
things. The world view that forms the background for Malay
magic is probably, with some variations in detail, public knowledge. Most Malays would understand what the magician tries to
do, but probably not the exact means by which he does it. It is
the latter subject that must now be examined.

The power in the Malay system of ideas seems to lie ultimately
with the ubiquitous vital principle. It is the force that, differentiated into *sěmangat* in the narrow sense, maintains the existence
of material 'things', and it is also the force, in the form of spirits,
that threatens their existence. The power is manifest, in other
words, as both the ability to maintain boundaries in the material
world and the ability to violate them. Although the power of
essences inside bodies is similar to that of ones outside, the two
kinds of power are not used in the same way. Because a *sěmangat*
uses all of its power to control and maintain the thing with which
it is conjoined, it has no power in its own right, no freedom or
independence like that of a *hantu*. The power of *sěmangat* in the
narrow sense can be seen simply as the capacity of things to exist,
specifically, the ability of a category of matter to resist the invasion
of free spirits and to retain the aspects of the soul that are partially
independent of the body. At this level of analysis, the opposed
forces are the power of essences and the power of the categories
that the culture imposes on the world. The task of the magician,
I suggest, is to gain control of these two kinds of power in order to
manipulate them in his own interest. This entails knowing how to
persuade and coerce essences and how to modify categories,
mainly to strengthen or weaken their boundaries to resist or facilitate the passing of essences through them. This chapter will

describe how the Malay magician performs these two operations, both through spells and through magical equipment, and will interpret some important magical rites in this light.

## I. THE SPELL

Magicians' spells present a rather confusing appearance, as they often incorporate references to concepts from many or all of the religious traditions that have influenced Malay magic. They are also sometimes extremely abbreviated and distorted by faulty transmission or deliberate efforts, in the interest of secrecy, to disguise their content and meaning. Still, it is possible to go beyond the diversity and distortion of specific content to isolate some general features of spells. It is then possible to discern some basic principles behind the supposed power of the spell.

I shall begin by presenting a sample of spells from the various areas of Malay magic as recorded and translated by Skeat.[1] The spells chosen are ones for which Skeat has given a complete or nearly complete translation; otherwise the selection is quite random.

The following spell is intended to counteract the effects of illness caused by an encounter with the Spectre Huntsman:

> In the name of God, the Compassionate, the Merciful,
> Peace be on thee, O Si Jidi, husband of Mah Jadah.
>
> Go thou and hunt in the forest of Ranchah Mahang.
> *Katapang* is the name of thy hill,
> *Si Langsat* is the name of thy dog,
> *Si Kumbang* is the name of thy dog,
> *Si Nibong* is the name of thy dog,
> *Si Pintas* is the name of thy dog,
> *Si Aru-Aru* is the name of thy dog,
> *Timiang Balu* is the name of thy blow-pipe
> *Lankapuri* is the name of thy spear,
> *Singha-buana* is the name of its blade,
> The peeling-knife with a long handle
> Is to split in twain the fibrous betel-nut.
> Here is a knife from Maharaja Guru,
> To cleave the bowels of the Hunter-Spirit.

[1] Skeat 1900.

I know the origin from which thou springest,
O man of Katapang.
Get thee back to the forest of Ranchah Mahang.
Afflict not my body with pain or disease.[1]

Spirits of the earth are addressed with the following charm when
the centre-post of a building is erected:

Ho, Raja Guru, Maharaja Guru,
You are the sons of Batara Guru.
I know the origin from which you spring,
From the Flashing of Lightning's spurs;
[I know the origin from which you spring.
From a drop of dew.[2]]
I know the origin from which you spring.
From the Brightening of Daybreak.
Ho, Spectre of the Earth, Brains of the Earth,
    Demon of the Earth,
Retire ye hence to the depths of the Ocean,
To the peace of the primeval forest.
Betwixt you and me
Division was made by Adam.[3]

The *badi* in the carcase of a newly killed elephant are addressed as
follows:

Badiyu, Mother of Mischief, Badi Panji, Blind Mother,
I know the origin from which you sprang,
Three drops of Adam's blood were the origin from which you
    sprang,
Mischief of Earth, return to Earth,
Mischief of Ant-heap, return to Ant-heap,
Mischief of Elephant, return to Elephant,
Mischief of Wood, return to Wood,
Mischief of Water, return to Water,
Mischief of Stone, return to Stone

[1] ibid., pp. 117–18.
[2] '*Aku tahu asal 'kau jadi:*
    *Deripada ambun sa-titek*'
    (Skeat 1900, p. 601).
    Skeat does not translate these lines. *Ambun* does not occur in my dictionary
    (Wilkinson 1964). Probably it is a corruption of *embun*, 'dew' (Wilkinson 1964,
    p. 69). *Titek* means 'a drop; fig. a point; an item; a full-stop; a dot,' and *sa*
    means 'one' or 'unity' (Wilkinson 1964, pp. 235, 292).
[3] Skeat 1900, pp. 145, 601.

And injure not my person.
By the virtue of my Teacher,
You may not injure the children of the race of Man.[1]

Crocodiles are attracted to the trap (a line attached to a fowl impaled on a hook-like device with the other end attached to a float) by the following charm:

Follow in procession, follow in succession,
The 'Assembly-flower' begins to unfold its petals;
Come in procession, come in succession,
King Solomon's self comes to summon you.
Ho, Si Jambu Rakai, I know your origin;
Sugar-cane knots forty-four were your bones,
Of clay was formed your body;
Rootlets of areca-palm were your arteries,
Liquid sugar made your blood,
A rotten mat your skin,
And a mid-rib of the thatch-palm your tail,
Prickles of the pandanus made your dorsal ridge,
And pointed bĕrĕmbang suckers your teeth.
If you splash with your tail it shall break in two,
If you strike downwards with your snout it shall break in two,
If you crunch with your teeth they shall all be broken.
Lo, Si Jambu Rakai, I bind (this fowl) with the sevenfold binding,
And enwrap it with the sevenfold wrapping
Which you shall never loosen or undo.
Turn it over in your mouth before you swallow it.
O, Si Jambu Rakai, accept this present from Her
    Highness Princess Rundok, from Java:
If you refuse to accept it,
Within two days or three
Mati mampek, mati mawai,[2]
You shall be choked to death with blood,
Choked to death by Her Highness Princess Rundok, from Java.
But if you accept it,
A reach up-stream or a reach down-stream, there do you await me;
It is not my Word, it is the King Solomon's Word;
If you are carried down-stream see that you incline up-stream,

[1] ibid., p. 156.
[2] This line is not translated by Skeat. Mati means 'dead' (Wilkinson 1964, p. 177), but I cannot find the meaning of mampek and mawai. Skeat says that spells are sometimes corrupt (1900, p. 581 n).

If you are carried up-stream see that you incline down-stream,
By virtue of the Saying of King Solomon, 'There is no god
but God'.[1]

Tin-ore can be drawn to the surface in a mine by the following
charm:

Peace be with you, O Tin-Ore,
At the first it was dew that turned into water,
And water that turned into foam,
And foam that turned into rock,
And rock that turned into tin-ore;
Do you, O Tin-Ore, lying in a matrix of solid rock,
Come forth from this matrix of solid rock;
If you do not come forth
You shall be a rebel in the sight of God.
Ho Tin-Ore, Sir 'Floating Islet',
'Flotsam-at-sea,' and 'Flotsam-on-land,'
Do you float up to the surface of this my tank,
Or you shall be a rebel to God.[2]

A soul that has left a person's body can be recalled in the following
way:

Peace be with you, O Breath [*rûh*]!
Hither, Breath, come hither!
Hither, Soul [*sěmangat*], come hither!
Hither, Little One, come hither!
[Hither, Bird, come hither!][3]
Hither, Filmy One, come hither!
Hither, I am sitting and praising you!
Hither, I am sitting and waving to you!
Come back to your house and house-ladder,

---

[1] Skeat 1900, pp. 298–9, 623–4.      [2] ibid., p. 265.
[3] *Mari Burong kamari* (Skeat 1900, p. 587).
Skeat omits this line in his translation. I noted in a previous chapter that
Skeat regards the 'bird soul' as merely a metaphor while Cuisinier, among
others, considers it the usual Malay conception of the soul (see p. 38 above).
A comment by Wilkinson helps explain Skeat's omission of this line from the
charm: 'Skeat's account of the Malay idea of the human soul as a sort of
"thumbling" or "manikin" (p. 47) is not supported by any other writer on
Malay magic, nor by anything that any Malay has ever told me, nor even by his
own quoted "charm" which addresses it as a "bird"—which it is. His diver-
gence from other writers seems to be due to a wish to make Malay ideas har-
monize with Professor Tylor's "classical definition" of the primitive man's idea
of what a soul is (Skeat, p. 49)' (Wilkinson 1932, p. 135).

To your floor of which the planks have started,
To your thatch-roof 'starred' (with holes).
Do not bear grudges,
Do not bear malice,
Do not take it as a wrong,
Do not take it as a transgression.
Here I sit and praise you.
Here I sit and drag you (home),
Here I sit and shout for you,
Here I sit and wave to you,
Come at this very time, come at this very moment.[1]

The following charm is recited as one buries the wax image of an enemy:

Peace be to you! Ho, Prophet 'Tap, in whose charge the earth is,
Lo, I am burying the corpse of *Somebody*,
I am bidden (to do so) by the Prophet Muhammad,
Because he (the corpse) was a rebel to God.
Do you assist in killing him or making him sick:
If you do not make him sick, if you do not kill him,
You shall be a rebel against God,
A rebel against Muhammad.
It is not I who am burying him,
It is Gabriel who is burying him.
Do you too grant my prayer and petition, this very day that has
    appeared,
Grant it by the grace of my petition within the fold of the Creed
*La ilaha.*[2]

The last charm I shall cite is allegedly a love charm working by soul abduction:

I know the origin from which you sprang,
From the glitter of the White Blood.
Come down then to your mother,
Stemming both ebb and flood tides,
Cluck! Cluck! souls of *Somebody*,
Come all of you together unto me.
Whither would ye go?
Come down to this house and house-ladder of yours.
This solitary taper is your house and house-ladder,

---

[1] Skeat 1900, pp. 454, 586–7.     [2] ibid., p. 571.

. Since already the liver, stomach, heart, spleen, and great maw
Of all of you have been given into my care,
So much the more have the body and life
Of all of you been given into my care.
Grant this by the grace of my use
Of the prayer called divination by (secret) cognizance (*tilek
ma'rifat*) of Somebody.[1]

What, then, do these examples of spells show? One thing that is
apparent is that the general features of spells are the same whether
the essences addressed are free spirits or *badi*, the souls of men or
the souls of animals and minerals. An explanation of the power of
the spell may be expected, therefore, to apply equally well to all
of these.

A substantial proportion of most spells consists of pleas, commands, and threats designed to persuade or coerce the essence to
do the magician's bidding. Simple requests sometimes contain
appeals to the sentiments or good nature of the essence and are
often, it will be shown, backed up by material offerings. Threats
and commands are usually coupled with assertions that the order
comes from or has the authority of beings superior in the spiritual
hierarchy to the essence addressed. Thus, orders to animals may
be alleged to come from the Prophet Solomon, to human souls
from Mohammed, and the disobedience of any essence may be
termed rebellion against God. The magician attempts to utilize
the power implicit in the ranking of essences to control them (see
p. 120 above), just as the politician manipulates the temporal
chain of command.

The remainder of most spells seems given over to recitation of
information about the essences addressed: naming and describing
the essences, their dwelling places, relatives, companions, equipment, and, most prominently, their origins (*asal usal*). There seems
to be a general consensus in the literature that this is no mere
formality, but rather that the knowledge gives the magician power
over the essence or at least reduces its potency. For example,
Skeat says that 'Malays believe Spirits to be extremely sensitive
as regards their origin and their habits, and any knowledge
possessed by a human being on these subjects renders the spirit
harmless' and adds that 'the same idea has been noticed *supra* with

[1] ibid., p. 578.

reference to animals, etc.'.[1] Winstedt points out that the belief in the power of knowing the name and origin of something goes back to Indian *mantra* and ritual.[2]

For all the comment on this subject in the literature, precious little is offered in the way of explanation of the supposed power of such knowledge. As far as I know, only Skeat has attempted to answer the question even partially. He suggests that the power of the ability to inform something of its origin might come from an idea that 'knowledge of another person's ancestry implied common tribal origin'.[3] This is possible, but I have seen nothing to suggest that Malays have such a belief, let alone that it is extended beyond human society to include all kinds of essence. In any case, the formulation would make the other information recited superfluous, since a knowledge of origin alone would be sufficient to ensure cooperation.

A better explanation can be made, I think, in terms of the conditions affecting the power of any essence. It was pointed out previously (Chapter IV) that the most powerful essences are only vaguely defined, while the more clearly defined essences are more vulnerable to the constraint of material boundaries. Free spirits, corresponding to vague anxieties, are much more powerful than *sĕmangat*, which are bound to the physical bodies from which their clear definition is largely derived. If permanent differences in the power of essences depend on the degree of definition of the concepts, it follows that to change the degree of differentiation of the vital principle composing an essence would affect the power of the essence. The process of heaping definition on an essence in a spell would be expected to constrain the essence by making its conceptual basis clearer and more rigid. Specification of the origin of an essence would be the most telling kind of definition, because it reveals the most basic features of the essence, those by which it originally attained its existence as an entity separate from the mass of the vital principle. I would interpret the recitation of information about the essence addressed in a spell, then, as being a tactic by which the freedom and power of conceptual obscurity are stripped from the essence, making it more susceptible to constraint by boundaries and more predictable in its behaviour.

---

[1] ibid., p. 506 n; see also Clifford, quoted in Skeat 1900, p. 156 n; Wilkinson 1906, p. 70; Winstedt 1925, pp. 32, 56–7; 1961a, p. 82.

[2] Winstedt 1925, pp. 56–7.     [3] Skeat 1900, p. 156 n.

## II. MAGICAL EQUIPMENT

The utterance of a spell in a specified manner may be considered a simple form of Malay ritual, but it seldom makes up the whole of the ceremony. Besides the manipulation of words, one must consider the manipulation of people and materials to understand the practice of Malay magic. The value of the materials used regularly in magical ritual seems to lie in their presumed special properties. These properties can be clearly understood, I think, in terms of the two basic operations the magician performs: manipulation of categories and persuasion of essences.

### Boundary Strengtheners

The magical power of iron is well known. 'The various forms of iron which play so conspicuous a part in Malay magic, from the long iron nail which equally protects the new-born infant and the Rice-Soul from the powers of evil, to the betel-nut scissors which are believed to scare the evil spirits from the dead, are alike called the representatives (symbols or emblems) of Iron (*tanda běsi*)'.[1] The power of iron seems to act as much to keep a person's soul in his body as to keep spirits out. Skeat says that a Malay will plant his wood-knife blade in the bed of a jungle stream before drinking from it and will sit on the blade while eating alone in the forest 'not only to drive away evil spirits, but to "confirm" the speaker's own soul (*měnětapkan sěmangat*)'.[2] Boundaries in the environment may be reinforced by iron just as the boundaries of the body are. For example, the scrap-iron and hatchet head deposited beneath the centre-post of a new house seem intended to 'seal' the boundary between the earth and house to prevent earth spirits from invading the latter.[3] The power of iron to ensure the integrity of bodies is implied in the belief that the iron (or steel) wrought into the clay body of Adam held it together when the spark of life was sent into it. The first attempt to create man, which lacked iron, exploded, and the fragments became the spirits.[4]

Gold and silver seem to have the same kind of power in ritual as iron, though they are used considerably less frequently, un-

---

[1] Skeat 1900, p. 274; see also Winstedt 1961a, p. 103.
[2] Skeat 1900, p. 274.    [3] See ibid., pp. 143, 144.
[4] Swettenham 1895, p. 199; Skeat 1900, pp. 19–20.

doubtedly because of their greater scarcity and economic value. Three rings of precious metals (gold, silver, and an amalgam of the two[1] are placed against an initiate's teeth before they are filed, a time when *badi* are feared to escape.[2] Rings of precious metal (presumably the same types) are attached to the seven tresses of hair cut at a girl's tonsure ceremony, possibly for the same reason.[3] A gold ring is included in the bag of things (including iron) that is shaken by a person seven times daily for three days to stop a soul in the act of escaping.[4]

Despite the great difference in the economic values of gold, silver, and iron, as ritual materials they seem to form a set. Annandale reports that in Perak an exorcised *pĕlĕsit* could be tied to a tree by a chain composed of strands of gold, silver, and iron. In fact a substitute was used, that being 'a hank of white cotton thread, [marked] in bars with wood from the fire and with grated turmeric; the thread itself will be silver, the black bars iron, and the yellow gold'.[5] Other cases tend to confirm these colour associations with the three metals,[6] but the Malays have many classifications by colour, and isolated connections might refer to any of them. The association of the three metals may tie in with the ancient Indian belief that 'the world was flat and circular, with a circumference of 22,500 miles. In the centre was a great mountain —Mount Meru—600,000 feet high with three peaks of gold, silver, and iron on which the gods dwelt'.[7]

Other materials used along with iron, gold, and silver, or in similar situations, seem also to have the power to reinforce boundaries. During the time a baby is fed on boiled rice (its first three months), the rice-jar must contain a stone, a big iron nail, and a candle-nut.[8] The water in which the new born baby is bathed contains 'a big iron nail (as a "symbol of iron")', "candle-nuts" and cockle-shells (*kulit k'rang*)'.[9] The 'rice-baby', which will be discussed presently, is protected by the same materials.[10] Along with the gold ring, the contents of the bag used to arrest an escaping soul include 'an iron nail, a candle-nut (*buah k'ras*), three small cockle-shells, three closed fistfuls of husked rice (*b'ras tiga gĕnggam bunyi*), and some parti-coloured thread'.[11]

---

[1] See Skeat 1900, p. 272. [2] ibid., p. 356 and n. [3] ibid., p. 353. [4] ibid., p. 455. [5] Annandale 1903, p. 101. [6] See e.g. Skeat 1900, pp. 33, 282. [7] Moorhead 1957, p. 32. [8] Skeat 1900, p. 338. [9] ibid., p. 340. [10] Skeat 1900, p. 237; Winstedt 1961a, pp. 51, 54. [11] Skeat 1900, p. 455; see also p. 454.

I think that stones, candle-nuts, and cockle-shells, form another set of boundary-strengthening substances. The associations here are with the earth, jungle (Skeat calls candle-nuts 'hard jungle-nuts'[1]) and water respectively. This classification may be symbolically associated with that of iron, gold, and silver, forming a single analogical classification, though the evidence is not clear. An informant told Skeat that iron was emblematic of earth[2] and spells quoted by both Skeat and Winstedt refer to genies of the earth as 'idols of iron'.[3] Skeat says that the gold spirit may take the form of a golden roe deer, an animal of the forest,[4] but admits that this is only an inference from a legend.[5] The colour of dry cockle-shells would be white, the colour associated with silver, but little importance can be attached to this isolated correspondence. The candle-nut (*Aleurites moluccana*) is 'olive' coloured,[6] at least before it is roasted, which might be within the range of colours associated with gold (and the jungle), but in the only case in which the particular kind of stone is specified, it is quartz, which would more likely be white than black, as one might expect for earth and iron. In any case, the main materials used for strengthening boundaries form two triadic sets; whether or not these two classifications are analogically associated is unclear.

What do these materials have in common that would suit them in Malay ideas to be boundary reinforcers? Probably their hardness is the important feature. The minerals used are all quite hard (gold in its unalloyed form would seldom be seen), the shell is also hard, and the Malay name for the candle-nut, *buah keras*, means literally 'hard fruit'.[7] The hardness of these materials could help define the boundaries to which they are applied. It has been seen that the sharper and firmer the boundaries of a category, the more constraint it exercises over essences. Well defined bodies hold their souls firmly and keep spirits out, but diffuse or fragmented bodies permit their souls to wander and admit alien essences easily. Some boundaries in the physical world are so poorly delineated that the category they define can hardly be called a body; such boundaries have almost no constraining

---

[1] ibid., pp. 236, 237.     [2] ibid., p. 629 n.
[3] ibid., p. 210; Winstedt 1961a, p. 40.
[4] Skeat 1900, pp. 52, 251, 271.     [5] ibid., errata.
[6] Ridley 1924, p. 253.     [7] Wilkinson 1964, pp. 36, 133.

power. Probably hard things, being especially firmly and clearly defined, are considered very resistant to the passage of essences. Their application to a less favoured boundary could seal it, protect it as a suit of armour would do. Apparently the materials used ritually for this purpose are thought especially to embody the quality of hardness and the accompanying strength of boundaries. A spell translated by Winstedt asks that the rice-soul be 'established as rock, firm as iron'.[1]

## Boundary Weakeners

Water seems to weaken the boundaries between many kinds of category, facilitating passage across them. Nearly all Malay rites of passage from one social status to another include ritual bathing. Bathing rites are especially prominent in the marriage and funeral ceremonies and in the installation of the king.[2] Even spirits cross boundaries with the aid of water. *Hantu bĕlian* inhabiting tiger-villages pass from village to jungle and change from human to tiger form and back again by passing through a body of water.[3]

Most important for the operation of magic is the weakening of boundaries of physical bodies to admit passage of essences. This seems to be the basic function of *tĕpong tawar*, a weak solution of yellow rice flour in water. *Tĕpong tawar* means literally 'flour without flavour or distinctive characteristics'.[4] This is sprinkled or daubed on people or things from which, it seems, an essence is to be extracted or into which one is to be inserted. Often this is done with a leaf brush which has the ability, as I shall explain, to absorb undesirable spirits, allowing them to be disposed of.

The quality that gives water the ability to weaken boundaries is probably its fluidity, its complete lack of 'hardness'. It will sustain no divisions or boundaries on its own. A charm quoted by Winstedt says of *tĕpong tawar*:

> It came down from Allah's presence,
> From a drop of dew descended!
> From the water whence eternal
> Life comes—that it's [sic] source of being.[5]

---

[1] Winstedt 1961a, p. 51.
[2] See Skeat 1900, pp. 380, 385–6, 387, 393, 399–401; Winstedt 1961b, p. 65.
[3] Skeat 1901, p. 26; Cuisinier 1936, p. 52; see Rentse 1933a, p. 247 for a similar belief held by Negritos.
[4] Wilkinson 1964, pp. 279, 287.      [5] Winstedt 1961a, p. 150.

This may recall the Indian notion of the primordial sea, the undifferentiated fluid from which all things sprang.[1] This would not be subject to boundaries, being prior to them. The meaning of the rice flour in *tĕpong tawar* is not completely clear to me. Perhaps the neutrality of the rice flour, its lack of distinctive characteristics, deprives the object on which it is brushed of the qualities that tie it to one or another category.

Another material that weakens boundaries, in the sense of conveying essences across them, is multicoloured thread. Such threads are often used to connect things between which an essence is to be transferred. For example, the victim of a spirit may hold a multicoloured thread leading to a tray of offerings or substitutes, while the *pawang* tries to evict the spirit.[2] Conversely, the thread may be used to convey a lost soul trapped in a soul receptacle back to its owner.[3] Interestingly, multicoloured thread seems to act as a barrier or boundary maintainer when tied in a circle.[4] Apparently, an essence would be led round and round and make no progress toward crossing the boundary around which the thread is tied.

The combination of colours (usually seven) in multicoloured thread seems to give it the power to transcend distinctions based on differences in colour. Though the Malays seem to have no unified symbolic classification based on colour, differences of colour are often used to establish or indicate particular boundaries between significant categories (though a single category may be associated with different colours at different times). Whatever colours define a boundary, a multicoloured thread would be immune to the division. A similar notion may be one of the ideas behind beliefs that the rainbow is a bridge between heaven and earth. Such beliefs are common in Indonesia, Polynesia, and Australia, but are not held, as far as I know, by Moslemized Malays.[5] I have mentioned above (p. 100) the apparent fact that a division between earthly and celestial realms is not well developed with the Malays.

*Essence Receptacles*

Certain things seem especially well suited for absorbing spirits or for acting as a substitute body for a soul. Limes are used to

---

[1] See Bosch 1960, pp. 51–2, 60–1, and *passim*.
[2] See e.g. Skeat 1900, pp. 432–3.     [3] See e.g. ibid., p. 453.
[4] See ibid., pp. 242, 573.     [5] See Elkin 1964, p. 232; Winstedt 1961a, p. 151.

extract bad spirits in ritual bathing and the pulp is then thrown away.[1] Limes may also be used as the receptacle for a soul in soul-abduction magic.[2] A spirit may be enticed into a lime (or sometimes lemon) for purposes of divination; the spirit is then asked to give signs in answer to questions.[3] Limes are thought to be offensive to earth spirits; it is forbidden to take them into mines or mention them by their ordinary name, and even shrimp paste is forbidden in mines, because it is usually eaten with lime juice.[4] The spirits probably fear the possibility of their being absorbed in a lime. Eggs are also used to absorb undesirable spirits[5] and to catch errant souls for transmission back to their owners.[6] Sometimes a piece of cloth is used in similar ways. Skeat calls it a 'soul cloth' when used to retrieve a soul and says it may be white or, rarely, yellow.[7] Such a cloth seems capable also of absorbing spirits,[8] and one method of divination uses a white cloth stretched across a vessel of water much as a lime is used when a spirit is inside.[9] *Badi* may be removed from a person with the aid of a black or white cloth[10] and from the carcase of a dead animal with a black cloth.[11]

Another commonly used kind of essence receptacle is leaf or grass brushes. These may be used to extract *badi* from a sick person or an animal carcase,[12] spirits from any afflicted body,[13] and even a familiar from a non-working animal trap.[14] Sometimes *tĕpong tawar* or some other special solution is brushed on; this would weaken the boundary and make the extraction easier. Skeat seems to see the leaf brush as only a means of applying the 'neutralizing rice-paste', but I think there are cases in which the brush is clearly used to absorb an essence. For example, a victim of *badi* attack may be brushed with a leaf brush, and a spell is spoken that includes the lines:

I crave as a boon the leaves of these shrubs
To be a drug and a neutralizing (power)
Within the body, frame, and person of *So-and-So.*

[1] See Skeat 1900, pp. 278, 431.    [2] ibid., p. 575.
[3] ibid., pp. 205 n., 535-7.    [4] ibid., pp. 254, 255.
[5] ibid., pp. 356, 355-6 n., 410 n.    [6] ibid., pp. 453, 454, 455.
[7] ibid., p. 51; see also pp. 452, 453, 575, 576.
[8] ibid., pp. 419-20, 422, 441-2, 444.    [9] ibid., pp. 540-2.
[10] ibid., p. 449.    [11] ibid., pp. 155-6, 177, 178.
[12] See ibid., pp. 177, 178, 429-30.    [13] See e.g. ibid., pp. 133-4, 135-6, 314.
[14] Annandale and Robinson 1904, p. 44.

If you (addressing the leaves) refuse to enter (the body of
  So-and-So),
You shall be cursed . . .[1]

I doubt if the leaves are actually asked to enter the body, but the
*badi* could very well be commanded to enter the leaves. Sometimes
the brush does seem to be used simply to apply *těpong tawar*, but
in those cases the water is sprinkled rather than brushed on
(compare, for example, Skeat 1900, pp. 133–4 with Skeat 1900,
p. 221, where the boundary with earth is to be weakened, but
nothing extracted). The distinction is not always noticed by Skeat,
but sometimes it comes through. For example, when the fishing-
stakes have *těpong tawar* applied, in a ceremony that seems to be
designed to get bad spirits out of them, he says the *pawang*
'sprinkled, or rather daubed it upon the two "tide-braces" of the
stakes'.[2] Similar brushes are held by shamans during séances to
act, it seems, as the first stop for the spirits called in.[3] Similarly, a
sheaf of palm blossoms becomes possessed by spirits in some kinds
of dance.[4] A number of other things are used as essence receptacles
in particular rites, but limes, eggs, cloths, and leaf brushes are
distinguished by being used in a wide variety of ceremonies.

The reasons for these four being good essence receptacles are
not completely clear to me. One would expect them to be constraining categories with some special claim on essences or some
large class of essences. The last three may be seen as being 'origins'
of essences. Eggs are the origins of birds, of course, and the bird
is a common Indonesian conception of the soul, especially when
detached from the body. Cloths recall the shrouds so prominent
in imagery of ghosts and may represent the constraint of the grave
to spirits that have escaped it. Leaf brushes are made of a number
of materials (including grass and flowers), but they seem always to
be facsimiles of trees, the dwelling place of many kinds of spirit.
They usually consist of a bouquet of leaves 'bound round with
*ribu-ribu* (a kind of small creeper), or a string of shredded tree
bark (*daun t'rap*)',[5] the same materials that encompass trees. They
sometimes contain 'leaves of the grass called *sambau dara*, which
is said to be the symbol of a "settled soul"' and leaves of *kayu
asal* and *pulut-pulut* which are 'said to be used as a "reminder of

---

[1] Skeat 1900, p. 430.      [2] ibid., p. 314.      [3] Winstedt 1961a, p. 146.
[4] Skeat 1900, pp. 466–8; Winstedt 1961a, p. 147.      [5] ibid., p. 78.

origin"'.[1] These apparently act to subdue the essences once absorbed. The feature of limes that is said to be distasteful to *hantu* is its acidity.[2] Perhaps this acidity, like the special leaves in the leaf brush, incapacitates spirits that are drawn into the lime. If the power of each one of these to contain and constrain a particular kind of essence were extended in Malay thought to include all kinds of essence, the general absorptive property of them would be clearer. Whatever the mechanism involved, I think that the evidence strongly indicates that absorbing essences is at least one of the main functions of limes, eggs, cloths, and leaf-brushes in Malay magic.

### Communicators

Incense, usually benzoin, is used extensively in Malay ritual. It is burned on special stands at *kramat*, for example,[3] and is used to fumigate offerings,[4] ritual equipment,[5] and even the magician himself in a spirit-raising séance.[6] Its main function seems to be to make contact with essences, usually free spirits, in order to attract their attention to the thing fumigated or the spell recited. Some magicians say that the burning of incense should be accompanied by an invocation to the 'spirit of incense', but others slur over it or even omit it, though possibly it is recited silently in the latter instance.[7] One such invocation translated by Skeat shows clearly what the incense is expected to do. It begins:

Zabur Hijau is your name, O Incense,
Zabur Bajang the name of your Mother,
Zabur Puteh the name of your Fumes,
Scales from the person of God's Apostle were your Origin.
May you fumigate the Seven Tiers of the Earth,
May you fumigate the Seven Tiers of the Sky,
And serve as a summons to all Spirits, to those which have magic
    powers, and those which have become Saints of God,
The Spirits of God's elect, who dwell in the Halo of the Sun,
And whose resort is the "Ka'bah" of God,
At even and morn, by night and day;

[1] ibid., pp. 78, 79.
[2] Abraham Hale, quoted in Skeat 1900, p. 254.   [3] Skeat 1900, p. 67.
[4] e.g. ibid., pp. 312, 411, 419.   [5] e.g. ibid., pp. 61, 412, 511, 575.
[6] Cuisinier 1936, p. 69; Skeat 1900, p. 440.
[7] Skeat 1900, p. 75.

And serve as a summons to the Elect of God,
Who dwell at the Gate of the Spaces of Heaven.[1]

Sometimes the spirits to be summoned are invoked directly
during the fumigation of the audience-chamber prepared for them.
One such charm, used in a tin mine, concludes thus:

Peace be with you, O White Sheikh,
  wizard of the virgin jungle,
Wizards old, and wizards young,
Come hither and share the banquet I have prepared for you.
I crave pardon for all mistakes,
For all shortcomings I beg pardon in every particular.[2]

Candles seem to be used for a similar purpose. A tray of offerings
described by Skeat contained, 'five waxen tapers, to light the
spirits to their food'.[3] Candles are usually placed on or near a space
or thing into which spirits are invited to enter, often at the corners
of quadrangular spaces.[4] Spirits seem to be attracted and guided
by the burning candles, and possibly they actually enter the candles
when they first arrive on the scene. Flickering and flaring up of
the flame are sometimes said to be signs that a spirit has entered,
and the characteristics of the flame's variation may be used for
divination.[5] However, this effect may simply indicate a distur-
bance of the air caused by the arrival of the spirit.

Other things are used in a limited range of ceremonies to attract
essences. For example, the musicians at a shaman's séance make
their instruments resound (membunyikan), not necessarily following a common rhythm, in order to inform the spirits and call the
spectators.[6] The instruments used are usually drums or tam-
bourines or some similar percussion instrument.[7] In some magical
rites no special material or object is used to attract spirits. Apparently, merely the sound of the spell recited is enough to get the
attention of the essence.

---

[1] ibid., pp. 75-6.   [2] ibid., p. 268.
[3] ibid., p. 421; see also Winstedt 1961a, p. 65.
[4] See e.g. Skeat 1900, pp. 268-9, 312.
[5] Swettenham, quoted in Skeat 1900, pp. 445-6; Winstedt 1961a, p. 147.
[6] Cuisinier 1936, p. 50.
[7] See Maxwell 1883, p. 228; cf. Needham 1967.

The smoke and smell of incense, the light of candles, and the sound of drums and spells have one thing in common: they all have the ability to penetrate across space to wherever the spirits might be, even through some of the boundaries of the physical world.[1] The amorphous, ephemeral quality of these emissions contrasts with the bounded, localized, persistent nature of the objects that generate them and to which, therefore, they are continuously tied. This tie between the formed and the formless seems to be the quality of incense, candles, and drums that especially suits them to be communications between the material and essential planes.

There is some suggestion that incense and candles have a protective aspect as well. During a séance a candle must remain lit to prevent hostile spirits from 'throwing stones' at the shaman. If it goes out, the spirits will paralyse him until it is relighted.[2] Also the *bomor bĕlian* 'bathes' himself in incense smoke before contacting the spirits, supposedly to make a protective barrier (*pagar*) around himself.[3] This would seem to be a clear case of a material reinforcing the boundaries of a body, but such an interpretation would hardly fit the other uses of incense, for example, the fumigation of offerings from which the spirits are expected to extract the essence. I think the reasoning here is not quite so direct as that. I suggest that a part of the value of communicators is that they represent controlled access to essences as distinct from their unsolicited intervention when the result is nearly always harmful. The protection they offer is a guarantee that the contact will be on the magician's terms and not on those of the spirits. If the candle goes out, for example, the shaman loses control of the spirits called in.

## Offerings

The most prominent instruments of persuasion or propitiation are offerings, mainly of food. The particular things offered vary widely. Attempts to specify essential items are not very enlightening. Cuisinier claims that the minimal set of offerings includes a plate of 'saffron' rice (*kunyit*); a pancake of eggs, flour, and coconut

---

[1] The beating of drums before a séance in Kelantan is called *tabur*, which means 'to sow, to scatter seeds' (Cuisinier 1936, p. 50 n.). The 'scattering' of sound is like the common Indonesian practice of scattering rice to attract spirits, which is also the way fowls are fed.

[2] Cuisinier 1936, p. 64.        [3] ibid., p. 69.

oil (*dadar*); a bowl of parched rice (*berteh*); a betel plug (*sireh sa-piak*), and a half cup of water (*ayer sa-titek*),[1] but it is possible to find any if not all of these omitted in particular cases, and the *dadar* seems to be used little outside Kelantan. Common categories of offering are just as hard to establish. Maxwell says that the offerings put in a model mosque to entice a spirit of disease should include four classes of food: fat (*lemak*), sweet (*manis*), sour (*masam*), and pungent (*pedas*).[2] However, he did not actually see the representatives of the last two classes, and the scheme is undetectable in most inventories of offerings I have seen. Nor is Cuisinier's claim, discussed above (p. 36), that every set of offerings should include representatives of the three kingdoms of nature—animal, vegetable, and mineral, and of the four elements—earth, air, fire, and water[3]—borne out by the evidence. Cuisinier admits this, but says that the imperfect presentations she observed were degenerations from earlier, complete forms.[4] There is no direct evidence that this has happened, and there are reasons, which I have explained above (p. 36), to doubt the entire formulation. The procedure of seeking offerings or classes of offering common to all presentations does not reveal any indispensible items, with the possible exception of rice in some form, but it does show that certain things occur more commonly than others. In general, these include the things that the people themselves use and desire, such as chews of betel, cigarettes, water, money, meat, cakes, and rice, along with a few thought appropriate to less civilized creatures, for example, blood and innards.[5]

The principles of variation from one ritual setting to another are no easier to determine than are the basic categories of offering. At a very general level, it seems that the demands of spirits are determined by analogy with what people in similar positions would desire. Thus, one finds spirits in a mine being offered things 'similar in character to those usually deposited on the sacrificial tray (*anchak*), with the addition, however, of certain articles which are considered to be especially representative of the miners' food. These articles are sugar-cane, plantains, yams, sweet potatoes, and fish, etc.'.[6] At a more specific level, the principles of variation seem too numerous to predict or even to specify. Skeat says that

[1] Cuisinier 1936, p. 28.
[2] Maxwell 1883, p. 230.
[3] Cuisinier 1951, pp. 220, 221, 250.
[4] ibid., pp. 220, 251.
[5] See Skeat 1900, pp. 413–16.
[6] ibid., p. 268.

'the offerings placed on the sacrificial tray vary considerably, according to the object of the ceremony, the means of the person for whose benefit they are offered, the caprice of the medicine-man who carries out the ceremony, and so on'.[1] I confess that I have not been able to find correlations between specific offerings or combinations of offering and any classification of spirits or of ceremonies, much less the principles one would expect to find behind such correlations. This is not to say that they do not exist, however. Although there are wide variations in the offerings presented, a few simple distinctions within the sets of offerings recur. Most prominent are divisions between cooked and uncooked offerings and between black and white ones. Other less clear divisions occur less frequently. These divisions cut across each other, rather than align. Skeat says 'strictly speaking, a white and a black fowl should be killed, but only half of each cooked, the remainder being left raw';[2] the divisions may extend to rice, eggs, goats, and whatever else it is practical to divide in these ways. These distinctions are made when more than one class of spirits is being propitiated in the same ceremony. Interestingly, there are no fixed associations between particular forms of offering and particular classes of spirit. Skeat says of one tray of offerings: 'the cooked food is for the king of the spirits (*Raja Hantu*), who is sometimes said to be the Wild-Huntsman (*Hantu Pĕmburu*) and sometimes *Batara Guru*, and the uncooked for his following. But of the two eggs, the uncooked one is alleged to be for the Land-spirit (i.e. the Wild Huntsman), and the cooked for the Sea-spirit'.[3] He adds that this last assertion requires further investigation before it can be unreservedly accepted, but it is quite consistent with the apparent general use of such divisions, namely, to indicate any distinction among spirits that needs to be made. By contrast with the preceding example, divisions of rice and fowls by black and white and by cooked and uncooked are made in a mining ceremony in which spirits of jungle and soil and their respective servants seem to be the essences propitiated.[4]

Another division, into prime portions and refuse, sometimes occurs. Skeat says, for the tray of offerings mentioned immediately above, 'the things deposited in the tray are intended for the spirits (Hantus) themselves; the refuse on the ground beneath it for their

---

[1] ibid., p. 415.          [2] ibid., p. 416.          [3] ibid., p. 418.
[4] ibid., pp. 270–1.

slaves *(hamba)*'.[1] However, in a ceremony described by Blagden, the skin, head and horns, and entrails of a goat, along with a large iron nail, are buried two feet beneath the altar on which the more desirable parts are placed.[2] In this case the refuse seems to go to the earth spirits and the better parts to those of the jungle, though Blagden is not explicit on the matter. The ceremony is one to make padi-fields safe, and these are the two main classes of spirit usually dealt with in that context. It is interesting that blood is placed on the ground, between those under the ground and those on the raised altar.[3] This may be intended to emphasize the intermediate position of blood and the spirits for which it is probably intended: wandering vampires.

The property of offerings that gives them their ritual value, their ability to persuade essences, is obviously that they give them pleasure and also sustenance, I have suggested (p. 54 above), in the form of undifferentiated *sěmangat*. Although broad classes of spirit may have vague preferences, it seems that, in general, any spirit will accept any offering (all offerings would contain a portion of the vital principle). This allows particular divisions of the sacrifice to be distributed to different divisions of the spirit world depending on whatever distinctions are relevant and are to be expressed in particular ceremonies.

## Numbers

Before leaving the matter of magical equipment, it is necessary to mention a condition that affects all or nearly all objects used in Malay magical ritual, namely, that the quantity of each kind of item to be used is clearly specified. This seems to indicate the control that the magician has over his equipment and therefore over the power over essences and boundaries implicit in their special properties. This interpretation is supported by the fact that the particular numbers specified are clearly connected with the 'three' and 'four' which have been shown to express control in time and in space respectively. Where quantities of ritual equipment are specified in Skeat's *Malay Magic* (1900), the proportions are as follows:

9 cases of 'one'
16 cases of 'two'

---

[1] ibid., pp. 417–18.    [2] Quoted in Skeat 1900, p. 232.
[3] Blagden, quoted in Skeat 1900, p. 232.

44 cases of 'three'
20 cases of 'four'
17 cases of 'five'
2 cases of 'six'
46 cases of 'seven'

and 11 cases of other numbers including 6 of 'fourteen' as 2 sets of 'seven'. The cases in which 'five' is specified could be lumped with cases of 'four' (giving 37 total), since quantities of five nearly always mark the four corners and the centre of a bounded quadrangular space such as an offering tray.[1] Quantities of 'three' items would be especially well controlled in time, of 'four' and 'five' in space, and of 'seven', by a simple act of symbolic arithmetic, in both time and space. These 'controlled' quantities make up 127 of the 165 instances in which the number of ritual objects is specified.

This brief outline is not meant to be exhaustive either as an inventory of the equipment used in Malay magic or as an exposition of the full meaning of the things described. It is meant only to describe the basic magical qualities of the most commonly used objects and materials as a preliminary to examining the magical rites themselves.

### III. INTERPRETATION OF TWO RITES

With the properties of magical equipment and the powers of spells in mind, it is possible to begin to understand the ritual the magician performs. Practical considerations prohibit making detailed analyses of all the rites recorded in the literature, so I have chosen to examine two of the most widely known and fully documented ones and then to give a brief outline of the main kinds of rite, using the analyses for illustration.

*Taking the Rice-Baby*

One of the best-known Malay ceremonies concerns the taking of the first rice from each field.[2] This is usually called the taking of the 'rice-baby' or 'rice-soul', the first few ears being ritually cut

---

[1] See e.g. Skeat 1900, pp. 415–16.
[2] See Blagden 1897, pp. 301–4; Hill 1951, pp. 66–75; Shaw 1911, pp. 20–5; Skeat 1900, pp. 225–7, 235–45, 247–9; Wilkinson 1906, pp. 50–1; Winstedt 1925, pp. 84–9; 1961a, pp. 49–55.

and escorted to the home of the field's owner where they are received as a new-born baby. Similar ceremonies are performed throughout the Malay Peninsula and Archipelago, Shaw says,[1] except in Acheh. The ceremonies are usually interpreted as being intended to preserve the life or vitality of the rice, the *sĕmangat padi*, from one season to the next.[2] I think this is essentially right; the analysis that follows is simply an attempt to determine exactly what it means and how the feat is accomplished. I shall first describe one such ceremony, following Skeat's detailed account of his own observations[3] with the addition of information from other sources as it is needed to clarify particular points. I shall then attempt to bring out the ideas that lie behind the ceremony.

Sometime before the ceremony begins, a 'mother-sheaf' from which to cut the 'rice-baby' is selected. The criterion for selection is that the ears to form the rice-baby should be freaks of some sort.[4] The ceremony begins at a time fixed previously, probably by divination. The *pawang* or midwife assembles a tray of things, including bowls of parched rice, saffron rice, washed rice, oil of frankincense, oil of celebes, a bowl of incense, a bundle of incense, a candle-nut, a cockle shell, a hen's egg, a block of quartz, an iron nail, and three tiny reaping knives. A basket is prepared for the rice-baby containing a strip of white cloth, some multicoloured thread, and a length of red cloth with which to suspend the basket around a bearer's neck. Also a bowl of *tĕpong tawar* and a leaf brush are collected along with three rice baskets containing folded *sarongs*, a cord of tree bark, and the stem and leaves of a dark red or black variety of sugar cane.

A procession sets off for the field, the women in the lead carrying the baskets and the owner of the field holding the sugar cane. The composition of this entourage may vary somewhat, I think. On the way to the field, the *pawang* recites a prayer to the Prophet 'Tap, in whose charge is the earth, wishing him peace and claiming to know the origin of rice. This is not always done, and it does duplicate an invocation made later, within the field, accompanying an offering. On reaching the field a spell is recited telling troublesome spirits to depart. This does seem to be a regular feature of

---

[1] Shaw 1911, p. 20.    [2] See e.g. ibid., p. 20; Wilkinson 1906, p. 50.
[3] Skeat 1900, pp. 235–45.
[4] ibid., pp. 247–8; Winstedt 1961a, p. 49; Shaw 1911, p. 23.

the ceremony.[1] Then the baskets are put down, and the *pawang* takes a position in front of the mother-sheaf. In the ceremony Skeat saw, the *pawang* then covered her head with a white cloth, 'stood up facing the sheaf, and waved the ends of this cloth thrice upward to the right, thrice upward to the left, and finally thrice upward to the right again. Then for a few moments she stood still, close to the sheaf with her head bent forward and buried among the ears'.[2] This seems to be a rite to attract the 'rice-soul' into a soul cloth and deposit it in the rice-mother. This is optional; most *pawang* just wait until some sign reveals that the soul is present before cutting.

After this, the *pawang* sprinkles *tĕpong tawar* on the roots of the mother-sheaf, and sprinkles and fumigates with incense the sugar cane while a female bearer plants it in the centre of the sheaf. The *pawang* recites the following charm:

> Peace be with thee, O Prophet 'Tap!
> Lo, I plant this Sugar-cane
> For you to lean against,
> Since I am about to take away this Soul of yours, S'ri Gading,
> And carry it home to your palace,
> Cluck, cluck, soul! cluck, cluck, soul!
>     cluck, cluck, soul![3]

The sugar cane seems to be an offering, the *tĕpong tawar* being intended to ease it through the boundary of earth, and the incense to attract the spirit. Another version has the *pawang* placing a quid of betel in the centre of the sheaf and saying:

> Greetings. Jinns and Spirits of the Earth,
> Jinns and Spirits of the Soil,
> Jinns and Spirits of the Fields, with this I reward you for your forbearance.[4]

Then the sheaf is drawn around the sugar cane and tied with a few of its own outer stems. The *pawang* takes in one hand the stone, egg, cockle-shell, and candle-nut, and with the other plants the big iron nail 'in the centre of the sheaf close to the foot of the sugar-cane'.[5] I think this seals in the earth spirits as the first step in separating the rice-baby from the earth. The *pawang* then fumigates the cord of tree-bark and the vessels of rice and oil, and

---

[1] See e.g. Hill 1951, p. 69.    [2] Skeat 1900, p. 239.    [3] ibid., p. 239.
[4] Hill 1951, p. 69.    [5] Skeat 1900, p. 240.

tosses some rice around, probably as propitiation of the earth spirits or, again, to attract the rice-soul. Next she circles the sheaf with the bark cord, draws it slowly upward to the middle, and ties it after reciting a Moslem prayer. This probably confines the rice-soul, making the sheaf into a tree facsimile like a leaf brush, and at the same time advances the separation of the rice-baby from the earth. Winstedt records a version that would combine this step with the previous one of sealing the earth boundary. He says that the *pawang* 'ties seven stalks with bark and fibre and many-coloured thread having a nail attached to it, and slips the nail into the middle of the bunch'.[1]

When the sheaf is tied the *pawang* digs up a lump of soil with her left big toe and deposits it 'in the centre of the sheaf';[2] the exact position, top or bottom, is not clear. This is also done with the sheaves left when the three female reapers have filled their baskets following the taking of the rice-baby.[3] At that time the following words are recited:

> Peace be with you, Prophet 'Tap,
> in whose charge is the earth,
> Confirm this my child.
> Do it no harm or scathe,
> But remove it far from Demons and Devils.
> By virtue of, etc.[4]

This is probably also connected with the custom recorded by Winstedt of smearing 'the seven stalks from which the ears were cut with clay, "as medicine for their hurt from the knife" '.[5] The earth material seems to act as a substitute for the severed heads of rice, thus calming the earth spirits.

Next the *pawang* fumigates and anoints with oil the contents of the rice-baby basket and anoints the rice-cutter. She presses her right thumb against her palate for several seconds, withdraws it, and cuts the first seven heads of rice while repeating the Moslem prayer mentioned above (called the 'Ten Prayers').

In most cases the *pawang* waits for a sign of the presence of the rice-soul, the sound of a breeze[6] or a slight movement of the stalk,[7] before cutting. Use of a tiny, hidden knife reduces the chance of frightening the rice-soul away,[8] a practice probably related to the

---

[1] Winstedt 1961a, p. 49.   [2] Skeat 1900, p. 241.   [3] ibid., p. 244 n.
[4] ibid., p. 244 n.   [5] Winstedt 1961a, p. 51.   [6] ibid., p. 51.
[7] Hill 1951, p. 69.   [8] Wilkinson 1906, p. 50.

replacement altogether of iron by bamboo in the knife that cuts the umbilical cord. The Moslem prayer is probably an alternative or replacement for one more to the point. Hill says that the *pawang* repeats the following charm three times as he cuts:

> Greetings to you, my child that is named Seri Bumi
> [*bumi* = earth].
> I call you to your mother.
> Your age is seven months.
> Come let us return together to my home.[1]

The *pawang* kisses the newly cut heads of rice, rolls her eyes, and swallows, supposedly to make the rice smooth and white.[2] She anoints the bundle of rice ears, ties them around with multi-coloured thread, fumigates them with incense, throws rice of each kind on them, folds the cloth around them, and deposits them in the basket on top of the egg, stone, candle-nut, and cockle-shell. She tosses more rice over the sheaf and the people in the party and shouts '*kur sĕmangat*' ('cluck, cluck, soul') in a loud voice several times. All these precautions seem intended to keep the rice-soul in the bundle of rice-heads or attract one that is beginning to escape. Winstedt records that a ring of gold or silver is tied to the stalk when the stalks are cut.[3] Finally all traces of the ceremony are removed.

The basket with the rice-baby in it is slung around the neck of the first bearer, and it is covered by an umbrella, possibly a sign of civilization or man's domain. The *pawang* says a Moslem prayer, then sets the other bearers to reaping the rice to fill the other three baskets. The rest of the party (including the *pawang*) proceeds back to the house of the owner of the field where it is greeted by the owner's wife. After an exchange of verses, the rice-child is taken inside and laid, still in the basket, on a sleeping mat. When the other bearers arrive, their baskets of rice are deposited on the mat at the foot of the soul-baskets, and all are fumigated and covered over with the long white cloth, again, I would suggest, to help settle the rice-soul in the heads of rice.

For three days the wife of the master of the house must observe the prohibitions required at the birth of a child. The prohibitions include rules against the passage (especially out) of things, even

---

[1] Hill 1951, p. 69.     [2] Skeat 1900, p. 241 n.
[3] Winstedt 1961a, pp. 50, 54.

THE OPERATION OF MAGIC

voices, across the boundaries of the house, *kampong*, or field[1] as
if any violation of these boundaries might let the rice-soul slip
back to the fields or the earth. A light must be kept burning.[2]
Noise is prohibited, undoubtedly to keep from scaring the rice-
soul away.[3] Skeat adds that hair may not be cut,[4] an event which,
like the casting of one's shadow on the rice (which is forbidden
throughout the harvest), would threaten to infect the rice with
*badi*.

The rice-baby and the first baskets of rice (and sometimes the
last as well) are eventually mixed with the next year's seed, though
part is used in *tĕpong tawar*.[5] When it is stored in the rice-bin, it is
placed on or near brinjal leaves, a stone, a nail or other piece of
iron, a candle-nut, cockle-shells, and various spirit traps.[6]

The magician seems to do two main things in this ceremony;
he (or she) produces a confined body from a diffuse or scattered
body and a consolidated soul from a diffuse or scattered soul. The
two are created together by parallel differentiations from undifferentiated matrices of matter and essence. The body of the
rice-baby is made by ritually severing a distinctive part of the
rice-field, and the rice-soul is created by defining as a discrete
entity, in conjunction with the newly formed body, the most
concentrated part of the *sĕmangat* of the rice-field.

A similar kind of differentiation is presumed to have gone on
previously in the development of the rice-field itself. The physical
part of the field seems to be regarded as a differentiation of the
even less differentiated earth. Earth spirits are propitiated and
confined to the earth when the rice is cut, and the wound from the
cutting is treated with materials from the earth,[7] perhaps as a
substitute for the missing heads of rice. The *sĕmangat* of the rice-
field seems to develop from the previous year's rice-soul seen as a
free spirit of the earth (*Seri Bumi*), and it retains traces of that
phase of its existence after becoming the *sĕmangat* of the rice-field.
This process is probably set in motion during the planting cere-

---

[1] See Hill 1951, p. 75; Shaw 1911, p. 25; Skeat 1900, p. 244; Winstedt
1961a, p. 52.
[2] Shaw 1911, p. 25; Skeat 1900, p. 244.
[3] See Hill 1951, p. 74 for a legend in which the personification of the first
rice-soul is driven, by the noise of the harvest celebration, to fly away.
[4] Skeat 1900, p. 244.     [5] ibid., p. 249; Winstedt 1961a, p. 54.
[6] Shaw 1911, p. 25; Winstedt 1961a, p. 54.
[7] See Winstedt 1961a, p. 51.

monies in which the rice-soul is committed to the earth, although the mechanism is not clear.[1] It seems that either the rice-soul or the Prophet 'Tap is assigned the task, as an agent of the magician, of creating the rice-field.

Since the *sěmangat* of the rice-field is, from one point of view, like a free spirit flitting from one place to another, the ceremony for taking the rice-baby appears in one aspect to be the capture of a spirit in an essence receptacle. The ears of the 'mother-sheaf' are magically transformed into a trap, a firmly bounded body, which is separated from the rice field when the *sěmangat* is thought to be inside. Elaborate magical precautions are then taken to ensure that the rice-soul remains in the body created for it, to confine the essence so that it acts more like a *sěmangat* than a free spirit. It can easily be stored in this compact receptacle until it is replaced in the earth at the next planting.

Apparently the different kinds of freak ear have different inherent capacities to restrain the rice-soul. Hill says 'at one ceremony we attended the *bomor* claimed that the *sěmangat padi* was represented by three young sisters, the eldest Siti Mani, the middle Seri Mani and the youngest Nur Rani, any one of whom he could summon as the embodiment of the rice-soul. He called Siti Mani because, he alleged, she is always gentle. Seri Mani may turn into a malignant *pělěsit* or *polong* haunting the rice store after the harvest if the offerings are not to her taste or if she is offended by any slight mistake in the ritual. Nur Rani may even become a wild demon of the forest (*botaranggas*) scourging the village'.[2] These three sisters represent several degrees of constraint a body can exercise over an essence making it a *sěmangat* in the narrow sense, a familiar, or a free spirit.

The basis of the analogy between taking the first rice and the birth of a baby is now quite clear. The earth, like the blood, is the material out of which the body is formed. The process of creation is completed in both cases when the differentiated body and the *sěmangat* which is its vital reflection are severed from their undifferentiated matrices.

One limitation of the analogy is that the rice-baby, unlike the human baby, has a different mother before birth than it has after. Winstedt says that 'the most notable point in the Perak account is

[1] See e.g. Hill 1951, pp. 63–5; Shaw 1911, p. 15; Skeat 1900, p. 229.
[2] Hill 1951, p. 66.

that the farmer and his wife are regarded as the father and mother of the rice-soul. In Malacca the sheaf from which the baby is cut is called the mother, treated like a woman after childbirth and reaped by the farmer's wife'; he implies that this indicates some confusion on the part of the Malays.[1] In fact, the matter must be quite clear to them; each is the mother during part of the agricultural cycle. With this in mind, an otherwise confusing spell uttered when the rice seeds are planted makes sense. Addressing the rice-soul the *pawang* says:

Greetings to you, my child that is named Seri Bumi [*bumi* = earth] the child of Nur Rani Nur Mani. I call you to your mother. Your age will be seven months when the time comes (i.e., when the harvest is brought in). Listen to the voice of your father. Do not pine for your mother. Be at hand day and night, never failing in power and strength, until I bring you back to the portals of my house (*enjong istana*).[2]

The Malays have a myth to explain the apparent contradiction of a woman's child being born from the earth.[3] They say that Adam and Hawa had two sons and two daughters. Needing food, they chopped one son and one daughter into small pieces and scattered them on the plain. A golden harvest developed and 'all the grain became *sěmangat* or instinct with life, and then rising in the air like a dense swarm of bees, poured onwards with a loud buzzing noise until it entered the habitation of the first man and woman from whom it had its birth'.[4]

A further limitation of the analogy has to do with the degree to which the rice-baby is 'created' by the magician. In some sense the taking of the rice-baby seems more like the manufacture of a *pělěsit* than the birth of a baby, although those two processes, as I have pointed out, have much in common. It is said that 'the villagers may well be suspicious of the man who makes extra-special efforts to woo the rice soul, for they believe that he can turn it into a familiar spirit (*pělěsit*) which will go out at his bidding and torment his enemies gaining him power over them'.[5] The exact basis of the probably subtle distinction between the creation of *pělěsit* and of human babies is not apparent to me, and its discovery would probably require the questioning of ritual experts.

---

[1] Winstedt 1961a, p. 54.
[2] Hill 1951, p. 65.
[3] Cf. Levi-Strauss 1963, p. 229.
[4] Shaw 1911, pp. 21–2.
[5] Hill 1951, p. 66.

*Bĕrhantu*

The *bĕrhantu* or 'spirit-raising séance' is more complex, if not more elaborate, than the ceremony for taking the rice-baby. The *bĕrhantu* consists of a number of subrites whose exact form and order vary depending on the purpose of the ceremony and the particular kind of séance performed. The simplest séance is the *gebiah* performed by certain female shamans of Kelantan with the aim of gaining the assistance of the tiger spirit. It takes little equipment and can be completed in just one session.[1] The most common type of séance seems to be a more elaborate version of the *gebiah*, usually lasting three nights and involving other spirits besides the *hantu bĕlian*. The most elaborate is that in which the spirits of the state are called in, and only a member of the royal house can act as shaman. Despite the differences, the essential features of the séance, such as invocation of spirits, 'possession' of a person who speaks for a spirit, and a final breaking off of contact with the spirits, are common to all forms.

Spirit-raising ceremonies are well reported in the literature,[2] and I shall describe the most common form of the ceremony, that in which the *hantu bĕlian* and other spirits are called in to help perform a cure. I shall use the reports of Cuisinier[3] to give the broad outline of the ceremony and Skeat's personal observations[4] for a detailed description of the last night's ritual.

Though Cuisinier's description of most phases of the ceremony is clear and detailed, the account of the third day's rites[5] is abbreviated. This is probably because the performance she witnessed was staged for her benefit as a demonstration,[6] and there was no real patient to cure. Skeat saw only one night of a performance, but it was an authentic attempt to restore a victim of disease.[7] Skeat does not explicitly state that he saw the third night's performance, though he makes clear that it was not the first,[8] but it does fit closely the pattern for the third night outlined by

---

[1] Cuisinier 1936, pp. 74–6.
[2] See e.g. Annandale 1903, pp. 100–2; Cuisinier 1936, pp. 30–83; Gimlette 1929, pp. 80–95; Maxwell 1883, pp. 222–8; Skeat 1900, pp. 436–48; Swettenham 1895, pp. 153–9; Wilkinson 1932, pp. 94–95; Winstedt 1925, pp. 97–106; 1961a, pp. 56–63; 69–71; Zainul-Abidin bin Ahmad 1922b, pp. 378–80.
[3] Cuisinier 1936, pp. 38–73.  [4] Skeat 1900, pp. 436–44.
[5] Cuisinier 1936, pp. 68–73.  [6] ibid., p. 39.
[7] Skeat 1900, p. 436.  [8] ibid., p. 437.

Cuisinier[1] and reaffirmed by Winstedt.[2] I shall draw on a number of sources besides those mentioned to generalize the description in an attempt to reveal the basic features of the ceremony and their meanings. Following the description, I shall attempt to bring out the ideas behind the practice of spirit-raising.

A séance is usually performed in some kind of building or, if outside, in a specially constructed shelter. Such shelters are rectangular (4–6 metres wide and 5–8 metres long) and made of 6 or 8 bamboo posts supporting a palm thatch roof.[3] They are oriented on an east-west axis, perpendicular to the usual orientation of houses (in Kelantan); the long side on the south is closed in with a plaited bamboo mat and the other sides are open.[4] Stretched around the shelter, two and a half or three metres outside the posts, is a fence made of a white cotton cord.[5] The fence marks the boundary that ordinary spectators should not cross; only the performers, sponsor and his family, a few privileged guests, and, presumably, the patient can go inside it.[6] This, and the disposition of the shelter at right angles to ordinary houses, seems to set off the area of the ceremony as a special space. Probably an ordinary house is made special in some way during a séance, though I have found no explicit statement of this. Special regulations apply, at any rate, such as the rule that the same number of guests (an uneven number) must be present each evening.[7]

A large amount and variety of equipment is used in *bĕrhantu* ceremonies. Examination of the equipment used in the *gebiah* is useful in determining what is basic, since the *gebiah* is the séance stripped to its bare essentials. Cuisinier says that the bundle of leaves held by the shaman while dancing is the most important part of the *gebiah* paraphernalia.[8] It is also necessary to have a tray of the minimal offerings: parched and saffron rice, a pancake, a little water, and a plug of betel.[9] Also candles are needed, a bowl of charmed water, a skein of untwisted cotton, incense, and a drum.[10]

---

[1] Cuisinier 1936, pp. 68–71.    [2] Winstedt 1961a, pp. 61–2.
[3] Cuisinier 1936, p. 41.    [4] ibid., p. 41.
[5] ibid., p. 41. This is not absolutely clear. Winstedt seems to think that the corded-off enclosure is inside the shelter (1961a, p. 60), but the dimensions given and the activities performed within the shelter make this seem highly improbable. The actual text says: 'Un cordon de fil de coton blanc est tendu tout autour de l'abri, à deux mètres cinquante ou trois mètres environ des pieux' (Cuisinier 1926, p. 41).
[6] Cuisinier 1936, p. 41–2.    [7] Skeat 1900, p. 437.
[8] Cuisinier 1936, p. 75–6.    [9] ibid., p. 76.    [10] ibid., pp. 76–7.

The shaman's leaf bundle may vary in composition. Maxwell mentions two kinds of leaves used by different shamans,[1] and the shaman Skeat observed used a sheaf of palm blossom.[2] Winstedt says the switch may also be grass.[3] If this is simply a variety of the leaf brush, as I suspect, one might add some of the combinations of leaves used for those.[4] The offerings used can range from the simple assortment described above to the feast presented to the state spirits which is arranged on a nine-tiered stand.[5] Any number and size of candles may be required depending on specific circumstances. The simple bowl of charmed water used in the *gebiah* is replaced by six kinds of special water in the standard *bĕlian* dance,[6] contained in a variety of vessels including large earthenware jars.[7] I do not know the equivalents to the skein of untwisted cotton, because Cuisinier does not explain how it is used in the *gebiah*. The incense used could certainly vary, but it is usually benzoin in Malay ritual. The musical instruments can vary as well. For example, Maxwell gives the tambourine as an alternative to the drum.[8] This is only a bare outline of the equipment used in séances, but it does show what seems to be basic and gives some idea of the range of possible variation of each item. The uses and meaning of the equipment will become apparent in the description that follows.

On the afternoon before the first performance of a standard *bĕlian* dance, the musicians, even before going into the shelter, play their instruments to inform the spirits and to call the spectators.[9] The minimal set of offerings is prepared and a number of knots of bamboo constructed, to be untied when the spirits are released.[10] Just before the performers go to the shelter, the candles to be used are censed; a few are lighted and held up while the head shaman (*To' Bĕlian*) recites a short invocation.[11] A bowl of charmed water is also censed. Then a procession forms with the man carrying the incense in the lead followed by bearers of offerings and other equipment, the dancers and musicians, and finally the questioner (*pengantin*).[12] When the procession crosses the cotton cord fence (*pupu*) a small candle is lighted and attached to

[1] Maxwell 1883, p. 228.   [2] Skeat 1900, p. 442.
[3] Winstedt 1961a, pp. 56, 59.   [4] See Skeat 1900, pp. 78–80.
[5] Winstedt 1961a, p. 70.   [6] Cuisinier 1936, p. 48.
[7] See ibid., pp. 65–6.
[8] Maxwell 1883, p. 228.   [9] Cuisinier 1936, p. 50.
[10] ibid., pp. 50–1.   [11] ibid., p. 51.   [12] ibid., p. 51.

each object carried.[1] The members of the procession walk around the shelter three times, inside the *pupu* cord, singing and scattering parched rice.[2] The candles and rice, like the drum-beating, would attract the spirits.

Then a basin of special water (*ayer pelapik*) is censed and placed in the shelter; the members of the procession enter, the bearer of parched rice now leading, stepping first into the basin of *ayer pelapik* and then into the building.[3] Probably this is to mark and facilitate the crossing of a significant boundary; once inside, the performers cannot leave until the full ceremony is completed, except for their two daily baths.[4] Finally the performers and privileged spectators are seated, the *To' Bĕlian* facing east just inside the centre-post on the east side (the principal post), the *pengantin* in the southeast corner, the drum (*ketubong*) players along the palisade on the south side, and the spectators scattered about, mainly along the west and north sides.[5]

After a pause, the first night's séance is begun. The initial act each evening is to hang up the overturned water (*ayer sungsang*), whose vessel is upside down, stoppered with a plug of cloth.[6] This symbol of reversal seems to further emphasise the extraordinary nature of the shelter. The *To' Bĕlian* begins to prepare an offering, first separating out the food he will need during the performance, and blows toward the four cardinal points invoking the four sheikhs, Nenek Manjah (who is supposed to have taught the magician's ancestors), and Dato' Brahil (Gabriel).[7] He puts a small offering on a tray of banana leaf and presses it into the ground, before the principal post, for the genies of the soil (*jin tanah* or *jin bumi*).[8]

The *To' Bĕlian* prepares the special water and tests the drums, and his assistant censes all the equipment[9]. A rite is then performed to 'marry' the hands and voices of the musicians to their instruments, so all will act as one.[10] Then the *To' Bĕlian* recites a list of the ancestors of his lineage, probably better understood, I have suggested (p. 18 above) as the series of masters through whom the *ilmu* has passed (the sense of guru as 'master' rather than 'ancestor').[11]

[1] ibid., p. 52.          [2] ibid., p. 52.          [3] ibid., p. 52.
[4] ibid., p. 42.          [5] ibid., p. 52.          [6] ibid., p. 68.
[7] ibid., p. 53.          [8] ibid., p. 53.          [9] ibid., p. 54.
[10] ibid., p. 54.          [11] ibid., pp. 55–6.

When this is finished, the music for the first dance begins, and the *To' Bĕlian* sings in a strained tremolo voice.[1] The assistant *bĕlian* dons his ceremonial clothes and ornaments, and takes up in his hands a bunch of fragrant leaves (*daun chalong*).[2] He gestures in homage to the earth and touches it with the leaves,[3] seemingly paying further tribute to the earth spirits. Then he pays homage to the *To' Bĕlian* who places a hand on his neck in return.[4]

The assistant *bĕlian* then faces east and, as the drums accelerate their rhythm, begins to invoke the *penggawa*, the most eminent among the minor spirits (what Gimlette calls 'control spirits'[5]). *Penggawa* is a term used for chiefs of important villages.[6] The assistant begins a slow dance, which is really just a hopping on his bottom (une suite de sauts . . . sur le séant).[7] Genuine *lupa* is not sought, since no questions are to be asked,[8] and a succession of *penggawa* are called in, but immediately dismissed.[9] A palm-leaf knot is broken after each spirit is invoked in order to release it.[10] This goes on for about three hours, the first half with the *To' Bĕlian* and assistant *bĕlian* taking turns and the second half with them dancing at the same time, both standing up.[11] The dancing is interspersed with short rests, but becomes more frantic toward the end when a large number of *penggawa* are called in, in rapid succession.[12] Suddenly, the dancing stops for the night.[13]

The first night's session is intended simply to make contact with the spirits.[14] The purpose seems to be to get as many spirits interested in the proceedings as possible on the assumption that one or more of them might be willing to help overcome the misfortune.[15] This is not explicit in Cuisinier's account, but it will be recalled that the performance she witnessed was a demonstration with no practical purpose.

During the following day, more offerings and palm leaf knots are prepared, and a structure called *panchur nibong* is constructed, decorated with branches of trees, ferns, pineapple leaves, coconuts, flowers, sugar-cane, bananas, and other titbits.[16] The *panchur nibong* seems to be the full sized equivalent of the pleasure garden

[1] ibid., p. 56.    [2] ibid., p. 57.
[3] ibid., p. 57.    [4] ibid., p. 57.    [5] Gimlette 1929, pp. 84–5.
[6] Cuisinier 1936, p. 57 n.; cf. Wilkinson 1964, p. 205.
[7] Cuisinier 1936, p. 58.    [8] ibid., p. 58.    [9] ibid., p. 58.
[10] ibid., p. 68.    [11] ibid., p. 58.    [12] ibid., p. 59.
[13] ibid., p. 59.    [14] ibid., p. 59.
[15] See e.g. Wilkinson 1932, p. 95.    [16] Cuisinier 1936, pp. 59–61.

of artificial flowers and ornaments in a large jar seen by Skeat in a séance conducted inside a house.[1] Besides this, a tray of offerings, more elaborate this time, with three earthen jars of water with a plug of betel at the bottom of each, and a tree branch decorated with ferns, to which the knots of palm leaf are attached, are all prepared for the evening's ceremony.[2]

In the afternoon a simplified version of the ritual of the previous night is performed. This seems intended to maintain or re-establish contact with the spirits in preparation for the evening.[3] Homage is paid to the branch, before it is placed among the jars, which holds the *lepas* knots and is said to represent a tree ('la branche figurant un arbre'),[4] and then to the ancestors at the same time as the equipment to be used is censed. *Nenek Manjah* is again invoked, and also *Nenek Logang* and *Nenek Uban di Kadang*,[5] though I do not know who these would be. The incense burner is carried thrice around the shelter, inside the *pupu* enclosure, and the shamans take their places.[6] The *To' Bĕlian* and his assistant dance several times in turn, but without trying actually to achieve *lupa*.[7]

The second evening is when the tiger spirit is supposed to appear, and before the séance begins, candles are lit on all the accessories.[8] The first part of the ceremony is called *gĕrak guru*, the movement of the ancestor.[9] The assistant *bĕlian* recalls the creation of the world in seven days,[10] and then describes the journey of the first magician (*hala*) through the forest where he first saw the bamboos, ferns, and other leaves that are now arrayed in and around the shelter. This is the first *bomor bĕlian*, and he must be brought back to help his descendant.[11]

The chorus begins to sing as the *To' Bĕlian* puts on his costume, and then he and his assistant again walk, with the incense burner, around the enclosure, reciting formulas to the ancestors.[12] Then the *To' Bĕlian* sits down, scatters some rice, draws a scarf over his head, and meditates with closed fists on temples, soon bringing his

---

[1] Skeat 1900, p. 438.  [2] Cuisinier 1936, p. 61.
[3] ibid., p. 61.  [4] ibid., p. 61.  [5] ibid., p. 61.
[6] ibid., pp. 61–2.  [7] ibid., p. 62.  [8] ibid., p. 62.
[9] ibid., p. 63.
[10] Winstedt claims that this is a trace of a tantric rite; these should always 'begin with the story of the creation and go on to deal with the worship of the gods' (1961a, p. 60).
[11] Cuisinier 1936, p. 63.  [12] ibid., pp. 63–4.

hands down in front and opening them with palms up to receive the spirits.[1] He begins to hop on his seat and is supposed to lose consciousness. A second lamp must then be lit behind him, and as his agitation increases he wails, but eventually calms down and stops moving at the sound of the voice of the *pengantin*.[2] The *pengantin* asks who he is and where he comes from, but receives no intelligible answers. Soon the dancer's agitation increases again, and he throws himself on the ground, biting, leaping, and clinging to the posts. He leaps onto the water jars, squats on all fours, and leaps down again.[3] Gradually he becomes quiet, pours some water beside the pots and breaks a leaf knot of release, and then prepares and smokes a pipe of opium and resumes the dance.[4] He reaches a peak of excitement leaping and climbing about on the *panchur nibong*. Soon he calms down and is questioned by the *pengantin*, though Cuisinier was unable to find out what passed in the conversation.[5]

This dance is followed by a pantomime recalling an episode from the life of one of the *guru*, and these mimed scenes are interspersed between the dances both this and the following night.[6] The alternation of dancing and pantomime finally comes to an end. A bowl of charmed water is passed from the musician to the *pengantin*, who gives it to the *To' Bĕlian* whose assistant receives it from him and passes it back to the musician.[7] The session is over.

For the events of the third day I follow Skeat,[8] referring back to Cuisinier and other sources on specific points. The séance Skeat observed took place in a house. The patient's bed lay in one corner with the head against the wall. Out in the room running parallel to the bed was a row of four large jars, the three toward the head of the bed containing water and the one adjacent to the foot holding a 'pleasure-garden' of artificial flowers and other ornaments. In line with the jars, against the wall on which the bed headed, was the magician's wife with a tambourine. The magician sat beside the bed, and a censer was between him and the row of jars. The spectators were arranged across the end of the room beyond the feet of the patient, closest to the pleasure garden jar.[9]

[1] ibid., p. 64.  [2] ibid., pp. 64–5.
[3] ibid., p. 65.  [4] ibid., p. 66.  [5] ibid., pp. 66–7.
[6] ibid., p. 67.  [7] ibid., p. 68.  [8] Skeat 1900, pp. 436–44.
[9] ibid., pp. 437–8.

The preparations of the third afternoon seem to be much the same as those of the two preceding.[1] In the evening when all the guests are assembled, the shaman and his wife appear and take their places. The woman begins to chant the following invocation:

Peace be unto you, Pĕnglima Lenggang Laut!
Of no ordinary beauty
Is the Vessel of Pĕnglima Lenggang Laut!
The Vessel that is called 'The Yellow Spirit-boat',
The Vessel that is overlaid with vermilion and ivory,
The Vessel that is gilded all over;
Whose Mast is named 'Prince Mĕndela',
Whose Shrouds are named 'The Shrouds that are silvered',
Whose Oars are named 'The Feet of the Centipede'
(And whose Oarsmen are twice seven in number).
Whose Side is named 'Civet-cat Fencing',
Whose Rudder is named 'The Pendulous Bees'-nest',
Whose Galleries are named 'Struggling Pythons',
Whose Pennon flaps against the deckhouse,
Whose Streamers sport in the wind,
And whose Standard waves so bravely.
Come hither, good sir; come hither, my master,
It is just the right moment to veer your vessel.
Master of the Anchor, heave up the anchor;
Master of the Foretop, spread the sails;
Master of the Helm, turn the helm;
Oarsmen, bend your oars;
Whither is our vessel yawing to?
The vessel whose starting-place is the Navel of the Seas,
And that yaws towards the Sea where the 'Pauh Janggi'[2] grows,
Sporting among the surge and breakers,
Sporting among the surge and following the wave-ridges.
It were well to hasten, O Pĕnglima Lenggang Laut,[3]
Be not careless or slothful,
Linger not by inlet or river-reach,
Dally not with mistress or courtesan,
But descend and enter into your embodiment.[4]

[1] See Cuisinier 1936, p. 68.
[2] 'Pauh Janggi' is a legendary tree at the navel of the sea (Skeat 1900, p. 6).
[3] *Pĕnglima* or *panglima* means a military leader (Wilkinson 1964, pp. 165, 197), *lenggang* means rocking or swaying (Wilkinson 1964, p. 161), and *laut* means sea (Wilkinson 1964, p. 156). *Pĕnglima Lenggang Laut* could be translated roughly 'General Rocking Sea'.
[4] Skeat 1900, p. 439.

This invocation obviously is asking a sea spirit to come up the river to the place of performance and to enter the shaman or possibly the jars of water. Cuisinier mentions that the third session begins with greetings to the spirits and demons of the sea (*hantu shaitan laut*), but, not understanding why this is done, she says the practice is almost certainly a foreign addition to the original dance.[1] In fact this is an integral part of the ceremony, as will soon be apparent.

While his wife chants the invocation, the shaman 'bathes' himself in a cloud of incense, inhales some, and announces 'in the accents of what is called the spirit-language (*bhasa hantu*) that he is going to "lie down"',[2] which he does, and covers himself completely with his long plaid *sarong*. The invocation goes on until suddenly the shaman is jolted by a violent spasm, followed by a less violent spasm; he coughs, sits up facing the musician, and then turns to face the water jars.[3] He seems now to be 'possessed' by Pěnglima Lenggang Laut.

The shaman removes the yam leaves covering the water jars and plants lighted candles on the rims of each; then he chews some betel. When he finishes, he rubs the patient over the neck and shoulders with a bezoar stone. Bezoar stones are considered powerful curatives; possibly they are mildly *kramat*, being very unusual. He then proceeds to dress himself in a white jacket and head cloth, putting his plaid sarong around his waist. He takes out his *kris*, fumigates it, and returns it to its scabbard.[4]

The shaman next takes three silver coins, recites a charm over them, and drops one in each water jar. He inspects them to see how they lie relative to the candles on the rim and from this can divine how serious the illness is, what is causing it, and how it can best be cured.[5] It is undoubtedly through the power of the water spirit that this divination by water is accomplished. Cuisinier says that when the divination by water is completed, a leaf knot is broken over the pots,[6] as if a spirit were being released.

The magician then scatters some parched, washed and saffron rice around the jars and, from blossoms of the areca-palm and sprays of *champaka*, makes bouquets, one of which is placed in

[1] Cuisinier 1936, pp. 68–9.          [2] Skeat 1900, p. 440.
[3] ibid., p. 440.          [4] ibid., pp. 440–1.
[5] Skeat 1900, p. 441; see also Cuisinier 1936, p. 70.
[6] Cuisinier 1936, p. 70.

each water jar,[1] which seems to transform those jars as well into pleasure-gardens. On the floor behind the jars he deposits a white cloth which has been fumigated. The *pawang* then plunges his *kris* into each of the bouquets to get rid of any hostile spirits.[2] He takes a sheaf of palm-blossom, removes its casing, and fumigates it. Working himself into an intense state of excitement, he begins to stroke the patient with this, brushing downward toward his feet and beating the blossom out on the floor.[3] This seems to be an attempt, possibly with the help of the water spirit, to get a spirit out of the patient, into the brush, and then onto the floor where the rice would attract it and the soul-cloth or pleasure-gardens capture it. The *pawang* continues the brushing and beating out for some time and then sinks back exhausted on the floor, where he lies face down, his head again covered by the *sarong*.[4] Apparently Pĕnglima Lenggang Laut has now left, if he had not already done so.

After a long interval, the shaman begins to twitch and then rises up, 'possessed' by the tiger-spirit. Growls are heard, and the *pawang* begins to scratch the floor, leap around, and lick up the rice on the floor.[5] He then stoops forward and licks the body of the patient all over, as a tigress might lick her cub.[6] Licking up the rice, which may contain a spirit brushed out of the patient, and licking the patient himself, who may still harbour the malefactor, seem intended to transfer the offender into the shaman's own body. The licking finished, the shaman sits back and with his *kris* draws blood from his own arm. This could be to bring the bad spirit outside again. The *pawang* begins to fight with an invisible foe, first with the dagger and then with the sheaf of areca-palm blossom.[7] Perhaps the iron of the dagger is supposed to weaken it so the blossom brush can absorb it. The fighting gradually diminishes, and the *pawang* returns to brushing the patient and beating out the sheaf of blossom on the floor. He sits down, crooning charms to himself, chews some betel, passes his hands over the patient, and plunges the *kris* once more into the bouquets in the jars.[8] This could be to demobilize anything trapped inside. 'Finally he clapped his hands, removed his headcloth, "stroked" the patient over and flicked him with the corners of it, and then

[1] Skeat 1900, p. 441.  [2] ibid., pp. 441–2.  [3] ibid., p. 442.
[4] ibid., p. 442.  [5] ibid., p. 442–3.  [6] ibid., p. 443.
[7] ibid., p. 443.  [8] ibid., pp. 443–4.

shrouding himself once more in the *sarong*, lay down at full length in a state of complete exhaustion'.[1] The clapping and removal of the headcloth may release the *hantu bĕlian*, but this is not completely clear. After a pause, during which the shaman is subject to some convulsive twitching, he regains consciousness and the séance is over.[2]

For the *bĕlian* dance, a final ceremony to dismiss all spirits takes place on the morning following the last séance.[3] The cord around the shelter is cut, the *panchur nibong* is split open, and the water in it poured on the performers and the family of the sponsor. Water from all the pots is also sprinkled on the company, and some drunk. A knot of coconut leaf is broken while a formula of release is recited, and a whole coconut is split in two and the halves thrown in the river. The spirits are all dismissed by the *To' Bĕlian*; he does it silently in his thoughts.[4] This rite seems to both release the spirits that had been called up and release the performers from the special space, with water again acting to dissolve the boundary.

It can be seen that the *bĕlian* dance may be divided into three sub-rites: the procedure for making contact with the spirits, divination, and the cure. This seems to be true also for the other kinds of *bĕrhantu* ceremony except, of course, those in which only information of some kind is sought. It will be useful for purposes of discussion to separate the three sub-rites indicated; it would be possible to divide the ceremonies further or in other ways, but I think that the division proposed fits the Malay categories quite closely.

The aim of the séance method of making contact with the spirits is to be able not only to communicate with them, but to work together with them without being harmed. One aspect of the method is that the shaman exercises complete control over the conditions of meeting; the danger of the arbitrary actions of spirits in their accidental contact with man is diminished. The space in which the meeting takes place is in itself constraining to essences because it is clearly and rigidly bounded. Inside that space spirits are further confined; rather than wandering freely, they are absorbed in various containers or 'bodies' and transferred from one to another at the wish of the shaman. Such things as leaf

---

[1] ibid., p. 444.     [2] ibid., p. 444.     [3] Cuisinier 1936, p. 71.
[4] ibid., pp. 71–3.

brushes and other tree facsimiles (decorated branches, pleasure gardens, etc.), trays of offerings (quadrangular spaces), soul cloths, and possibly candles, hold spirits while they are consulted. During *lupa* ('possession'), the spirit is said to sit on the shaman's shoulders[1] or on his 'back, neck or shoulder'[2] to direct his body. It seems very likely that the special head cloth and jacket worn by shamans during *lupa*[3] is a form of soul-cloth which holds the helper spirit during the 'trance'.

Besides being able to confine and control spirits within the ritual space, the shaman knows how to get rid of them when they are no longer needed, usually by breaking a leaf-knot to symbolize breaking off the relationship. The shaman's control of the ritual space is important but not alone sufficient to permit safe inter-action with the spirits. If this were the case, anyone, or at least any magician, could conduct a séance. The shaman must also have a powerful spirit accomplice to police the other spirits that are brought in and to help accomplish the cure. The importance of the tie with the spirit helper is emphasized in the tribute paid the 'ancestors' through whom the relationship is validated.

Apart from the creation of a special space in which people and spirits can come together and the use of a spirit helper, the shaman's séance shares much with the less dramatic methods of communicating with the essential plane. Essences are attracted with candles, incense, and sound (of voice and musical instruments), and they are rewarded with offerings. The séance differs from most sacrifices and prayers, however, in the comprehensiveness of its appeal; it seeks to make contact with a large number of spirits from many different places. It will be recalled that, in Cuisinier's séance, the first night's ritual included a sacrifice to the earth spirits, the second night's ritual centred on the spirits of the jungle, or at least their representative the *hantu bělian*, and the third night's ritual began with an invocation to the water spirits. Thus, while the *běrhantu* is a specialized form of communication in terms of who can perform it, it is unspecialized in terms of the spirits with which it can make contact.

The kind of divination used in a séance varies according to the nature of the spirit consulted. Often the divination is done by

---

[1] Cuisinier 1936, pp. 35-6.     [2] Winstedt 1961a, p. 59.
[3] See Cuisinier 1936, pp. 47, 57, 63-4, 75; Skeat 1900, p. 441; Swettenham, quoted in Skeat 1900, pp. 444, 445.

examination of variations in a candle flame,[1] or the knowledge desired is transmitted in some secret way from the spirit helper to the shaman. Similar kinds of divination depending on signs from spirits are found outside the séance situation.[2] In most of these cases, the spirits are merely invoked; no formal séance is necessary to get them into the water, candle, lemon, soul-cloth, or whatever is used to transmit the knowledge of the spirits. It seems that the methods of divination used in the séance are merely part of a much broader class of divination techniques; one could expect to find any one of those techniques used in a séance, given a suitable combination of magician and spirit.

The curing segment of the běrhantu also has a number of alternatives. Some seem to use the spirit helper directly and others do not. Annandale witnessed a ceremony in which the bomor sniffed a pělěsit out of the patient into his own body where his spirit helper, which was called Nenek (grandmother), was able to overpower it. It was then possible to tie the pělěsit to a tree with a cotton cord marked with bars of charcoal and turmeric.[3] On the other hand, the cure used in the séance described by Maxwell (1883) did not make use of a spirit helper. A model mosque was built and filled with food, and the several shamans involved, 'armed with a bunch of leaves dipped into a bowl of těpong tawar, guided an indefinite number of evil ones into the place where the feast had been spread for them'.[4] When all were aboard, the mosque was set adrift in the river.[5] Winstedt says the pawang may 'brush and sprinkle the sick man, suck at his body or rub it with medicinal leaves and a bezoar stone. He may tell the patient to drink charmed water from an inverted jar for seven days'.[6] Only the cures that use a spirit helper are unique to the běrhantu ceremonies; the other techniques mentioned may be used outside of the běrhantu ritual, as well as within it. It is likely that nearly any curing technique could be used in conjunction with a séance depending on the cause indicated for the disease, the shaman's special abilities, and other specific circumstances.

The běrhantu ceremonies, then, are unique in their form and the combination of sub-rites, but the sub-rites themselves are quite

---

[1] See Cuisinier 1936, p. 81; Winstedt 1961a, pp. 61, 147.
[2] See e.g. Skeat 1900, pp. 411–14, 535–42.
[3] Annandale 1903, pp. 100–1.     [4] Maxwell 1883, p. 231.
[5] ibid., p. 231.          [6] Winstedt 1961a, p. 61.

clearly members of larger classes of ritual, and members of those classes that do not depend on the unique characteristics of *bĕrhantu* ceremonies often occur in place of ones that do.

## IV. SURVEY OF MAGICAL RITES

The two ceremonies described provide examples of most of the basic processes in Malay magic. It would be impossible in this study to describe and interpret all of the Malay magical rites, but it is possible to outline the main forms of ritual using the preceding ceremonies as examples, and to show where most rites fit in.

### (a) DIFFERENTIATION MAGIC

Examination of the rice-baby ceremony suggests that the magical creation of a 'thing' may be seen as resulting from the simultaneous differentiation of a 'body' and a 'soul' out of a formerly undifferentiated category of matter and vital principle. The magic involves ritually severing distinct portions of matter and essence from their diffuse sources and then magically ensuring that the newly created body and *sĕmangat* remain together. These features can be seen as diagnostic of a small but important class of Malay magic which I shall call 'differentiation magic'.

The magic needed to produce human babies must obviously be of this sort, since the rice-baby ceremony is apparently modelled after its human counterpart. In fact, however, the differentiation magic is less clear with human birth because the ritual is complicated by rites to protect the mother and child and by rites of passage that apply to both. Nevertheless, the form is present, as the baby's body must be differentiated from the mother's blood[1] and its soul from her supply of the vital principle.[2] The umbilical cord is ritually severed with a bamboo knife, to avoid frightening the *sĕmangat* as an iron one would do,[3] and efforts are made to confirm the soul in the body by such devices as including candlenuts, cockle-shells, and iron nails in the baby's bath.

The creation of a *pĕlĕsit* also entails some differentiation magic, though the body created is not completely independent of that of

---

[1] Annandale and Robinson 1904, p. 65.
[2] Cuisinier 1951, p. 207.
[3] Annandale and Robinson 1904, p. 47.

the owner. Methods of making *pĕlĕsit* have been described pre-viously (Chapter IV). In every case, the essence is differentiated from the owner's *badi*.

Oddly enough, differentiation magic seems to be involved in a rite performed by toddy collectors when they cut off the blossom sheaths of the coconut palm, apparently to drain the toddy which will be boiled down to sugar.[1] The operator begins by reciting the following lines as he stands at the base of the tree:

> Peace be with you, O Abubakar!
> Drowse not as you keep watch and ward in the heart of this tree
> (*umbi*).[2]

When he has climbed half-way up he says:

> Peace be with you, Little Sister, Handmaiden Bidah,
> Drowse not as you keep watch and ward in the middle of the trunk,
> Come and accompany me on my way up this tree.[3]

Upon reaching the leaf stalks, he shakes the central shoot three times and says:

> Peace be with you, Little Sister, Youngest of the Princesses,
> Drowse not as you keep watch and ward over the central shoot,
> Do you accompany me on my way down this tree.[4]

The last lines seem to imply that the tree soul, which has been herded up the tree, will be confined to the central shoot which is cut off and taken back down the tree. Unfortunately Skeat does not say what is actually done, but only gives the spells.

After this, the operator bends down a blossom-sheath, takes hold of the central shoot, and repeats thrice:

> Peace be with your Highnesses, Princesses of the Shorn Hair and (perpetual) Distillation,
> Who are (seen) in the curve (lit. swell) and the ebbing away of the Blossom-sheath,
> Of the Blossom-sheath Si Gĕdĕbeh Mayang,
> Seven Princesses who are the Handmaidens of Si Mayang,
> Come hither, Little One, come hither,
> Come hither, Tiny One, come hither,
> Come hither, Bird, come hither,

---

[1] See Skeat 1900, pp. 216–17.     [2] ibid., p. 216.
[3] ibid., p. 216.     [4] ibid., p. 216.

Come hither, Filmy One, come hither.
Thus I bend your neck,
Thus I roll up your hair,
And here is an Ivory Toddy-knife to help the washing of your
    face.
[Sweet afterbirth, sweet caul,
Sweet reaching to (or hanging loosely from) the ring finger;
Sweet afterbirth, sweet caul,
Sweet reaching to (or hanging loosely from) the palm blossom's
    face][1]
Here is an Ivory Toddy-knife to cut you short,
And here is an Ivory Cup to hold under you,
And there is an Ivory Bath that waits below for you.
Clap your hands and splash in the Ivory Bath,
For it is called the 'Sovereign Changing Clothes'.[2]

The lines Skeat leaves untranslated further confirm the connection of this rite with those previously described. They also
suggest that the toddy is seen as a by-product of the birth of the
central shoot of the tree which holds the blossom-sheaths. Why
the idiom of birth is used in the operation of tapping toddy is
not clear unless the shoot with the blossoms is, or once was,
planted as one way of starting new trees. Unfortunately, I cannot
find out the botanical or agricultural facts of this matter. In any
case, the magic used in cutting the central shoot is very similar
to the other kinds of differentiation magic, and it is not too far-
fetched to see this as a mature tree giving birth to a baby one.

There is some reason to believe that the miraculous births
recorded in the literature are examples of differentiation magic.
The two forms usually reported are the discovery of a child inside
an unusual stalk of bamboo or other tree and the appearance of a
child in the foam generated by a river.[3] These supernatural
children may be seen as differentiations of trees and rivers or even
of the broad realms of jungle and water.

The recurrence of the idiom of birth in the various kinds of
magic that can be interpreted as differentiating diffuse matter and
essence into more specific parts suggests that this is the basic

---

[1] '*Uri manis, tembuni manis,*
    *Manis sampei* [*sampai?*] *ka jari manis;*
    *Uri manis, tembuni manis,*
    *Manis sampei ka muka mayang!*'
    (Skeat 1900, pp. 612–13).
[2] ibid., pp. 216–17, 612–13.          [3] See e.g. Skeat 1900, pp. 16–19.

image the Malays have of the process. It would be tempting to say that changes from more to less differentiated categories are described in terms of an idea of death, but the almost total adoption of the Moslem funeral makes it difficult to see how even death itself is conceived. Perhaps the disappearance of the *sĕmangat* at death should be seen as a merging with some less differentiated order of essence just as the body merges with the soil.

## (b) SPIRIT CONTACT MAGIC

When spirits are deliberately brought to the habitation of man, they are kept under strict control. The magic used to accomplish this is what I call 'spirit contact magic'. Typically, the spirits are attracted into a well defined rectangular space, which is capable of restraining them, by the use of such things as incense, candles, and percussion instruments. Inside that space, they are often further constrained by various spirit receptacles.

The most common kind of spirit contact magic is the ritual used to make offerings to spirits while protecting the congregation from them. The offerings are nearly always placed in rectangular or square offering trays (*anchak*) or on similarly shaped altars,[1] and the spirits are called in by the burning of incense and the recitation of spells.

The shaman's séance operates similarly, though a more intimate contact between the spirits and certain people is achieved by including the latter within the space prepared for the spirits. Additions are made to the basic magical complex to protect the persons so exposed.

Rites of the same form as the shaman's séance are used in a number of Malay entertainments. Performers of traditional dances, whether human or inanimate (such as a sheaf of palm blossom or a 'scare-crow' made of fish trap), must be 'possessed' by an appropriate spirit, and the shelter used and the means of attraction employed fit the pattern of the séance.[2] The same is true of theatrical performances, whether the players are human or shadow puppets.[3] Even story-tellers in Patani must be possessed,[4] though unfortunately, I know none of the details of the story-teller's performance.

The ritual performed during the transitional stage of certain

---

[1] See Skeat 1900, pp. 231, 260, 414–18.    [2] See ibid., pp. 457–68.
[3] See ibid., pp. 503–21.    [4] Annandale and Robinson 1904, p. 33 n.

Malay rites of passage fits the general scheme of spirit contact magic, suggesting that persons in transition are regarded as exposed to the spirits. The installation of the king (sultan) exhibits the basic characteristics of a séance,[1] and it is said that the new king is the receptacle of a god[2] and that the guardian genies of the state light on his sword during the ceremony.[3] Interestingly, the Malay marriage ceremony, which is very similar to the installation of the king (the couple is regarded as royalty for a day[4]), displays some characteristics of a séance, although the coming of spirits is not explicitly reported.[5] On the second night of the wedding, a ceremony for publicly staining the fingernails of the couple with henna is performed.[6] The bride and groom are seated on an enclosed rectangular dais between two candles, and a tray of offerings is placed nearby. Incense is burned and handfuls of rice are thrown around the sitting couple. Their foreheads and hands are then 'painted' with *tĕpong tawar* and the henna is rubbed on their hands. This rite is performed in succession by an odd number of relatives of the couple. Nearby, a dance called the Henna Dance (*mĕnari hinei*) is performed. The dancer rapidly rotates a brazen cup containing a small cake of henna and several lighted candles. The use of henna and of this particular dance occur in Muslim weddings as far away as Morocco.[7] However, the form of the Malay rite suggests that at one time spirits were believed to attend this ceremony, though the purpose of the visit is not clear. At least the practices accompanying the henna staining are hard to explain in terms other than those of spirit contact magic. Under the circumstances, it is difficult to tell why spirits are called in at these rites, if indeed they are. Possibly the marginal state of the people involved exposes them to spirit contact, and the magic is merely intended to protect them in this inevitable association. On the other hand, it may be that spirit helpers are called in to protect the couple from other spirits which have gained access to them because of their position between clear social categories.

(c) ESSENCE TRANSFER MAGIC

A major class of Malay rites comprises procedures intended to transfer essences from one category of matter to another. The basic

[1] See Winstedt 1961a, pp. 10, 35–37.
[2] Winstedt 1961a, p. 36.      [3] ibid., pp. 11, 146.
[4] Skeat 1900, p. 388.      [5] See ibid., pp. 368–94.
[6] ibid., pp. 376–7.      [7] Winstedt 1961a, p. 123.

features of these ceremonies are simple and few. The categories involved must be connected or brought into direct contact, their boundaries must be weakened, and the essence must be persuaded to move from one to the other. The relative emphasis on the different features varies, and occasionally one or more seem to be eliminated altogether, although this would be expected to diminish the effectiveness of the rite. There are no systematic differences in the rites depending on whether it is the extraction or insertion of the essence that is desired, or whether the aim is beneficent or evil.

Probably the largest body of spirit transfer magic aims to extract an essence from one category of matter by transferring it to another. The essence removed can be any kind of spirit or *badi* that is afflicting a 'body', or it may be part of a soul as in certain 'black magic rites'. The category of matter from which the essence is removed can be the individual body of a person, animal, or in-animate object, a diffuse body such as a village during an epidemic, or even a whole state when misfortune is widespread. Special essence receptacles such as limes, soul-cloths, and leaf brushes can be used either as the final container for the essence or as an inter-mediate vessel for further transfer. Much 'black magic' uses the receptacle as final container, attempting to entice a person's *sěmangat* into it, leaving the victim helpless.[1] An example of the receptacle as intermediary is the case described above (p. 166) in which shamans transfer spirits in leaf brushes (dipped in *těpong tawar*) to a model mosque. Commonly the final container is a tray of offerings that is disposed of in jungle or stream when the spirit has been transferred into it. These may be simple *anchak*, fanciful forms such as palaces and mosques, or the well-known 'spirit-boats'.[2]

Magic that aims simply to expel an essence from something usually has the form of essence transfer magic. The reason is probably that even the most general categories of matter, the three natural realms, are body-like in some ways, and simply to expel an essence from a confined body injects it into a natural realm. Spirits driven out of fields or foundations, for example, are driven into the earth or jungle.

[1] See Skeat 1900, pp. 575–577.
[2] See e.g. Maxwell 1883, pp. 229–32; Maxwell 1886, pp. 80–81; Skeat 1900, pp. 418–24, 433–6; Wilkinson 1932, pp. 96–7; Winstedt 1961a, p. 68.

Frequently, the object of essence transfer is to get an essence into its proper body. This applies mainly to the processes used to retrieve a straying soul. The soul may be called directly back into the body, but it is usually transferred through one or more intermediaries.[1] For example, one ceremony to recall a soul entails placing seven quids of betel and plates of saffron-rice, parched rice, and washed rice at the feet of the sick man, attaching seven strands of multicoloured thread to an egg, and giving the patient the other end of the strands to hold. The soul is then called by a spell, 'caught in a soul-cloth, and passed (it is thought) first of all into the egg, and thence back into the patient's body by means of the thread which connects the egg with the patient'.[2]

## (d) ESSENCE CONTROL MAGIC

Probably the simplest kind of Malay magic is that designed to control the actions of essences, either souls or spirits. This depends basically on spells to persuade or frighten the essences and offerings to reward their obedience.

One class of this magic aims, by controlling certain essences, to control the bodies to which they are attached. The hunter tries to communicate with the *sĕmangat* of his prey and often with the spirits or deities in charge of the animal's environment, so that they will guide the whole animal into his hands.[3] 'Love magic' seems to work in this way as well, consisting predominantly of spells addressed to the *sĕmangat* of the beloved, entreating it to come to the petitioner or to be dazed with affection at the sight of him.[4] Skeat calls love magic 'soul-abduction', but it is likely that the intent is for the soul to bring the body as well, since to extract a person's *sĕmangat* would cause illness rather than love. In a few cases, the essence that controls a body is a spirit, not a *sĕmangat*, but the procedure for magically controlling the body is the same. A good example is the practice of attracting a spirit into a suspended lemon and using its motion for divination.[5]

In another class of essence control magic, the magician requires essences to act as free spirits, not as *sĕmangat*. The use of familiar spirits to afflict one's enemies and of spirit helpers in the séance are examples of this kind of magic. One interesting rite reported

[1] See Skeat 1900, pp. 452–6, 577.     [2] Skeat 1900, pp. 453, 454.
[3] See ibid., pp. 132–41, 171–81, 296–301.
[4] See ibid., pp. 569–70, 574–9.     [5] ibid., pp. 535–7.

by Skeat,[1] used either to extract a person's soul or to gain control
of it and thereby of the person (the meaning is not clear), seems to
operate by the sending out of one's own *badi* as a quasi-familiar.
The magician beats his shadow with a cane three times a day while
reciting the following spell:

> Ho! Irupi,[2] Shadowy One,
> Let the Queen come to me.
> Do you, if *Somebody* is awake,
> Stir her and shake her, and make her rise,
> And take her breath and her soul and bring them here,
> And deposit them in my left side.
> But if she sleep,
> Do you take hold of the great toe of her right foot
> Until you can make her get up,
> And use your utmost endeavours to bring them to me.
> If you do not, you shall be a rebel to God, etc.[3]

Much of the 'sympathetic magic' that Skeat says underlies the
'Black Art' of the Malays[4] seems to work by control of spirits.
Various kinds of image and materials that have been part of or in
contact with the body of an intended victim, often incorporated in
wax figures, can be used to harm an enemy.[5] The objects used are
whipped, burned, or stabbed with pins or palm twigs. This would
fit Frazer's notion of sympathetic magic except that the objects
are usually buried afterward, and the Prophet 'Tap or another
earth spirit is invoked and asked to harm or kill the intended
victim.[6] Wilkinson says that the manipulation of wax figures is not
sympathetic magic as Skeat says, but that it serves instead to give
the spirits an example of what is expected of them; if it were based
on a 'certain physical sympathy between the person and his
image', it would be unnecessary to invoke spirits at all.[7] It is
perfectly possible that some parts of what I have called Malay
magic work directly, although the great bulk of it quite clearly
works through essential intermediaries. This suggests the possi-

---

[1] ibid., p. 575.

[2] *Irup* means 'to suck up liquor from a spoon or cup; to lap up' (Wilkinson
1964, p. 100). I have suggested that this is what spirits do to the soul substance
of their victims and what familiars and vampires in particular do to get blood.

[3] Skeat 1900, p. 575.          [4] ibid., p. 82.

[5] See ibid., pp. 568–9, 573.          [6] ibid., pp. 569, 571, 573.

[7] Wilkinson 1906, p. 73.

bility that the few rites that seem to work directly are actually intended to instruct the essences that control the situation.

## Summary

The practice of Malay magic depends basically on the manipulation of essences and of the categories imposed on the physical world. In general, the spell operates on essences, being the means of reasoning with them and of changing the degree of their definition which, in turn, changes their susceptibility to boundaries in the material world. The ritual manipulation of people and special materials operates mainly by changing the strength of those boundaries. The material and essential planes are interdependent at some levels and in opposition at others. The several kinds of magic discussed express different aspects of this relationship and the ways the magician attempts to control them.

# VII

## CONCLUSIONS

SOME aspects, at least, of the order in Malay magic can now be seen. It has been found that the Malays distinguish material and essential planes of existence, and that the two planes interact in several ways. The most profound interconnection concerns the very existence of discrete material and essential entities. Both planes seem to be seen as divided into a hierarchical set of categories, a common substance being differentiated into particles at several levels of distinctiveness. Homogeneous matter is divided first into the realms of earth, water, and jungle which are further divided, where they concern man, into roughly bounded classes of matter such as mines, fishing grounds, and fields. More specific classes of things are distinguished within the various realms: the fish, the coconut trees, or the barking deer of limited areas. Under some circumstances, individual bodies are distinguished from each other: the animal killed, the unusual tree, the particular human being. The differentiation of *sĕmangat*, the ubiquitous vital principle, closely parallels this. Vague free spirits, identified only with the division of the world that is their habitat, roam widely. Some spirits are associated with more specific classes of matter and are sometimes called their 'souls'. Some, such as the souls of animals, are quite distinct and are attached to particular classes of body. Finally, individualized particles of the vital principle exist in conjunction with particular human beings.

The correspondence of the divisions of the two planes is no mere coincidence. Each member of an associated pair of such divisions contributes fundamentally to the definition of the other, to setting it off from similar divisions in its own plane and, thereby, to its existence as a discrete entity. This conceptual interdependence is expressed as a physical interdependence, mainly as the reliance of material categories on essences to defend their boundaries and the complementary need of essences for bodies to supply them with undifferentiated *sĕmangat*.

This conceptual interdependence is also expressed in the idiom of power. The fact that essences are partially defined by the categories of matter that they inhabit and that they, in turn, help define those categories means that the essences most closely associated with clearly defined categories of matter are themselves clearly defined. In one frame of reference, the powers of essences are seen as being opposed to those of bodies, and, in terms of this scheme, the well defined bodies appear to constrain well defined essences much more than vaguely defined categories of matter constrain their poorly defined inhabitants. This seems to be interpreted as indicating both that the power of categories of matter varies directly with their clarity of definition (degree of differentiation), and that the power of essences varies inversely with conceptual clarity. In other words, *sĕmangat* are less powerful in relation to boundaries than spirits, and clearly defined bodies are more powerful in relation to essences than bodies with vaguely defined boundaries.

In general, the most powerful spirits are associated with broad categories of matter, while weak essences are attached to constricted, localized bodies, since less differentiated bodies encompass the more differentiated ones. This produces a 'political' hierarchy of essences in which superiority roughly correlates with the extent of the category of matter to which the essence is attached. Thus Allah, whose domain is the universe, is superior to the prophets 'Tap, Solomon, and Khizr, lords of the three natural realms, who in turn rule the more localized spirits within those realms. The arrangement is similar to that of the political hierarchy in human society in that the higher positions are associated with wider territorial control than those below.[1] The similarity is expressed by the use of military and political terms, such as *raja* and *penggawa*, for important spirits.

The Malay magician attempts to make use of the power manifest in each aspect of the relationship between categories of matter and of essence. He manipulates their conceptual interdependence by adjusting their definitions, using material and verbal symbols. He intervenes in their physical interdependence, making offerings of the vital principle to spirits and using special materials to reinforce the boundaries of bodies, the usual task of *sĕmangat*. He also uses the 'political' hierarchy of essences to his advantage, employing

---

[1] See Gullick 1958, pp. 36, 37, and *passim*.

powerful spirits as spirit-helpers and invoking their names in spells to frighten lesser powers.

At each level within this hierarchical structure of matter and essence, there is a tendency to differentiate in sets of three. These divisions are truly triadic in the sense that the three parts are of similar status, and each is related to the other two in similar ways. Dyads often occur, defining the boundaries of the triadic classifications, but dual classifications do not seem prominent in Malay magical ideas. In fact, the same dualisms, such as 'raw-cooked' and 'black-white', may occur on more than one boundary in a triadic classification and are sometimes found on all three. In some cases an intermediate category is found between the two terms of a dyad. This seems to be an elaboration of the boundary, giving it the status of a category (usually a dangerous one)[1] in its own right, just as the transitional stage in a rite of passage can become an autonomous condition.[2] In other words, I would regard these triple divisions as special cases of boundary-defining dyads, not as triads like the others discovered. Perhaps they should be regarded as one kind of structure intermediate between the dyad and triad.[3]

Successive inclusion and triadic division seem, then, to be the basic ordering principles in Malay magical ideas, although the triadically divided hierarchy that would be the expected form of Malay classifications is sometimes modified or embellished in empirical fact. Still, such classifications are common and, I have shown, basic to the Malay world-view.

Possibly the prominence of the triadically divided hierarchy in the Malay situation can be attributed to its ability to accommodate new and sometimes contradictory beliefs. Evans-Pritchard says that the Nuer are able to assimilate the spirits of their neighbours because all spirits are regarded as differentiations of an all-pervading spirit, Kwoth, and newly acquired spirits can be seen simply as new or formerly unnoticed refractions of Kwoth.[4] Something similar seems to be done in Malaya. It has been seen, for example, that spirits of Indian, Arabic, and Indonesian origin often occur in the same classifications and that all are regarded as differentiations of *sěmangat*, the vital principle. Triadic divisions

---

[1] Cf. Douglas 1966, pp. 39–40, 96–7, 122.
[2] See Van Gennep 1960, p. 11.
[3] Cf. Levi-Strauss 1963, pp. 132–63.
[4] Evans-Pritchard 1953, pp. 209–10 and *passim*.

also suit the syncretic condition of Malay ideas in that, while they form quite simple classifications, they admit contradictory ideas more readily than the simpler dual classifications. It is possible, for example, for a category to be considered both black and white, if it is 'black' in relation to one other category and 'white' in relation to another. In a dual classification, both categories would have both attributes, and the power of the distinction would be lost. Triadic structures help preserve, in the face of the conflicting qualities and associations of things brought on by massive cultural syncretism, the dual mode of distinction that so efficiently marks boundaries. Durkheim and Mauss say that complexity of structure helps to conceal contradictions.[1] In this regard, the triad exceeds the dyad in complexity far more than the difference between the quantities 'two' and 'three' suggest.

This study has shown that, despite the extensive mixing of traditions, a few simple principles of organization do underly the complex empirical reality that is Malay magic. The kind of order found seems well suited to situations in which several traditions are mixed and might be expected to be favoured in such situations elsewhere in the world.

[1] Durkheim and Mauss 1963, pp. 70–1

# BIBLIOGRAPHY

ANNANDALE, NELSON, 1903: 'A magical ceremony for the cure of a sick person among the Malays of Upper Perak', *Man iii* (1903), pp. 100–3.

ANNANDALE, NELSON, and ROBINSON, HERBERT C., 1903: *Fasciculi Malayenses: Anthropological and zoological results of an expedition to Perak and the Siamese Malay states, 1901–1902; Anthropology, part 1,* (London, The University Press of Liverpool, 1903).

— 1904: *Fasciculi Malayenses: Anthropological and zoological results of an expedition to Perak and the Siamese Malay states, 1901–1902; Anthropology, part 2,* (London, The University Press of Liverpool, 1904).

BLAGDEN, C. O., 1896: 'Notes on the folk-lore and popular religion of the Malays', *Journal of the Straits Branch of the Royal Asiatic Society* xxix (1896), pp. 1–12.

— 1897: 'An account of the cultivation of rice in Malacca', *Journal of the Straits Branch of the Royal Asiatic Society* xxx (1897), pp. 285–304.

BOSCH, F. D. K., 1960: *The golden germ: an introduction to Indian symbolism,* ('S-Gravenhage, Mouton and Co., 1960).

CHELOD, J., 1964: 'Contribution au problème de la prééminence de la droite, d'apres le témoignage Arabe', *Anthropos* lix (1964), pp. 529–45.

CLIFFORD, HUGH, 1897: *In court and kampong,* (London, Grant Richards, 1897).

CLIFFORD, HUGH, and SWETTENHAM, FRANK ATHELSTANE, 1896: *A dictionary of the Malay language: Malay-English,* (Taiping, Perak, The Government Printing Office, 1896).

CUISINIER, JEANNE, 1936: *Danses magiques de Kelantan,* (Paris, Institut D'Ethnologie, 1936).

— 1951: *Sumangat: l'ame et son culte en Indochine et en Indonésie,* (Paris, Gallimard, 1951).

DJAMOUR, JUDITH, 1959: *Malay kinship and marriage in Singapore,* (London, The Athlone Press, University of London, 1959).

DOUGLAS, MARY, 1966: *Purity and danger: an analysis of concepts of pollution and taboo,* (London, Routledge and Kegan Paul, 1966).

DUMONT, LOUIS, 1959: 'A structural definition of a folk deity of Tamil Nad: Aiyanar, the lord', *Contributions to Indian Sociology* iii, (1959), pp. 75–87.

DURKHEIM, EMILE, and MAUSS, MARCEL, 1963: *Primitive classification*, Rodney Needham, trans., (Chicago, University of Chicago, 1963).

ELKIN, A. P., 1964: *The Australian Aborigines*, (Garden City, New York, Doubleday and Company, Inc., 1964).

EVANS-PRITCHARD, E. E., 1937: *Witchcraft, oracles, and magic among the Azande*, (London, Oxford University Press, 1937).

— 1953: 'The Nuer concept of Spirit in its relation to the social order', *American Anthropologist* lv (2) (1953), pp. 201–14.

FORTUNE, R. F., n.d.: *Manus religion: an ethnological study of the Manus natives of the Admiralty islands*, (Lincoln, Nebraska, University of Nebraska Press).

G.C., 1885: 'Malay superstitions', *Notes and Queries* ii (1885), p. 53. Issued with *Journal of the Straits Branch of the Royal Asiatic Society*, No. 15.

GEDDES, W. R., 1961: *Nine Dayak nights*, (London, Oxford University Press, 1961).

GIMLETTE, JOHN P., 1929: *Malay poisons and charm cures*, (London, J. and A. Churchill, 1929).

GULLICK, J. M., 1958: *Indigenous political systems of Western Malaya*, (London, The Athlone Press, University of London, 1958).

HAMILTON, A. W., 1922: 'Points of the compass in Kedah', *Journal of the Straits Branch of the Royal Asiatic Society* lxxxvi (1922), p. 385.

HILL, A. H., 1951: 'Kelantan padi planting', *Journal of the Malayan Branch of the Royal Asiatic Society* xxiv (1) (1951), pp. 56–76.

HUMPHREYS, J. L., 1926: 'A note on the north and south points of the compass in Kedah and Trengganu', *Journal of the Malayan Branch of the Royal Asiatic Society* iv (1) (1926), pp. 133–5.

LEACH, EDMUND, 1964: 'Anthropological aspects of language: animal categories and verbal abuse', in *New Directions in the Study of Language*, Eric H. Lenneberg, ed., (Cambridge, Massachusetts, M.I.T. Press, 1964).

LÉVI-STRAUSS, CLAUDE, 1963: *Structural anthropology*, Claire Jacobson and Brooke Grundfest Schoepf, trans., (New York, Basic Books, Inc., 1963).

LÉVY-BRUHL, LUCIEN, 1965: *The 'soul' of the primitive*, Lilian A. Clare, trans., (London, George Allen and Unwin Ltd, 1965).

McHUGH, J. N., 1955: *Hantu hantu: an account of ghost belief in modern Malaya*, (Singapore, Donald Moore, 1955).

MAXWELL, WILLIAM E., 1883: 'Shamanism in Perak', *Journal of the Straits Branch of the Royal Asiatic Society* xii (1883), pp. 222–32.

— 1885: 'Legend of Changkat Rambian', *Notes and Queries* i (1885), pp. 19–22. Issued with *Journal of the Straits Branch of the Royal Asiatic Society*, No. 14.

— 1886: 'Pelas negri', *Notes and Queries* iii (1886), pp. 80–2. Issued with *Journal of the Straits Branch of the Royal Asiatic Society*, No. 16.

— 1906: 'Mantra Gajah', *Journal of the Straits Branch of the Royal Asiatic Society* xlv (1906), pp. 1–53.

MOORHEAD, FRANCIS JOSEPH, 1957: *A history of Malaya and her neighbours*, vol. i, (Kuala Lumpur, Longmans of Malaysia Ltd, 1957).

NADEL, SIEGFRIED FREDERICK, 1957: *The theory of social structure*, (London, Cohen and West Ltd, 1957).

NEEDHAM, RODNEY, 1967: 'Percussion and transition', *Man* ii (4) (1967), pp. 606–14.

NICHOLSON, REYNOLD A., 1928: 'Sufis', in *Encyclopedia of religion and ethics*, James Hastings, ed., (New York, Charles Scribner's Sons, 1928).

POTT, P. H., 1966: *Yoga and yantra: their interrelation and their significance for Indian archaeology*, Rodney Needham, trans., (The Hague, Martinus Nijhoff, 1966).

RENTSE, ANKER, 1933a: 'Notes on Malay beliefs', *Journal of the Malayan Branch of the Royal Asiatic Society* xi (2) (1933), pp. 245–51.

— 1933b: 'The points of the compass in Kelantan', *Journal of the Malayan Branch of the Royal Asiatic Society* xi (2) (1933), p. 252.

RIDLEY, H. N., 1924: *The flora of the Malay Peninsula*, vol. iii, (London, L. Reeve & Co., Ltd., 1924).

SHAW, G. E., 1911: *Papers on Malay subjects: Malay industries, part III, rice planting*, (Kuala Lumpur, Federated Malay States Government Press, 1911).

SKEAT, WALTER WILLIAM, 1900: *Malay magic: an introduction to the folklore and popular religion of the Malay Peninsular* [sic], (London, Macmillan and Co., Ltd, 1900).

— 1901: *Fables and folk-tales from an eastern forest*, (Cambridge, Cambridge University Press, 1901).

SKEAT, WALTER WILLIAM, and BLAGDEN, CHARLES OTTO, 1906: *Pagan races of the Malay Peninsula*, vol. ii, (London, Macmillan and Co., Ltd, 1906).

SWETTENHAM, FRANK ATHELSTANE, 1895: *Malay sketches*, (London, John Lane, 1895).

TURNER, VICTOR, 1967: *The forest of symbols: aspects of Ndembu ritual*, (Ithaca, New York, Cornell University Press, 1967).

VAN GENNEP, ARNOLD, 1960: *The rites of passage*, M. B. Vizadom and G. I. Caffee, trans., (London, Routledge and Kegan Paul, 1960).

WAVELL, STEWART, 1958: *The lost world of the East: an adventurous quest in the Malayan hinterland*, (London, Souvenir Press, 1958).

— 1964: *The naga king's daughter*, (London, George Allen and Unwin, Ltd, 1964).

WEHR, HANS, 1961: *A dictionary of modern written Arabic*, J. Milton Cowan, ed., (Ithaca, New York, Cornell University Press, 1961).

WHITEHEAD, ALFRED NORTH, 1927: *Symbolism: its meaning and effect*, (New York, The Macmillan Company, 1927).

WILKINSON, R. J., 1901: *A Malay-English dictionary*, (Singapore, Kelly and Walsh, 1901).

— 1906: *Malay beliefs*, (London, Luzac and Co., 1906).

— 1907: *Papers on Malay subjects: Malay literature,* (Kuala Lumpur, Federated Malay States Government Press, 1907).

— 1932: 'Some Malay studies', *Journal of the Malayan Branch of the Royal Asiatic Society* x (1) (1932), pp. 67–137.

— 1964: *An abridged Malay-English dictionary* (Romanised), (London, Macmillan and Co., Ltd, 1964).

WINSTEDT, R. O., 1911: *Papers on Malay subjects: Malay industries, part II, fishing, hunting and trapping*, (Kuala Lumpur, Federated Malay States Government Press, 1911).

— 1922: 'A Malay pantheist charm', *Journal of the Straits Branch of the Royal Asiatic Society* lxxxvi (1922), pp. 261–7.

— 1924: 'Karamat: sacred places and persons in Malaya', *Journal of the Malayan Branch of the Royal Asiatic Society* ii (1924), pp. 264–79.

— 1925: *Shaman, saiva and sufi: a study of the evolution of Malay magic*, (London, Constable and Co., Ltd, 1925).

— 1954: 'A Malay Kramat', *The Straits Times Annual for 1954*, (Singapore, The Straits Times).

— 1961a: *The Malay magician: being shaman, saiva and sufi*, (London, Routledge and Kegan Paul, 1961).

— 1961b: *The Malays: a cultural history*, (London, Routledge and Kegan Paul Ltd, 1961).

ZAINUL-ABIDIN BIN AHMAD, 1922a: 'The tiger-breed families', *Journal of the Straits Branch of the Royal Asiatic Society* lxxxv (1922), pp. 36–9.

— 1922b: 'The *akuan* or spirit-friends', *Journal of the Straits Branch of the Royal Asiatic Society* lxxxvi (1922), pp. 378–84.

# INDEX